THE MAGILL BIBLIOGRAPHIES

The American Presidents, by Norman S. Cohen, 1989
Black American Women Novelists, by Craig Werner, 1989
Classical Greek and Roman Drama, by Robert J. Forman, 1989
Contemporary Latin American Fiction, by Keith H. Brower, 1989
Masters of Mystery and Detective Fiction, by J. Randolph Cox, 1989
Nineteenth Century American Poetry, by Philip K. Jason, 1989
Restoration Drama, by Thomas J. Taylor, 1989
Twentieth Century European Short Story, by Charles E. May, 1989
The Victorian Novel, by Laurence W. Mazzeno, 1989
Women's Issues, by Laura Stempel Mumford, 1989
America in Space, by Russell R. Tobias, 1991
The American Constitution, by Robert J. Janosik, 1991
The Classic Epic, by Thomas J. Sienkewicz, 1991
English Romantic Poetry, by Brian Aubrey, 1991
Ethics, by John K. Roth, 1991
The Immigrant Experience, by Paul D. Mageli, 1991
The Modern American Novel, by Steven G. Kellman, 1991
Native Americans, by Frederick E. Hoxie and Harvey Markowitz, 1991
American Drama: 1918-1960, by R. Baird Shuman, 1992
American Ethnic Literatures, by David R. Peck, 1992
American Theatre History, by Thomas J. Taylor, 1992
The Atomic Bomb, by Hans G. Graetzer and Larry M. Browning, 1992
Biography, by Carl Rollyson, 1992
The History of Science, by Gordon L. Miller, 1992
The Origin and Evolution of Life on Earth, by David W. Hollar, Jr., 1992
Pan-Africanism, by Michael W. Williams, 1992
Resources for Writers, by R. Baird Shuman, 1992
Shakespeare, by Joseph Rosenblum, 1992
The Vietnam War in Literature, by Philip K. Jason, 1992
Contemporary Southern Women Fiction Writers, by Rosemary M.
   Canfield Reisman and Christopher J. Canfield, 1994
Cycles in Humans and Nature, by John T. Burns, 1994
Environmental Studies, by Diane M. Fortner, 1994
Poverty in America, by Steven Pressman, 1994
The Short Story in English: Britain and North America, by Dean Baldwin
   and Gregory L. Morris, 1994
Victorian Poetry, by Laurence W. Mazzeno, 1995

Human Rights in Theory and Practice, by Gregory J. Walters, 1995

Energy, by Joseph R. Rudolph, Jr., 1995

A Bibliographic History of the Book, by Joseph Rosenblum, 1995

Psychology, by the Editors of Salem Press (Susan E. Beers, Consulting Editor), 1996

The Search for Economics as a Science, by the Editors of Salem Press (Lynn Turgeon, Consulting Editor), 1996

World Mythology: An Annotated Guide to Collections and Anthologies, by Thomas J. Sienkewicz, 1996

Art, Truth, and High Politics: A Bibliographic Study of the Official Lives of Queen Victoria's Ministers in Cabinet, 1843–1969, by John Powell, 1996

Popular Physics and Astronomy, by Roger Smith, 1996

Paradise Lost, by P. J. Klemp, 1996

The Kings of Medieval England, c. 560–1485, by Larry W. Usilton, 1996

Propaganda in Twentieth Century War and Politics, by Robert Cole, 1996

Social Movement Theory and Research, by Roberta Garner and John Tenuto, 1997

Social Movement Theory and Research

An Annotated Bibliographical Guide

Roberta Garner
and
John Tenuto

Magill Bibliographies

The Scarecrow Press, Inc.
Lanham, Md., & London
and
Salem Press
Pasadena, Calif. / Englewood Cliffs, N.J.
1997

SCARECROW PRESS, INC.

Published in the United States of America
by Scarecrow Press, Inc.
4720 Boston Way
Lanham, Maryland 20706

4 Pleydell Gardens, Folkestone
Kent CT20 2DN, England

British Cataloguing-in-Publication Information Available

Library of Congress Cataloging-in-Publication Data

Garner, Roberta.
Social movement theory and research : an annotated bibliographical
guide / by Roberta Garner and John Tenuto.
p.   cm. — (Magill bibliographies)
1. Social movements—Bibliography. 2. Ideology—Bibliography.
3. Social change—Bibliography. 4. Collective behavior—Bibliography.
I. Tenuto, John. II. Title. III. Series.
Z7164.S66G38   1996   016.30348'4—dc20   96–26900   CIP

ISBN 0-8108-3197-X (cloth : alk.paper)

⊗™ The paper used in this publication meets the minimum requirements of
American National Standard for Information Sciences—Permanence of
Paper for Printed Library Materials, ANSI Z39.48–1984.
Manufactured in the United States of America.

Ref.
Z
7164
.S66
638
1997

Contents

FIFTY YEARS OF SOCIAL MOVEMENT THEORY: AN INTERPRETATION

by Roberta Garner

Introduction

This essay reviews social movement theory from the end of World War II to the mid-1990's, focusing primarily on the United States, with some attention to European scholarship as well. It divides the history of the field into three major periods with distinct paradigms, key concepts, and patterns of research. For each period, a number of key themes, works, and terms are discussed. The shifts are related to the internal development of the field, intellectual currents in the larger culture, and changes in movements themselves. The basic premise of this essay is that the story of social movement theory can be told only together with the story of social movements themselves. Perhaps more than any other field of sociology, the study of social movements is volatile because the phenomena under consideration change so rapidly. Despite the existence of distinct periods in the postwar history of the field, there are also major continuities in theory and value orientations, and these are summarized in the conclusion.

This essay focuses on social movement theory, the project of creating a unified and coherent definition and explanation of social movements and related phenomena. Social movements are usually defined as collectivities engaged in noninstitutionalized discourses and practices aimed at changing the existing condition of society. This definition is itself subject to some controversy, but enough agreement exists within the field to make it a useful starting point. To say that discourses and practices (or behavior) are not institutionalized implies that they are not recognized as recurrent, widely diffused, and legitimate in a society. Among the adherents and supporters of a social movement, however, these discourses and practices are defined positively; this consensus is one of the characteristics that makes a movement different from criminal behavior and other forms of deviance. In movements, the challenge is always explicit and collective.

Explaining the emergence and consequence of movements is a theoretical problem that has undergone considerable change in the last fifty years. This essay looks at the ways in which sociologists approach general, theoretical issues. The bibliography, in contrast, covers research studies of specific movements and research methods for studying movements, as well as activists' memoirs of their experiences in movements.

1

Change in Fields of Knowledge

This essay begins with a consideration of how fields of knowledge change and why change is especially dramatic in social movement theory. This discussion of change in fields of knowledge provides a background for understanding the rapid shifts that took place in social movement theory in the second half of the twentieth century, which are the subject of the remainder of the essay.

A paradigm is an approach that scientists use to understand the subject matter of their field (Kuhn, 1962). (Citations are to items in the "Works Cited" section at the conclusion of this essay.) A paradigm includes concepts and theories, research methodologies, a body of knowledge, and a sense of the major solved and unsolved problems in the field. A field can have one single paradigm, when there is consensus in the community of scientists, or multiple competing paradigms. Most fields of study at some point undergo paradigm shifts, when the community of scientists changes its basic approach (or approaches) to the subject matter of the field. These shifts are responses to internal and external pressures.

Internal Imperatives

Internal imperatives are unsolved puzzles within the existing paradigms of the field (Kuhn, 1962). The existing theories and their accompanying research methodologies appear to be unable to explain some part of the phenomena at hand. Consensus builds within the community of scientists that a new approach is necessary to solve these puzzles. New paradigms are formulated (or borrowed from related fields) to provide tentative theoretical explanations and research approaches to these unsolved puzzles. For example, biology as a field was transformed after World War II by the introduction of the theories and methods of chemistry; these new approaches were associated with the discovery of the structure of DNA.

Puzzles are recognized and paradigms are formulated, revised, and replaced by new paradigms within a set of social relations of scientific and scholarly production—university teaching, mentorship, colleagueship, government and foundation funding processes, coauthorship, the refereeing of scholarly journals and grant proposals, the formation of research teams and organizations, and so on. Most scholars within a field are familiar with the paradigm shifts in their own field; some may defend the existing paradigms, others may be eager to develop new ones. The teaching of graduate students, the funding of proposals, the assessment of institutional prestige, and the selection of articles in refereed publications are all sites of controversies associated with the rise of new paradigms.

When asked to provide a narrative of the history of the field, scholars often reconstruct such histories in terms of internal problems, puzzles, and paradigm shifts.

External Pressures: Intellectual Currents

Fields also respond to external pressures, which may be experienced directly or may operate indirectly to change the field by influencing the perception of puzzles and paradigms. The external pressures are far more varied in nature than are the internal processes of change and can be understood only by examining societies and cultures within which the community of scientists functions.

At least two distinct types of external pressure can be identified. One type is composed of shifts in larger intellectual fashions and currents. Scientific fields, despite all their arcane terminology, elaborated theories, and specialized research techniques, are not immune to these changes in the larger social and intellectual climate. These fashions, which often are based on the popularization and expansion of scientific theories, like Darwinism at the beginning of the twentieth century and psychoanalysis at mid-century, can influence the direction of scholarly work. Whatever their point of origin, expanding intellectual currents come to influence the formation of paradigms in many areas of scholarly inquiry, especially in the humanities and social sciences.

External Pressures: Changes in the Phenomena Themselves

A second, distinct external pressure in some fields (but not all) comes from changes in the phenomena themselves. Fields in which the phenomena are likely to change are termed historical or evolutionary. These include fields as different as astrophysics, evolutionary biology, and the social sciences (because all human action is historically situated). Other fields (such as physiological psychology or organic chemistry) appear to be more protected from such changes in the "real world" of the phenomena that they examine; the phenomena themselves are unlikely to change within the time frame of scientific inquiry. Changes in these fields cannot be explained in terms of changes in the phenomena; for example, the discovery of DNA was not caused by a change in the molecular structure of genes.

In practice, often it is difficult to divide inquiry so neatly into fields that are historical (subject to a linear, nonreversible flow of time, constituted by nonrepeatable changes in phenomena, and generally not subject to experimentation) and those that are not historical. Although the social sciences are concerned with historically situated human behavior, many social science paradigms proceed as if time is not a relevant dimension;

for example, neoclassical economics, behavioral psychology, small group research in sociology, and some ethnographic research in anthropology choose to set aside the consideration of the historical dimension. Other areas of the social sciences—for example, studies of regimes and voting behavior in political science and social movement research—must respond to historical change in the phenomena themselves.

The Volatile Nature of the Social Movements Field

All three of these pressures are experienced in the study of social and political movements: internal paradigm shifts found in all fields of inquiry; external shifts associated with larger intellectual fashions and currents; and external shifts associated with the phenomena themselves, which I will henceforth refer to as historical circumstances. The interaction of all three pressures—and the major impact of historical circumstances—results in a highly volatile field.

Movements—by definition—are processes of change (or, at least, attempted change). Compared to the subject matter of many other social science fields and subfields of sociology, they shift quite rapidly. The study of movements is embedded in history to an exceptional degree and must respond to changes in movements themselves, in contrast to many other areas of sociology that examine either large, stable, institutional structures or the relatively invariant formal properties of interactions in small groups. In contrast to scholars involved in both the sociological micro and macro perspectives, the student of social movements can count on significant change in the phenomena on a scale of years or decades.

The volatility of the field is compounded by the intricate relationship between intellectual fashions and social movements themselves; the phenomena to be studied (movements) have direct and indirect impacts on intellectual activity. For example, Marxism and feminism are not only ideologies of movements but also ways of thinking that have impacts in the social sciences. The boundaries between ideology and theory, intellectual trends and movement perspectives, and activism in the society and activism in the discipline are blurred. The neat boundaries between knower and known that characterize many sciences are difficult to sustain in the study of social movements.

Overview of the Analysis

I propose to trace paradigm shifts in the social movement field over a fifty-year period, roughly from the end of World War II to the mid-1990's. The rhythms of paradigm shifts in the field of social movements are complex, as each source of change has its own trajectory that is somewhat but not entirely independent of the others. Three distinct periods, however, can be identified. Each period has its set of paradigms, not a single dominant one but a linked set of leading paradigms. Each period has distinct themes conveyed by key terms, objects of research, research methods, and value orientations toward social movements. The periods overlap somewhat, and as each period reaches culmination, its dominant paradigms are already being challenged by forerunners and prototypes of the paradigms that characterize the following period.

The first period was characterized by negative orientations toward social movements and a tendency to explain them in terms of social psychology. In the 1940's and 1950's, responding to the intellectual popularity of psychoanalysis and the "real world" impact of Nazism, fascism, Stalinism, and lynchings and race riots, social movement theory pointed to the irrational origins of movements, using the paradigms of psychoanalytic theory, social psychology, collective behavior, and mass society theory. In the 1950's, McCarthyism (unintentionally) stimulated theories of status politics that persisted into the 1960's. Structural strain theories that focused on individual and collective interpretations of societal problems began to emerge around 1960 and formed a bridge to the social movement theories of the second period.

In the second period, social movement theories were based on more positive orientations toward movements. More emphasis was placed on movements as organizations undertaking rational strategies to change structural conditions. In the 1960's, social movements emerged that stimulated movement theorists to take a more favorable look at the phenomena they studied. The Civil Rights movement, anticolonial independence movements, and the Prague Spring drew support from academics; so too, though perhaps with less consensus, did the New Left, student movements, and the movement against the war in Vietnam. All these movements were interpreted as forces for progress toward democracy, inclusion, and equality or more equity among global regions. Rational choice models and a revived interest in Marxism became fashionable in the general intellectual environment; social movement theorists developed Marxist and resource mobilization theories to integrate these trends into their field. These theories emphasized rational action undertaken in the effort to change structural conditions.

By the 1970's, the New Social Movements appeared in Europe. They were characterized by fragmentation of movement structure, an ambiguous class base, and antigovernment left-libertarian ideologies. With these new social movements of environmentalists, feminists, gay persons, peace activists, and urban grassroots mobilizations came New Social

Movement theory, forming a bridge from the second to the third period.

The third period could be labeled the period of deconstruction. From the late 1970's to the 1990's, new movements emerged that were less in concert with the liberal, democratic, pluralist, and/or left-wing values of social movement scholars. These new movements could not be seen as embodying progress toward inclusive, egalitarian, and democratic societies. Ultranationalist movements in the post-Communist regions, a new right, the resurgence of Nazism and ethnoracism, religious fundamentalism in both the Christian and Islamic worlds, identity politics and racial politics in the United States, and the deteriorating conditions of Third World socialist states all led to a more negative assessment of movements.

Intellectual fashions had shifted to poststructural theory and deconstructionism, often pursued most vigorously in feminist studies and cultural studies. According to these new intellectual currents, all human phenomena are socially constructed in ongoing processes of cultural discourse and interaction; hence, there is no bedrock for human society, either in the individual or in social structures. What theorists in the past had viewed as stable structures of society and individual personalities are now understood to be processes of discourse and interaction through which "society" and "the individual" are constituted. The fixity, stability, and coherence once associated with terms such as "society," "social structure," and "the individual" (or "the subject") are now viewed as illusions produced by these discursive formations.

Social movement theorists responded to new realities and new intellectual fashions by proposing theories based on concepts such as culture, framing, and the construction of identity. Increasing attention was given to the dynamics of movements and countermovements, to transnational activism and cross-border issues, and to the relation of movements to media. There was a revived interest in social psychological theories, now focused on the process of forming collective identities.

The new value orientation, in social movement scholarship as well as in the larger currents of cultural studies and postmodern philosophy, is increasingly self-reflective and ironic. Movement research carries a subtext that movements are both manipulative and manipulated forms of social action, and that all collective identities are arbitrary.

Despite these discontinuities in the social movements field, there are also continuities: Some theoretical and research questions persist throughout. So does a value orientation toward an open and self-reflective society, even though a belief in progress has become problematic. This underlying value orientation will be explored in the last section of the review essay.

The First Period: Emphasizing the Irrational

Overview

The first period, running roughly from 1945 to 1960, can be characterized as the period during which the irrationality of movements was the focus of attention. Some analysts term this the classical period (Mayer, 1991). Social movement studies were dominated by several related paradigms: a general social psychological paradigm, a more specifically psychoanalytic paradigm (in turn influenced by popular culture and intellectual fashions of the period), a mass society paradigm, and a collective behavior paradigm. Most of these paradigms contained the theme of irrationality in movement participation, and several of the paradigms place considerable emphasis on social psychological factors in movement emergence.

In terms of historical circumstances, theory in this period was influenced by Nazism, fascism, Stalinism, and McCarthyism. In the United States, lynchings and race riots directed against African Americans and Hispanics were a matter of concern and were studied as major prototypes of collective behavior. The general value orientation of the period is negative toward social movements.

In terms of intellectual currents, the field was influenced strongly by psychoanalysis, which reached it through several channels. The influences came directly from the role of psychoanalysis in American popular culture and intellectual fashion, as well as from the impact of European psychoanalytic theory on sociology. Psychoanalysis reached sociology through the adaptation of the Frankfurt Institute scholars to the United States. The Frankfurt Institute in pre-Nazi Germany had been a social science research institute that brought together psychoanalysis, Marxism, and the analysis of culture. When most of its leading scholars were forced into exile during the Nazi regime, they adapted their research to the atmosphere of the United States, highlighting their interest in psychoanalysis, culture, and the formation of individual attitudes while downplaying the influence of Marxism.

Internally, the development of social movement theory and research in this period was influenced by the long-standing postclassical micro shift in sociology. In the decades after World War I, sociology turned away from the grand historical theories of Auguste Comte, Karl Marx, Émile Durkheim, and Max Weber and began to focus more on small-scale phenomena. Larger structures, institutions, and organizations increasingly were analyzed in terms of small-scale processes, informal groups, and individual motivations. Examples of these small-scale approaches include the Chicago School's view of city structure in terms of neighborhoods and the human relations researchers' studies of worker interaction in factories. These approaches focused attention on informal processes within larger formal organizations. The growing sophistication of survey research methods also contributed to the development of individual-level data as the bedrock of sociological analysis.

Historical Circumstances

The study of social movements expanded in the United States and Western Europe in the 1940's and early 1950's, at precisely the historical moment when antidemocratic and repressive movement-regimes were major geopolitical forces. The character of movements and movement-regimes was one reason why movement studies in this period emphasized the irrationality of movements.

World War II was the result of the militarization of the competition and conflict among three major movement-states, types of states and societies formed by movements that had attained state power. The oldest of these states were the market democracies, states and societies such as Great Britain, France, and the United States that had formed with the emergence of industrial capitalism, the triumph of liberalism in the classical sense of the term (that is, the separation of state and civil society), and the successes of nationalist movements. These states usually were grouped together loosely as the West. The second type of state involved in this conflict was the Soviet Union, a movement-based regime experimenting with socialism in one country. The third force was the Axis, composed of regimes formed by fascist movements in Japan, Italy, and Nazi Germany, along with their allies and puppet regimes. In these societies, a capitalist economy was combined with a repressive, activist state.

The alliance that won the war—the Western market democracies and the Soviet Union, with its aligned Communist movements—did not survive the end of the conflict. The emergence of conflict between the victors took the form of the Cold War, a nuclear arms race accompanied by regional conflicts in the "Third World." Within a few years of the end of World War II, China and Eastern Europe had been absorbed into the Communist bloc, and war had spread across the Korean peninsula. Within the core nations of each bloc, actual and suspected supporters of the "other side" were purged. The purges generally were more violent in the Communist nations, but with a few exceptions (France and Italy), the market democracies were as thorough in eliminating Communist parties and movements from the political arena as the Communist states were in eliminating "bourgeois" movements and parties.

These historical circumstances gave a somber shading to social movement studies in the West. Political movements were at the heart of the emergence of fascism and Nazism. Genocide, total war, and totalitarianism were seen as the major consequences of the formation of movement regimes.

The repressive nature of the Soviet regime made it more difficult to build a democratic socialist movement in the West, a source of frustration for scholars sympathetic to socialism. Within the market democracies, anti-Communism had taken on a movement character, especially in the form of McCarthyism in the United States (purges of leftists from unions, government agencies, the film industry, and other institutions). Anti-Communism as a mass phenomenon narrowed the limits of political discourse.

Another historical impetus toward movement theory was the phenomenon of crowd behavior. Especially in the United States, crowds were associated with race riots and lynchings. Lynchings and riots perpetrated by whites against people of color—for example, African Americans in Chicago (1919), East St. Louis (1917), and Detroit (1943), and Mexican Americans in Los Angeles (1943)—were a persistent feature of American society in the twentieth century. By the 1930's, the racist nature of Nazism gave a new context to these acts of violence in the United States; they were seen as part of the same larger phenomenon. Social scientists felt impelled to understand the irrational and intolerant side of crowd behavior in order to combat racism in all of its forms. The study of collective behavior (crowds, mobs, panics, fads, riots, hysterias, and so on) became associated with the study of movements. The brutality of many instances of collective behavior contributed to the negative orientation of the researchers toward the phenomena they studied.

Intellectual Fashions and Sociological Paradigms

Work on movements in this period also was influenced by intellectual currents and the paradigms of sociology itself. Sociology and the social sciences had begun in an attempt to answer questions about the nature of modern society as a whole. In its first century, the field bore the stamp of Enlightenment thought and the notion of progress. The important phenomena were those associated with large-scale, irreversible changes in social institutions and the structure of society. Although classical theorists such as Auguste Comte, Karl Marx, Émile Durkheim, and Max Weber conceptualized modern society in different ways, they agreed that the large-scale and irreversible process of modernization was the crucial subject matter of social inquiry. Comte was a positivist who believed in an orderly and cumulative pattern of progress. Marx was influenced by Hegelian thought, which posited a discontinuous flow of history that, nevertheless, ultimately moved toward a higher level of social organization and consciousness. Thus, both Comte and Marx viewed the process of modernization with considerable optimism. Durkheim and Weber were more cautious in their judgment, yet they too saw a definite direction in social change and a cumulative, irreversible movement in history.

After World War I, the intellectual tide turned, perhaps because the slaughter of hundreds of thousands of young men shook faith in progress and the forward motion of history. Smaller-scale processes and individual-level phenomena became the focal point of inquiry and were seen as the fundamental level of analysis. The individual, interaction between individuals, and small groups constituted society. Society was a summation of processes within and between individuals, not a grand structure. Empirical studies in the 1920's and 1930's focused on neighborhoods within cities, the adaptation of individuals to immigration, and the workings of small groups within institutions such as factories. This small-scale focus continued in social movement theories during and after World War II.

Two other intellectual forces contributed to the development of small-scale and individually oriented paradigms. One was the influence of psychoanalysis. The second was the growing sophistication of survey research.

Psychoanalysis had survived the flight from Nazi Germany into exile in England and the United States, but it had suffered a sea change. From an intellectual venture that questioned the foundations of bourgeois morality, it became a professional practice that helped individuals adjust to society. It came increasingly under the aegis of the medical profession. In Europe in the 1920's, a number of intellectuals influenced by psychoanalysis were also influenced by Marxism, in both its orthodox Communist forms and more heterodox perspectives. Wilhelm Reich and Otto Fenichel as individuals and the Frankfurt Institute as a collective enterprise looked for the links between psychoanalysis and Marxism as radical and subversive visions of human society. The scholars and analysts who migrated to the United States were forced by direct and indirect pressures to abandon this line of inquiry. The "Americanization of the unconscious" did not, however, completely disrupt the effort to use psychoanalytic insights to understand social phenomena; many scholars turned first to fascist and Nazi movements as the objects of psychoanalytically influenced research (Jacoby, 1983; Seeley, 1967).

The micro-emphasis of sociology in the immediate postwar period was accelerated by the availability of new research tools, especially survey methods and the growing sophistication of multivariate analysis. Researchers in many subfields of sociology (not only social movement theory) became intrigued with the possibility of understanding culture and social processes as the outcome of the sum total of individual attitudes.

The first period thus is marked by a convergence of several forces: a negative orientation toward movements associated with the role of Nazism, fascism, Stalinism, and McCarthyism, as well as scholars' opposition to race riots, lynchings, and ethnocentric prejudice; the influence of micro paradigms in sociology; the influence of psychoanalysis on the study of intrapersonal processes, with a consequent emphasis on the irrational roots of human action; and the growth of survey research, which also focused on individual attitudes as the fundamental object of study.

Themes of the First Period
Each period has its distinct analytical themes that guided empirical research. These themes are associated with key terms and concepts, which are emphasized for the reader's convenience. In the first period, these themes included the following.

1. The object of analysis in the study of social movements is first and foremost the *individual*. Research needs to focus on why and how individuals join social movements and on characteristics that distinguish those individuals who join a movement from those who do not. Cultural forces become manifest and subject to empirical research as they are transformed into individual *motivations*, predispositions, and propensities. The concept of *personality* is a useful and valid way of referring to consistency in individuals' motivations, attitudes, beliefs, and predispositions, consistency that persists over time and across social roles. The study of social movements is closely linked to social psychology.

2. Ideology—the belief system of a movement—is secondary, a determined rather than determining element. Individuals' beliefs are shaped by their personality, that is, by their *psychological propensities*, or are formed by *informal micro-pressures* in the individual's immediate personal environment. Attitudes held by individuals, rather than the ideas of the belief system as an abstract system of thought, are the key focus for the study of beliefs.

3. The phenomenon of *mass society*, a state of society in which individuals are dislodged from stable social groups and made more vulnerable to movement appeals, is a useful concept linking the study of individual behavior to analysis of larger social changes. Analysis should focus on examining how individual conditions such as *alienation* and cultural conditions such as *anomie* (normlessness) are connected to the emergence of social movements. Mass society generates social movements—they are a response to a loss of traditional anchors, because individuals who are detached from stable communities seek new forms of collective commitment.

4. Social movement theory is closely connected to *collective behavior theory*. Phenomena such as panics, hysterias, fads, and crowd behavior

are related to movements and probably represent early stages of movement formation that later expand and stabilize into movements. Movements are closely associated with the irrational phenomena studied by collective behavior researchers—fads, panics, hysterias, lynchings, and other crowd behavior. Crowds and mobs bring about, on a small scale, what mass society does on a large scale. They separate the individual from anchoring in primary groups such as the family, stable secondary relationships (such as residential communities and trade unions), and normal routines, including conventional political behavior, and thereby make him or her more susceptible to irrational pressures. Conditions of mass society, in turn, make individuals more susceptible to pressures to participate in collective behavior.

5. An underlying orientation of most researchers toward the movements they study is that movements are related to threats against liberal democratic institutions and democratic pluralism, whether these originate largely outside the liberal-democratic societies (fascism, Nazism, and Communist movements) or within them (McCarthyism, lynching, race riots, and movements based on ethnocentrism and prejudice). Movements threaten the functioning of public institutions in liberal democracies. Movements are associated with authoritarian individual predispositions and with intolerant attitudes and actions. Movements on both the left and the right ends of the spectrum can be labeled as authoritarian and even totalitarian (Arendt, 1951; Christie & Jahoda, 1954).

6. Social movement theories need to examine *attitudes*, especially antidemocratic ones, held by individuals. Social movement research should examine the extent of attitudes that are antidemocratic, anti-Semitic, racist, or authoritarian and explore the question of the social strata or social milieus and life experiences with which these attitudes are associated. Attitudes are a basic object of survey research. Survey research clarifies what beliefs are held by *elites* and in *mass publics*. The concept of attitude also can be used to analyze how individuals organize their personal belief systems, including the resolution of *cognitive dissonance* (holding two or more inconsistent beliefs).

Major Theoretical and Empirical Studies

Analysis of social movements and collective behavior as a modern field of study has origins in the late nineteenth century. It began with a negative orientation toward crowd behavior and movements. Gustave LeBon's (1897) and G. Tarde's (1903) negative assessment of crowds and Sigmund Freud's dismissive views of group psychology (1921/1959) were echoed in the early twentieth century in the work of Robert Park and E. Burgess. Park is credited with first using the term "collective behavior."

His writing with Burgess shows the influence of LeBon in the use of such concepts as suggestibility, contagion, and the crowd's submission to a leader. Park and Burgess also saw that collective behavior was a force for change. As early as 1903, Park had suggested that crowds and publics dissolve old ties and bring individuals into new relationships (Turner & Killian, 1987).

Park and the Chicago School had an important role in shifting the emerging academic field of sociology away from large-scale theories of social structure and social change toward small-scale empirical studies of social processes. With this general shift came a first definition of the collective behavior and social movements field that oriented it toward crowd behavior and social psychological factors in movement formation rather than toward the role of movements in political reform and historical change.

Hadley Cantril's *The Psychology of Social Movements* (1941) marks the beginning of the first period. It offers an explanation of social movements in largely psychological terms and continues to make use of the concept of suggestibility.

Theodor Adorno, E. Frenkel-Brunswick, D. Levinson, and R. Sanford's *The Authoritarian Personality* (1993/1950) is the key work of the first period. To describe it as a social psychological or psychoanalytically influenced research project is accurate but understated; the first author, Adorno, was associated with the Frankfurt Institute and critical theory, so the study develops a philosophy of history and society as well as an application of psychoanalysis and social psychological perspectives to the study of movements and ideologies. Adorno and his coworkers set out to understand the sources of fascism. They saw the appeal of fascism in the interaction between cultural themes and individual predispositions. Blind submission to the charismatic leadership of the Führer or Duce, the desire to submerge the self in the group, the distrust of ambiguity and complexity, the passion for scapegoating, a mystique of strength and toughness, the constitution of all relationships in terms of command and subordination, and deep fears of sexual deviance and contamination all are elements of this predisposition. Adorno saw fascism and related movements as both drawing on and amplifying these predispositions. These characteristics of individuals, cultures, and movement ideologies made possible the horrors of the Third Reich, especially genocide based on virulent racism and justified by obedience to the Führer and to the hierarchy of the regime as well as the predisposition to "follow orders." The researchers developed a scale, the F-scale, to measure authoritarian tendencies. Adorno believed that these predispositions could be found in many modern societies and had by no means been brought to an end with the military defeat of the

Axis; this premise was connected to Adorno's pessimism about modern society. This apparently most psychological of studies also was a questioning of the structure and culture of modern societies; like other leading thinkers in the social sciences, Adorno was able to encompass individual and cultural levels of analysis.

In *Social Change and Prejudice* (1964), a study of veterans, Bruno Bettelheim and Morris Janowitz examined downward mobility and prejudice in the United States, developing a similar analysis of authoritarianism, racism, and anti-Semitism as rooted in individual experiences and personality characteristics. While these researchers looked for the explanation of Nazism and fascism in cultural and individual propensities, Edward Shils and Morris Janowitz (1948) supplemented these perspectives with sociological micro-analyses, based on interviews with Germans who had fought in the Wehrmacht. They found that willingness to fight was not so much a result of ideological indoctrination or belief in the Nazi state as it was the result of personal ties, both hierarchical ties to noncommissioned officers and more egalitarian ones to other enlisted men. The functioning of the Nazi movement-state had to be understood in terms of networks of cohesive personal relationships.

As public concern shifted from Nazism and fascism to Communism in the Soviet bloc, the topics of social movement analyses also shifted, but many of the explanatory frameworks remained the same. The Korean War experience of brainwashing generated a number of studies that searched for psychological and social sources of susceptibility to ideological as well as physical pressures to cooperate with captors. Gabriel Almond's *The Appeals of Communism* (1954) related ideological motivation to individual motives. The individual within a national political culture was the focus of Almond and Sidney Verba's *The Civic Culture: Political Attitudes and Democracy in Five Nations* (1963), which examined the orientations and ideological dispositions of individual citizens toward the political order. Richard Christie and Marie Jahoda's edited volume, *Studies in the Scope and Method of "The Authoritarian Personality"* (1954) included efforts to define authoritarianism on the Left as well as on the Right, encompassing Communism and especially its Stalinist variant, as well as the radical right. Robert Lane's *Political Ideology* (1962) presented in-depth analyses of individual attitudes toward the political system. Harold Lasswell and Daniel Lerner's *World Revolutionary Elites* (1966) gave more attention to demographic and structural variables in the formation of the elites associated with Soviet, fascist, Nazi, Kuomintang (Chinese Nationalist), and Chinese Communist movements and states, but it was also informed by Lasswell's interest in the social psychology of political action.

Anti-Communism became a focus of sociological analysis when it took on some movement characteristics in the form of McCarthyism and the activities of the House Un-American Activities Committee in the United States. Constriction of civil liberties, loyalty oath requirements, witch-hunt-like purges of institutions, the execution of Julius and Ethel Rosenberg on the basis of ambiguous evidence, and the absence of critical voices in the major media all suggested that anti-Communism had developed characteristics akin to panics, hysterias, and mob action. Today, social movement theorists might prefer the term "countermovement" to describe these behaviors, which were on the borderline between mobilizations and institutionalized social control, but at the time it was not yet in use. In a cautious and subdued study, *Communism, Conformity, and Civil Liberties* (1955), Samuel Stouffer turned survey research methods on these problems to discover the social sources of support for civil liberties. The research team found that established elites were more respectful of these rights (although in hindsight, it is difficult to avoid the conclusion that these elites did little to support civil liberties until very late in the process). Although this study was less an inquiry into micro and irrational sources of movements than an analysis of sources of opposition to top-down mobilizations, it shared with such studies a focus on individual-level data; the propensities, experiences, demographic characteristics, and attitudes of individuals—not characteristics of social structure—were the object of analysis. Edward Shils's *Torment of Secrecy* (1956) was an essay about the importance of insulating decision-making elites from mass pressures and gave more attention to contrasting institutional structures, not only attitudes, in England and the United States.

Not all studies focused on geopolitical movements and mobilizations. An influential study of the period was Leon Festinger, Henry Riecken, and Stanley Schachter's *When Prophecy Fails* (1956), a participant observer study of a cult. The focus was how individuals in the cult coped with cognitive dissonance, reconciling their beliefs in the end of the world with the fact that it had not come to an end on the appointed day. The analysis gave powerful insights into intrapersonal processes of constructing ideologies.

Amid all these studies of specific cases of ideologies and movements primarily focused at the level of analyzing individual attitudes (or demographic background characteristics of individual activists), Herbert Blumer (1946) published a key article about symbolic interactionist approaches to the field of social movements and collective behavior. For Blumer, as for other symbolic interactionists, movements and collective behavior were to be understood as collective enterprises to establish a new social order. All social phenomena must be understood as actions—

ongoing, processual, and shared constructions of the social world. These actions are based on communication in symbols. Through these actions and interactions using symbols, individuals constantly renegotiate the symbolic representations that they make to themselves and to others. Blumer and other social interactionists did not make a neat distinction between institutionalized and noninstitutionalized behavior, between movements and collective behavior on one hand and structures on the other hand; collective behavior, like all human action, is situated and spontaneous—it is more spontaneous and less programmed by customs or rules than other human action. Blumer differed from many of the social psychological theorists in that he "did not regard collective behavior as pathological, destructive behavior" (Turner & Killian, 1987, p. 11). The representations that form the basis of collective behavior are not necessarily irrational, and the associated actions could be pragmatic. In many respects, Blumer's perspective was ahead of its time, not fully coming into its own until the third period. Symbolic interactionists' emphasis on the social construction of social reality remained something of a subterranean tradition of sociology in the 1950's and 1960's.

Characterizing the first period as concerned with social psychological paradigms should not lead one to overlook the importance of mass society theory. Adorno's work had already pointed to the dialectic of culture and individual propensities; the mass society theorists, drawing on the same traditions of European critical theory as Adorno, elaborated the cultural side. Modern society is conceptualized as mass society. It is characterized by states of alienation and anomie, of disintegration of traditional social ties and weakening of the normative order. As the fabric of social ties to communities, classes, and families shreds and the moral order "thins out," individuals become susceptible to ideological appeals, promises to reconstitute social relationships and moral order in a new, politicized, and anti-institutional framework. Elements of mass society theory appeared in the work of Hannah Arendt (1951), in conservative social thought, in the work of Harold Lasswell and Daniel Lerner, and most explicitly in William Kornhauser's *The Politics of Mass Society* (1959).

Some of the influence of psychology and psychoanalysis waned during the 1950's, and within academic sociology, the field of social movements became increasingly identified with the analysis of collective behavior, especially in key works of synthesis such as Turner and Killian (1957) and Lang and Lang (1961).

McCarthyism was one of the phenomena analyzed in theories of the first period, which focused on the irrational and antidemocratic themes of social movements, but it later became the basis for new directions in social movement theory. The study of anti-Communist mobilizations in the

United States stimulated the search for new perspectives, most notably the concept of *status politics*. Interpretations of political behavior by Seymour Martin Lipset (1960), Joseph Gusfield's study of Prohibition (1963), and the analysis of the authoritarian right edited by Daniel Bell (1964) began to focus attention on ways in which strains associated with social status, instead of class, could generate movements, especially those on the conservative end of the spectrum. The work of historians of American social movements raised similar questions about antidemocratic or right-wing tendencies in populism in the United States. Social scientists read Richard Hofstadter's *The Age of Reform* (1955) and a new edition of C. Vann Woodward's study of Tom Watson (1963), a southern populist, to gain insight into why class discontent was translated into right-wing rather than left-wing activism. These studies began to point the way toward the analysis of structural pressures in the emergence of movements. They form a bridge to the second period.

The Second Period: Movements as Rational Actors Within Social Structures

Overview

The second major period became identifiable in the 1960's and persists to the present, although after the mid-1970's, its leading paradigms were modified by the themes of the third stage. The second period was characterized by emphasis on rational action within structural constraints. It involved three distinct paradigms. Early in the period, when formulations were still influenced by social psychological models, the *structural strain* paradigm emerged; later it was joined, and to some extent replaced by, *Marxist* and *resource mobilization* paradigms. These paradigms were influenced by larger currents such as the revitalization of Western Marxism and a growing interest in rational choice models and organizational behavior studies in the social sciences. The relevant historical phenomena were the Civil Rights movement, the national liberation or decolonization movements, the student movements, the Prague Spring, and (somewhat later) the women's movement and environmental movements. The general orientation of scholars toward the movements they studied began in a favorable light, but the positive orientation trailed off toward a more negative one after the mid-1970's.

Historical Circumstances

By the late 1950's and decisively by the 1960's, new movements had emerged in the United States and the world scene that contributed to new theoretical and research perspectives in the field. Several types of move-ments were crucial to the reassessment of movements in academic soci-ology and political science. The Civil Rights movement in the United States and the decolonization movements in the colonial empires were among the most important movements for redefining social movement theory as the analysis of how movement organizations undertake to reform or abolish oppressive institutions. The Civil Rights movement was the key factor in swinging emphasis in the social movements field from an analysis of the largely irrational characteristics of participants to a focus on rational actions aimed at reforming or transforming limiting social structures. Also important was a growing peace movement directed against the arms race and atomic testing. In the United States, the move-ment against the war in Vietnam drew together peace activism and support for decolonization.

Not only did specific movements shift the focus of analysis in the field, but intellectual currents among political elites and in the general culture also produced a sense that reform was both legitimate and rational. Welfare state activism in Europe, as well as the Great Society and War on Poverty programs of the Kennedy and Johnson administrations in the United States, contributed to the reform climate. The 1959 Bad Godesberg program of the SPD (the Socialist Party of West Germany) marked the willingness of socialists to make ideological concessions in return for involvement in building West German institutions.

At the same time that these reform agendas were set in motion, more radical movements and intellectual currents questioned the very structures that were being reformed. Whether they defined themselves as Marxist or not, component movements of the New Left began to use terms such as "capitalism" and "power structure" to define the source of social prob-lems. Western Marxism enjoyed a major revival, especially in Western Europe, where it became the leading ideology of younger intellectuals (Anderson, 1976). Its influence remained more limited in the United States. Journals of independent socialist thought were founded in this period, the most notable and lasting of which were the *New Left Review* and *Monthly Review*.

All these intellectual activities, even if they did not directly involve social movement theorists, created an atmosphere of legitimacy for social movements. Social movements were not problems but instead were the source of solutions to problems.

Intellectual Currents and Internal Paradigm Changes

These external forces were combined inextricably with internal pro-cesses in the social movements field, namely the coming of age of a new generation of sociologists, part of the general expansion of graduate education and universities in both the United States and Western Europe. The 1960's was a growth period of the profession, associated with the Baby Boom, social mobility into academia, and the expansion of graduate programs. Thanks to the economic boom and government support for educational opportunities, children and grandchildren of the European ethnic working class were able to attend colleges and universities, and they brought a new ferment to academic life in the United States. It was an exciting period of intellectual conflict and dissent, as well as a period of expanding opportunities to publish and teach. Graduate students and young academics made a large volume of contributions to social movement theory after 1960; some of them were themselves movement activists. Those who were not activists—probably the majority, according to Margit Mayer (1991)—were nevertheless sympathetic to the goals of many movements, especially the Civil Rights movement and other movements directed at extending citizenship rights.

These internal developments were not unique to the social movement field. All of sociology shifted to more attention to social structure and away from the individual as the unit of analysis. The themes of social structure and macro processes that had absorbed the classical theorists—Marx, Weber, and Durkheim—reappeared in the teaching of sociology and in new developments in sociological theory. *Structure* became a key concept of the whole field. It referred to the patterning of activities and relationships, abstracted from and existing independently of individual motivations. Structure can be thought of as a set of limiting conditions on individual action. For the new wave of structural theorists, structure was seen as a phenomenon that existed objectively and could be studied objectively.

The emphasis on structure rather than individual motivation was associated with the belief that institutions had to be changed in order to change society. As C. Wright Mills (1959) had defined it, the sociological imagination was the ability to see personal troubles as public issues. The new wave of social movement theorists saw social movements as the most powerful way to translate the sociological imagination into collective action.

Three major paradigms characterize the second period of postwar social movement theory: *Structural strain*, *resource mobilization*, and *structural Marxism*. Although in some respects these paradigms are opposed to one another, they converged on several major assumptions and themes concerning social movements.

Themes of the Second Period

The second period of social movement theory encompassed a variety of themes, including the following.

1. Movements are best understood in terms of *organizations* and organizational behavior.

2. Whatever one might think of the goals (or ends) of movements, their strategies (or means) usually are *rational*. The means-rationality of strategies is embodied in movement organizations that behave much like any organization.

3. A major activity of movement organizations is *mobilizing* different types of constituencies in a variety of ways in order to obtain needed resources. *Resources* can be construed very broadly to include the time and energy of activists, funds, arms, media support, and so on.

4. The *organizational form* and *resource mobilizing strategies* of movements make them quite similar to *institutionalized* forms of action.

5. Collective behavior phenomena (crowds, mobs, panics, rumors, and so on) are associated with movements because they are deliberately produced elements of movement tactics. They are not the "primordial matter" of social movements (a raw material from which movements eventually form) but a "manufactured product" of social movements (incidents that movements plan to generate as part of their strategies and tactics).

6. Movement actions take place within *structures* that limit but do not completely or mechanically determine actions. These structures can be studied as objectively existing conditions. A major factor in movement behavior is the *political opportunity structure*, or form of political institutions, which may constrain movement strategies.

7. Movements have complex relationships to one another (as competitors for resources, coalition partners, and mutually opposing *countermovements*) and to societal elites. They operate in *multiorganizational fields* formed by many organizations including other movements, interest groups, and government agencies.

8. Although the Marxist paradigm diverges markedly from resource mobilization in many fundamental respects, it converges with it in seeing movement behavior as generally a set of rational responses to an environment conceptualized in social structural terms. Although resource mobilization theory remains silent on the ultimate rationality of any given movement, Marxist theories evaluate movements in terms of their ideological goals. Resource mobilization theorists tended to be most favorably disposed toward movements that sought to expand civil rights for their members and constituents, movements such as the Civil Rights movement and the farmworkers' union that sought reform within the market democ-

racies. Marxist theory leaned more toward a revolutionary than a reformist view of the social structure of capitalist society.

The Structural Strain Paradigm

The structural strain paradigm was chronologically the first of the second-period paradigms and in many respects bridges the earlier social psychological approaches and the second-period structural models. The varieties of the structural strain paradigm focused on the interrelationship between a problem in society—the structural strain—and the formation of movements to address the problem. Unlike many of the collective behavior and social psychological paradigms, the structural strain paradigm posits a considerable degree of "out-there-ness" to the strain. The strain is, at least in part, an objectively existing condition as well as a state of tension among social actors. Given this objectively existing strain, what needs to be explained is how and when actors come together to form a movement. Different forms of structural strain models were proposed to explain how strains are perceived and communicated. T. R. Gurr (1970) emphasized the anger and frustration caused by macro-social strain and began to develop quantitative measures for instances of strain and rebellion. Also important was a relative deprivation model that suggested that strain is perceived in a process of comparison; movements are formed when people see themselves as deprived relative to a reference group. In the model proposed by James Davies (1962), the trajectory of reform itself is part of the strain; initial efforts by elites to undertake reforms create higher expectations, and when these expectations are not met or even are reversed, social movements emerge. Here the perceived deprivation and point of comparison lies in the future.

The most inclusive and elaborated of the structural strain models was proposed by Neil Smelser in *Theory of Collective Behavior* (1963). His six-stage value-added theory includes structural strain as an explanatory factor as well as more psychological, ideological, and processual components, termed "generalized beliefs," "leadership and communication" and "precipitating incidents." Smelser also included another structural factor, structural conduciveness, as the first element of the model; it referred to the possibilities for movement organization inherent in the political and social circumstances of the society. Smelser's sixth stage, "response of social control agents," also pointed to the limitations and possibilities for a movement in a specific political system. In all these models, there was some ambiguity about the structural strain, about the extent to which it was really there or existed only as a causal force identified in the belief system of movement participants, not necessarily corresponding to an objectively present characteristic of society.

Although not directly identified with the structural strain paradigm, Joseph Gusfield's *Symbolic Crusade* (1963) uses a similar model, bridging structural and social psychological elements. In his study of the prohibition movement in the early part of the twentieth century, Gusfield applied the term "status politics" to refer to the response to structural strain experienced by the Anglo/Protestant middle classes, especially in small towns, as the United States absorbed increasing numbers of immigrants from Eastern and Southern Europe at the same time that it moved from an agrarian to a manufacturing economy, with accompanying urbanization and industrial concentration. This complex structural strain—with its economic, spatial, and cultural dimensions—was condensed and given symbolic form in the demand for prohibition of alcoholic beverages. Daniel Bell's *The Radical Right* (1964) is an influential edited collection that also explores the structural strains and status anxieties that contributed to movements and currents of opinion on the right end of the spectrum in the United States.

Resource Mobilization and Related Theories

By the mid-1960's, the resource mobilization paradigm had emerged as a major breakthrough. It virtually eliminated the ambiguity inherent in the structural strain model. For resource mobilization theory, it did not matter whether the structural strain existed objectively or only in the minds of participants, whether the perception of strain and the goals of the movement were rational or not, or what symbolic form movement participants gave to the (real or perceived) strain. What mattered were the actions—generally rational actions—undertaken by movement participants to make their movement successful. To be effective, these actions almost always had to be undertaken by movement *organizations*. Resource mobilization pushed toward replacing the study of social movements (seen as currents, ideologies, discourses, and motivations and actions of individuals) by the study of *social movement organizations*. In Max Weber's terms, resource mobilization theory put a premium on *means-rationality*, on the conscious and purposive matching of organizational forms, strategies, and tactics to the desired goals.

The key elements of movements are social movement organizations; these, rather than individuals, are the acting units of the movement and the single most important object of research (Zald & Ash, 1966). Research carried out within the resource mobilization paradigm (and related paradigms) often consisted of studies of specific movement organizations. The case study of a movement organization, or the comparative study of several such organizations, rather than the survey of individual attitudes, was the leading method of the second period.

Movement organizations attempt to reach *constituencies* and assemble possible participants. Resource mobilization theory distinguishes different levels and types of involvement in a movement, differentiating adherents (members and participants), constituencies (the source of resources), and beneficiaries; these types of involvement do not necessarily overlap. Individuals need to be mobilized to take part in the activities that form part of the movement organization's strategies and tactics, but members qua "bodies" are not the only resource that is mobilized; money, arms, elite sponsorship, and media support and the molding of favorable public opinion also are resources. For example, the generally favorable coverage that national media gave the Civil Rights movement was crucial to its success; so was the favorable tilt of the Kennedy Administration, perhaps under Cold War pressure to change the racist image of the United States in the decolonizing regions of the world.

Movement organizations differ in the types and relative proportions of resources they mobilize and in the strategies and tactics they use to accomplish these mobilizations. The effectiveness of different strategies and organizational forms is the focus of William Gamson's *The Strategy of Social Protest* (1975), which suggests that success of a movement is associated with the pursuit of narrow goals, bureaucratic structure, and disruptive methods; large organizations with formal structures are more likely to be coopted (defined as acceptance and legitimacy without tangible benefits); preemptive outcomes (benefits without acceptance) are associated with small, centrally controlled movements. The internal structure of movements is an ongoing topic of resource mobilization theory, beginning with Zald and Ash's (1966) challenge to Robert Michels' "iron law of oligarchy" as far too unilinear a conceptualization of movement structure. The concept of internal structure was reviewed and further developed by Curtis and Zurcher (1974).

Movement professionals have an important role in movement organizations, because all societies by the end of the twentieth century are "organizational societies," in which action for social change requires a high level of technical expertise, especially in the management of resources, strategic planning, fund-raising, pressure on elites, and contact with the media (Zald & McCarthy, 1979, 1987). Movements also may form within organizations; such movements usually are not linked to larger political and ideological issues of the society but are focused on intraorganizational authority (Zald & Berger, 1971).

Resource mobilization theory gives careful attention to *movement environments*. In the broadest terms, an environment includes all the preexisting social infrastructure, including the opportunities and constraints afforded by the political system, other movement organizations,

institutions such as churches and media, and networks of partially institutionalized activists and organizations. A major component of the environment is the *political opportunity structure*, which includes the form of
political institutions in the society, the behavior of incumbent elites, the
level of social control and repression of movements, and intended and
unintended reductions in the level of social control exercised against
movements (Eisinger, 1973; Tarrow, 1988, 1991, 1994; Blackmer &
Tarrow, 1975). In a broad interpretation, it also includes the society's
political culture, which may be supportive for movements or repressive.

Recent work has given attention to comparisons of the same movement
in different national settings—for example, to the antinuclear movement
in different countries—to observe the effects of political cultures and
opportunity structures on movement organization and outcomes. This
method has brought together the study of movement organization and
strategy with an analysis of political opportunity structures and political
cultures (Kitschelt, 1986). In a related development, cross-boundary
issues (and movements targeted at these issues), such as nuclear fallout,
acid rain, and flows of migrants and refugees, also point to the increasing
complexity of political opportunity structures as both national and transnational systems.

Another important component of the environment of any given movement is formed by other movements (which may be in relations of
competition, cooperation, and coalition) and countermovements (if the
relationship is one of conflict and opposition). The term "countermovement" came into prominence after its use by Tahi Mottl (1980). It was
then used by, among others, Mayer Zald and Bert Useem (1987) in the
discussion of the pronuclear power movement as a countermovement to
antinuclear environmental movements, and Useem (1984) in the analysis
of antibusing mobilization in Boston.

The political opportunity structure, political culture, and the dynamics
of movements and countermovements are important factors in determining the size of the social movement sector or social movement industry,
the sum total of such partially institutionalized action and organization in
a given society (Garner & Zald, 1985; McCarthy & Zald, 1987). Some
countries have exceptionally active sectors, with movements and countermovements as a major force in the political arena; other societies, no
less democratic in formal terms, have only intermittent or highly concentrated activism.

The interaction over time of movements with states, nonstate elites
(such as the private media), and countermovements sets in motion cycles
of protest, waves of activity followed by reduction of such activities,
lowered levels of resources for movements, and (in some cases) height-

ened efforts at social control. The tracing of waves of movement activity, or more broadly, collective action, accompanying political change in Europe was the subject of Charles Tilly's research (1978). Using a shorter time frame, Tarrow (1988) analyzed cycles of protest in contemporary Italy. Both scholars refined the method of using newspaper archives to identify incidents of social protest and collective action; when it is applied to a sufficiently long time period, this method creates a large database of incidents that makes possible quantitative analysis.

Some observers of resource mobilization theory point to two slightly different versions of the paradigm. For example, Margit Mayer (1991) distinguishes resource mobilization in the strict sense from a larger, more broadly focused view of movements as rational actors within opportunity structures. According to her, resource mobilization theory sees movements as organizational entrepreneurs that seek to mobilize and routinize resources, including support from elites; this view emphasizes the professionalization of movement organizations. The second, and larger, approach sees movements largely in terms of indigenous protest mobilizations and the political opportunity structures in which they act. This position, exemplified by Aldon Morris' studies (1981, 1984) of the Civil Rights movement, accords such protest movements more authenticity, in the sense of seeing them as more genuinely based in a community rather than created by movement professionals.

The fact that one or another form of resource mobilization theory has been the dominant paradigm of the field since the late 1960's means that there is a very large body of theory and empirical research based on this perspective. Many of the key works of the resource mobilization paradigm took the form of articles in scholarly journals and collections of theoretical and empirical studies. This format was in keeping with the explosive growth of publishing in the social sciences during this period, a surge that was better accommodated in periodicals than in the slower and less expansive book market, although eventually many of the periodical articles were anthologized in book-length collections. Among these studies are Jo Freeman on the formation of second wave feminism and the relationship of the movement to incumbent political elites and institutionally anchored networks of female activists, as well as her editorship of a major collection on movements of the 1960's and 1970's (1973, 1975, 1979, 1983); J. Craig Jenkins and Charles Perrow (1977) on farmworker insurgency and the role of elites in supporting the goals of the movement (1973); Aldon Morris' (1984) study of the internal structure of the Civil Rights movement and the relationship between the Civil Rights movement and preexisting structures and institutions in the African American community, most notably African American churches; and Anthony Oberschall's (1973) general exposition of the resource mobilization framework. John McCarthy and Mayer Zald have a leading position in resource mobilization theory, developing new key terms of the field, carrying out empirical studies of mobilizations that illustrated and refined conceptual development, identifying new directions for empirical research, and publishing major collections of theoretical papers, of which *Social Movements in an Organizational Society* (Zald & McCarthy, 1987) is a prime example.

At the peak of the second period, in a 1983 publication, Jo Freeman pointed out that ideology was a relatively unexplored topic of the period; she astutely connected this conceptual absence to the theorists' positive attitude toward the movements they were analyzing. Her remarks are worth quoting at length, and this issue will come up again in the discussion of the third period.

> More contemporary social movement analysts have tended to downplay the importance of ideology, and like interest-group theorists, to view it as an optional tool in the organizer's arsenal. . . . With a few notable exceptions, the belief systems of most movements in the sixties and seventies were extensions of basic liberal concepts that dominate our public philosophy. Contemporary analysts have simply not seen their motivating force as requiring an explanation. *As movements develop whose ideology is inconsistent with liberal values, we can expect to see greater attention paid to belief systems.* Perhaps the next generation of theorists will agree with Smelser that "beliefs on which collective behavior is based . . . are . . . akin to magical beliefs." (Freeman, 1983, p. 3; emphasis added)

Marxist Theory and Historical Analysis

The Marxist paradigm was the third paradigm of this period. It shared with resource mobilization theory an emphasis on the rationality of movement actions, the need to analyze the structures within which movements acted, and an interest in movement organizations. It differed from the resource mobilization paradigm in three significant respects. One was that it gave more attention to existing structures, not merely as movement environments but as the underlying cause of movements. Movements were not merely means-rational in their relationship to the environment as a source of resources or of opposition but also ends-rational in their attempt to reform or transform these structures. Second, Marxist theories in the final analysis related these structures to capitalism as a social formation; even when analyzing the state or local power elites or colonial situations, they connected these structures to the larger system of capitalism. Third, Marxists tended to be more favorable toward revolutionary movements, whereas resource mobilization theorists were more inclined to study reform movements.

Marxism in the West was not a single undisputed system of ideas (Anderson, 1976). Marxists were divided over many issues, including foundational philosophical questions such as the tensions between the dialectical thought of the Hegelian heritage and structuralist and determinist interpretations of history. The Hegelians gave more attention to the formation of consciousness, the discontinuous flow of history, the idea of society as a totality, and the complex relationship between the knower (or subject) and the known, the social world of which the knower is also a part. The structuralists emphasized the objective nature of social structure, which exists and changes independently of the consciousness of a human subject; their position on the nature of social reality was closer to that of the natural sciences, and they did not find the Hegelian notion of dialectic a useful concept for understanding social change and revolution. Marxists also had more concrete disagreements among themselves about the analysis of socialism in the Soviet Union and China. Both epistemological and substantive divisions were reflected in Marxist theories of social movements in ways that require a more detailed discussion than is possible in this essay. At the same time, many theorists who would not label themselves as Marxists were influenced by Marxist concepts. Thus, it is important to understand that Marxist social movement theory is not a single body of ideas but many overlapping currents. Because Marxist theory cut across many academic disciplines, key works in the Marxist paradigm were not confined to sociology. Some examples of works in this period that used elements of a Marxist analysis follow.

Alice and Staughton Lynd's *Rank and File* (1973) provided eloquent testimony from workers and rank-and-file union members and organizers that gave insight into why people participate in working-class movements. The oral histories begin in the 1930's. The time frame and the authors' orientation place the analysis solidly within a socialist perspective on workplace struggles. Herbert Aptheker's *American Negro Slave Revolts* (1943), widely read in the 1960's, was influential for the generation of young scholars that emerged in the 1960's. In books addressed to a readership of nonspecialists, authors such as Sidney Lens (1966) and Jeremy Brecher (1974) described labor history, radical movements, and working-class insurgencies in the United States.

Marxist historians contributed to theoretical innovation in the social movements field. Eric Hobsbawm's studies of bandits and rebels (1959) show how movements formed as capitalist development penetrated agrarian societies, such as southern Italy and Brazil. E. P. Thompson's detailed *The Making of the English Working Class* (1963) traces the evolution of working-class organizations as the class was transformed from artisans into an industrial proletariat and transformed itself into a political force in society. James Weinstein's *The Decline of Socialism in America* (1967) suggests that the weight of evidence indicates that the socialist movement declined later than had been previously thought and that its decline was more a result of organizational and ideological splintering than of the external force of government repression.

Class relationships and class structure became leading variables for explaining the rise and form of movements, even among scholars who were not inclined to label their work as Marxist. For example, Barrington Moore (1965) used concepts such as class conflict and class structure to explain why societies arrived at liberal-democratic, revolutionary social-ist, or fascist political systems in the twentieth century. Neither was Arthur Stinchcombe a Marxist, but his "Agricultural Enterprise and Rural Class Relationships" (1967) explains the emergence of different types of agrar-ian movements in terms of the class structure of agrarian production; for example, sharecroppers engage in types of movements markedly different from those of farmers who own small amounts of land. Eric Wolf (an anthropologist), in *Peasant Wars of the Twentieth Century* (1969), ana-lyzes how the major revolutions of the twentieth century—in Mexico, Russia, China, Cuba, Algeria and Vietnam—were the results of capitalist development in the countryside and the consequent transformation of the relationship between peasants and landed classes. Theda Skocpol was probably influenced as much by Weber as by Marx; her work on the French, Russian, and Chinese revolutions (1979) was a milestone in explaining the linkages among social structures, state formation, and revolutionary movements.

Many of the Marxist studies were beginning to grapple with the fact that movements increasingly were taking place in city streets and on college campuses and not on the shop floor. As Marxist-influenced theorists turned their attention to the current scene in the United States, rather than historical examples of movements, they found themselves challenged by new conceptual problems. A number of analyses tried to retain the concept of capitalism as the determinant of movement activity while explaining why movements were becoming less frequent at the point of production (the workplace) and more frequent at sites of social reproduction, such as residential neighborhoods, educational institutions, and the government. When theorists moved away from the major histori-cal focal points of Marxist analysis (union movements and workplace struggles, opposition to slavery, the history of anticapitalist mobilizations, and the emergence of socialist movements) and gave attention to the way in which advanced capitalism shifts the site of class conflict off the shop floor into institutions of social reproduction, including cultural institu-tions, the state, and family and consumer behavior, they had to revise

Marxist theory in order to explain the complex ways in which classes and class culture are formed in advanced capitalism.

For example, Stanley Aronowitz's *False Promises* (1973) combines a personal memoir of growing up in the Jewish American working class with an analysis of unions in the United States, the increasing colonization of working-class culture by commercial forms of culture, and the transformation of the working class in advanced capitalism. Roberta Garner (1977) traces the varieties of movements that were generated in successive phases of capitalist development in the United States, giving attention to how nonclass movements (as well as class-conscious ones) can be explained in terms of changes in the capitalist mode of production. She also comments on the way in which the institutions of advanced capitalism tend to diffuse, defuse, displace, and refract class conflict. It is no longer experienced and expressed directly as workplace struggles between labor and capital but instead appears as well in more refracted and less transparent forms in other institutional settings. Both the state and the media have become points at which these shifts and refractions take place.

The increasingly complicated and refracted character of class conflict was also the theme of studies of urban movements. Ira Katznelson's *City Trenches* (1981) recalls the theoretical work of Antonio Gramsci, an Italian Marxist. Writing in the 1930's, Gramsci (1971) suggested that in the West (in contrast to prerevolutionary Russia), capitalist rule is not merely lodged in the coercive powers of the state but also is protected by an effective system of fortifications, the institutions and associations of civil society. Katznelson uses this metaphor (fortifications or "trenches") in his discussion of how radical class and race-based movements of the 1960's (as well as earlier periods) became bogged down in the details of ethnic politics and local politics in New York. Ethnic politics and local issues are the trenches in which movements against capitalism and the capitalist state lose their transformative energy. Manuel Castells (1983) explores the new grassroots urban movements that sprang up in opposition to top-down urban planning; these movements brought together currents of opposition to capitalist developers and technocratic government intervention. John Mollenkopf (1983) shows how the city became the site of conflict between different stakeholders of the capitalist state with different levels of commitment to central city redevelopment. This conflict eventually spread to populist outsiders and neighborhood movements, opposed to urban renewal of city centers.

Frances Fox Piven and Richard Cloward (1977) offer a thought-provoking criticism of both the Leninist and the resource mobilization models of movements. Leninist analysis and resource mobilization theories privilege the role of organization in movement success. Piven and Cloward argue that it was precisely the opposite type of mobilization—based on spontaneity, unpredictability, and action from below—that contributed to the successes of poor people's movements.

Toward the later part of the second period, some Marxist analysis became to reframe itself in terms of world systems theory. Movements were seen as responses to long-term processes in the configuration of the global system that included markets and nation-states. Immanuel Wallerstein (1974, 1980) and a large number of researchers using the world systems paradigm began by tracing the formation of a system in which production is organized by global markets and political processes are controlled by nation-states. The overall system is highly unequal, with some nations associated with the core of capitalism and others relegated to the semi-periphery and periphery. Movements and ideological currents of opposition are a way in which the subaltern regions and classes challenge the system. Wallerstein increasingly turned his attention to the discourses of these movements (1990).

In addition to individual scholars, journals of socialist and Marxist thought provided ongoing analyses of movements, situating them in terms of a global struggle to curb and eventually end the capitalist system. Articles in the journals that flourished in the 1960's and 1970's updated information on anticolonial movements, working-class organization, and working-class history.

The Third Period: Deconstructing Movements

Overview
A gradual shift is under way toward a distinct third period of social movement theory. The historical circumstances causing this shift are the difficulties encountered by the movements of the 1960's and 1970's, the formation of countermovements, and the emergence of a large spectrum of new movements and ideologies that present problems for the theories and value orientations of the second period. Intellectual currents contributing to this shift include deconstructionism, postmodern philosophy, feminism, and cultural studies. Together, these trends spell the end of a sense of historical progress. They are forcing movement theorists to assess movement outcomes over longer time frames and to give more attention to belief systems and discursive framing.

The Historical Circumstances
The historical circumstances that gave rise to new paradigms by the 1980's can be summarized in terms of several developments, most of

which led to a less optimistic and less favorable assessment of movements among the scholars studying them. First, the movements of the 1960's encountered difficulties that led to a decrease in positive, optimistic assessments of movements and to the realization that movement success is a concept that requires long-term historical analysis; initiating reforms or forming a new regime are first steps in movement success but may be negated by subsequent problems faced in the implementation of reforms. Regimes constituted by revolutionary movements encounter problems, so that a revolutionary seizure of power is by no means a guarantee of movement success. Second, new types of movements appeared that challenged both Marxist and liberal-pluralist views of movements, such as religious fundamentalism, neo-Nazism, and ultranationalist movements. The circumstances of their emergence included new global economic and political trends. Together, these issues led to a more negative view of movements and to major modifications in the resource mobilization paradigm and Marxist paradigms.

Warning signs appeared quickly after the initial successes. The late 1960's and the 1970's were characterized by growing problems for movements. It appeared to be difficult for them to turn initial successes, especially in the political sphere, into ongoing changes in civil society, in social structure, and in the economy. These problems in accomplishing social transformations were associated with divisions in the support bases of movements. Groups that had provided unified support for movements now splintered, often along lines of ethnicity rather than class. Countermovements developed to halt or reverse the successes of earlier waves of movements. A few examples illustrate these types of problems.

The Civil Rights movement in the United States, having won civil rights in the political and juridical systems, found itself faced with the more intractable problems of black poverty and unemployment, de facto segregation, and pervasive racism. Black Power and black nationalism, Martin Luther King, Jr.'s increasing interest in unions and his growing criticism of both U.S. foreign policy and capitalism, and the Black Panther Party emerged as movements and ideologies that tried to address these problems. By the late 1960's, ghetto uprisings in Newark, New Jersey; the Watts area in Los Angeles, California; and (after King's murder) many other cities seemed to mark a turn away from the more disciplined and organized forms of protest. Both the new movements and the ghetto uprisings separated some African American constituencies from a liberal white support base and divided African Americans themselves.

On a global scale, the states formed by independence movements, with nationalist or socialist orientations, entered a difficult phase of developing their economies within the limits of growing stagflation and continued dependence on the economies of the center. These problems also became acute in older states in the Third World, especially in Latin America. Some of the new socialist and postcolonial states became increasingly repressive in order to preserve and consolidate what the leadership defined as core institutions. The Cultural Revolution in China, the actions of the Khmer Rouge, and the closed and corrupt form of some African regimes suggested that the building of progressive alternatives to Western capitalism was a more difficult project than had been anticipated. These cases reawakened doubts about Stalinism and the violence of the Chinese revolution of 1949, suggesting once again that revolutionary "excesses" were not a chance or occasional occurrence but a fundamental feature of the revolutionary transition to socialism. In other instances—most notably the Allende government in Chile—movement-states attempted to preserve democratic institutions and were overthrown by military coups. By 1990, the destruction of the Sandinista revolution in Nicaragua in the contra war underlined the vulnerability of Third World socialism.

Movements of the 1960's and 1970's—socialist revolutions, decolonization movements, and the civil rights movements in the developed market nations—found that their initial successes precipitated a "backlash" and countermovements. The phenomena of backlash, counterinsurgencies, and countermovements showed that movements were not simply active agents setting out to solve structural problems (whether "objective conditions" or "structural strains"). The "structural problems" were in fact also actors with their own agendas (Mansbridge, 1986). These counteractors tried to prevent movements from attacking their privileges, power, or values, and they often did so by forming countermovements. Elites threatened by revolutionary movements (the bourgeoisie, in Marxist terms) initiated and supported counterinsurgencies; for example, through policies like the Reagan Doctrine (Halliday, 1989).

Social movement theorists had to understand the ideas and visions of the countermovements, not simply their organization and strategies. Resource mobilization theorists had given attention to countermovements but perhaps had treated them in too reductionist a way, seeing them either as structural obstacles for the movement to overcome or as organizational actors that could be analyzed in the same way as any movement organization. Resource mobilization theorists had given relatively little attention to the *ideology* of the countermovements or to their larger historical meaning. For example, the antiabortion movement was not only an organizational opponent of the prochoice forces, to be analyzed in terms of strategies and resources; it also was a movement that had an elaborated set of discourses that aligned with conservative religious traditions, so that an in-depth understanding of its appeals had to be based on an analysis of the clash between religious tradition and modern, secular culture. Structural strain theories had turned human agents into impersonal forces—"strains." Resource mobilization theory had seen them as human agents but had given little attention to their ideas; it had conceptualized them as means-rational organizations, similar to corporations engaged in short-term profit maximization, when they were in fact cultural forces, enmeshed in creating and transforming the ideas by which people live. These cultural conflicts are much longer historical processes than the short-term successes and failures analyzed by resource mobilization theorists.

The gaps in understanding left by resource mobilization's inattention to ideology could be filled only by the analysis of cultural discourses, a new paradigm in the humanities and the social sciences, as well as a return to two sociological traditions: Theoretical attention to long-term historical change and the paradigm of the symbolic interactionists, which emphasized understanding the ways that human beings interact with one another in ongoing processes of defining situations. All social processes involve human action, sometimes in concert and sometimes in contention over meaning. Jo Freeman's 1983 prediction was coming true: Social movement theorists had to include attention to ideas, belief systems, and the social construction of meaning in their paradigms.

These issues and problems for movements expanded in the late 1970's and the 1980's. Not only had the movements of the 1960's and 1970's encountered problems in sustaining their initial successes, but in addition, economic and social structures were changing and new types of movements were emerging. A shift in economic production and accompanying class structure became visible in the developed economies. The phenomena of "deindustrialization," "postindustrialization," "post-Fordism," "late capitalism," "high modernity," "advanced capitalism," and the "service/information economy" had implications for movements and movement theory. Whichever of these terms one might use, the underlying reality appeared to be a transformation away from mass production manufacturing industries in the developed market economies. Industrial production did not cease—on the contrary, the use of machinery penetrated new areas, such as information processing—but it became automated, reorganized, and shifted to new locations in the periphery and semiperiphery in newly industrializing nations.

With these economic changes came a decline in the cultures, communities, and organizations of the industrial working class in Europe and North America. In the United States, the New Deal coalition of labor, liberals, African Americans, the white ethnic working class, and Southern whites gradually fell apart. This decline of the New Deal coalition in the United States and the fading of traditional working-class culture and politics in Europe were accompanied by changes in collective identities and new types of activism.

Furthermore, the globalization of markets, technology, and media was associated with the globalization of culture and movements, as well as with increasing tendencies for both structural strains (for example, nuclear safety problems) and movements to spill across national borders (Appadurai, 1990; Wallerstein, 1990; Reich, 1992; Flavin, 1987). As markets expand and nation-states weaken, movements that target their reform efforts on the policies of any one nation-state seem increasingly futile.

These economic, cultural, and political shifts created a new landscape for movements and hence for movement analysis. They were associated with the decline in class-based politics. This decline was first observed in the *New Social Movements* in Europe. The term "New Social Movements" came to be used for a number of very loosely organized movements, vaguely on the Left, definitely antistatist, and associated with mobilizations for peace; for the autonomy of women and gay persons; and against environmental pollution. Unlike the older Left, these movements used strong libertarian or anarchist appeals directed not only against capitalism but also against the capitalist state, which was seen as rationalizing and enforcing the dominance of capital. Government was no longer seen as a force that could be on the side of working people by legitimating unions, regulating the private sector, providing social services, and expanding the welfare state. These functions were now seen as at best a way of ameliorating capitalism and at worst as highly intrusive forms of social control. The movements attacked the authority of experts and technocrats who had imposed their decisions on matters such as nuclear power development, North Atlantic Treaty Organization missile siting, and city-center urban renewal. The values of the New Social Movements were antithetical to economic growth and capitalist values. The movement participants undertook a search for new forms of culture and demanded new representations of marginalized social groups and of the body itself. The sites of struggle were no longer the workplace and the production process but instead were communities, cultural and aesthetic representations, and the practices that constituted the body and sexuality. Nonmaterial needs were highlighted. The movements engaged in small-scale, antihierarchical actions and experimented with direct democracy within shifting and loosely networked core constituencies (Klandermans, 1991; Beccalli, 1994). The support bases were difficult to define in class terms. They included both alienated young people in the "new middle classes" and members of the "new working class." These strata were increasingly blurred together and in both cases were composed of individuals who were likely to be disengaged from occupational anchors and stable career paths.

The New Social Movements were welcomed by a number of European social movement theorists (who were themselves sometimes activists in these movements), but they also presented problems for resource mobilization analysis. Many of them failed to form stable movement organizations. This acephalous or polycephalous ("headless" or "many-headed"), decentralized, and amorphous form had advantages in flexibility but disadvantages in its lack of a strategy for societal transformation. Disconnected from government, without a stable social base, and lacking organizational continuity, the New Social Movements produced mobilizations that could disrupt state and corporate functioning but gave rise to few organizations that could participate in the implementation of reforms. Although some theorists (Melucci, 1989; Touraine, 1981) hailed these movements as a flexible form of opposition to the rigidities of the technocratic-capitalist states in Europe, others began to question their efficacy and pointed to the shallowness of their roots (Beccalli, 1994).

While European scholars were observing and often welcoming the New Social Movements in the late 1970's and the 1980's, in the United States social scientists were looking at a related phenomenon that was, however, usually distinctly anti-Left and often antiliberal/pluralist: single-issue constituencies, mobilizations, and movements. Single-issue movements, constituencies, and interest groups emerged as a major force in political culture in the United States; among them were antibusing mobilizations, antitax property owners' associations, anti-gun control groups, and the antiabortion movement. Liberal reformers unintentionally had contributed to the opening up of party structures, most notably through increasing the importance of primaries, a reform that shifted power from stable party elites to more volatile forces that could aggregate primary votes and campaign funds around ideological issues. Many of these single-issue movements eventually were successfully aggregated by New Right movement organizations into a large, loosely coherent conservative front that contributed to Ronald Reagan's electoral victories and the Republican congressional majority in 1994 (Davis, 1981; Lo, 1990). Whereas the antigovernment networks of the New Social Movements in Europe had a left-libertarian tilt, in the United States, these formations were brought together by ideologues on the right end of the political spectrum.

The tilt of movement activity to the right became quite noticeable in the 1980's. Left and left-liberal reforms accomplished by the movements of the 1960's were challenged by growing countermovements and mobilizations on the political and cultural right, most notably the movement against the legalization of abortion after the *Roe v. Wade* decision. Like the New Social Movements, these mobilizations seemed to have an ambiguous class basis. As in the case of the New Social Movements, the weakening of stable political structures such as trade unions and political parties contributed to their emergence (Dalton, 1993). With two cultural and economic centers of the English-language global community governed with the support of New Right movements (in the United States and England), it appeared that countermovements to those of the 1960's were effective at influencing state institutions and the media (Levitas, 1986).

By the end of the 1980's, the decline in large, class-based movements seemed to give rise to identity politics and ethnonationalism. Beyond the New Right on the political spectrum, there was a resurgence of the extreme right—the neo-fascist, neo-Nazi, ultranationalist and nativist movements that emerged in both Western Europe and the post-Communist states (Denitch, 1994; Hockenos, 1994; Laqueur, 1993). Observing these movements forced intellectuals to realize that a collective fading of the memory of World War II was taking place; Nazi genocide and the struggles of the resistance were on the verge of becoming written history rather than lived experience. With this routinization of movement history and the passing of the generations, the unthinkability of ethnoracism and genocide (at least within Europe) was diminishing. The activities of the paramilitary right in the United States, such as the formation of antigovernment militias and the Oklahoma City bombing, highlighted the resurgence of the far right and its potential for terrorism.

The successes of what came to be called religious fundamentalism in both the West and the Islamic world (where "integralism" might be a more accurate term) also became a new focus of social movement theory. In these movements, rational resource mobilization strategies were associated with goals from which secular intellectuals felt alienated. Social scientists felt a cognitive dissonance when they saw resource mobilization practiced effectively by movements committed to antimodern and antipluralist values; movements that attacked pluralism and liberal ideals of religious tolerance were at least as effective as actors in the political arena as were movements that defended and expanded pluralist values. Movement theorists, among them scholars in the field of religious studies, tried to understand the rise of these distinctly postmodern movements, movements that attacked modern values while making use of modern methods of resource mobilization (Arjomand, 1988a, 1988b; Cohen, 1990; Hadden, 1993; Jelen, 1992; Marty & Appleby, 1992; Moaddel, 1993; Riesebrodt, 1993; Wilcox, 1992; Wills, 1990).

The collapse of Communism (with the exception of Southeast Asian states and Cuba) and its transformation in China became the most decisive sign of a new global structure and a new era for movements. The outbreak of ethnonationalisms, often in violent form, associated with the formation and disintegration of postcommunist and postcolonial states became a central topic for movement studies.

As Jo Freeman had predicted, these developments in the real world forced social scientists to reexamine the ideas of social movements. No longer were movements simply "good guys" pushing an agenda of liberal inclusion, pluralism, and civil rights for the marginalized; nor were they Marxist "good guys" involved in anticolonial movements, revolutionary transitions to socialism, and the New Left.

Intellectual Currents and Internal Developments

The intellectual atmosphere of the late 1980's and the 1990's is abuzz with concepts such as deconstructionism, postmodernism, the end of metanarratives, cultural studies, cultural feminism, and postcolonial discourse. The popularized net impact of these intellectual currents is distrust of larger, universalistic readings of history, especially those associated with concepts such as progress and science; Marxism and the ideals of the Enlightenment are suspect, both for their claims to truth and for their visions of progress. The critical stand toward institutions remains as part of the Enlightenment legacy, but critical discourse no longer is seen as a first step toward creating a better society. Past efforts to define progress, rationality, and universal values are believed to be tainted with racism and sexism, and in any case to be inherently futile and illusory. The Enlightenment itself is subjected to critical scrutiny for its discourses of classification and its claims to progress that underlay and continue to sustain racist, Eurocentric, and sexist practices (Foucault, 1973, 1977; Wallerstein, 1990).

On campuses, the boundaries of many departments such as English, sociology, and political science seem to be blurring, and the subject matter of these fields is diffusing into new areas such as women's studies, cultural studies, ethnic studies, and so on. The appearance of ethnic identity politics and the politics of cultural diversity on college campuses is influencing social movement theory. So is the way in which feminism veered from its liberal, equality-oriented initial goals and became a current of thought that poses fundamental challenges to the structure of existing societies. Sexual orientation, though involving a smaller support base, has a similarly radical potential as a basis of collective identity.

The most intense conflicts in these settings often focus on issues of *representation*, representation in the media, academic writing, and other kinds of discourses. Issues of representation are not seen as epiphenomenal (that is, the mere surface of deeper, more "real" conflicts over institutional power and resources); the discursive and representational issues are the real issues. Because inequality in power is not merely expressed in discourse but actually established in discourse, the cultural perspective gives priority to identifying and exposing these discursive power plays. For example, the images of women and people of color in the media continually establish and perpetuate sexism and racism. Images and representations precede and give rise to practices such as violence against women and job discrimination against women and specific ethnic groups. It is through images and representations that some categories of human beings are constituted as dominant and others as subaltern. The term "marginalization," referring to inequalities in power within a cultural process, is replacing words such as "oppression" and "exploitation," which refer to structural strains rooted in institutional political power and economic dominance.

Together, ethnicity, gender, and sexual orientation appear to be forming new bases of solidarity and activism that are not well theorized by either resource mobilization theory or Marxist analysis. It is difficult to discern the extent to which these forms of identity politics represent new ideological challenges or are ways of asserting the claims of corporate groups for a share of increasingly scarce resources such as faculty positions, student centers, and university funds. In any case, identity politics suggests that the liberal model of movements, in which movements were understood to be opening up opportunities for individual integration into the mainstream, based on an ethos of similarity and assimilation, is not matching new realities in which movements assert difference. Nor does identity politics match the Marxist emphasis on class-conscious movements, for which it is the capitalist system, not the straight white male and his disrespectful discourses, that is the source of alienation. Marxists from Gramsci to Katznelson noticed the problems posed for class-based movements by the deep and intricate "trenches" of advanced capitalism; the trenches of identity politics now seemed to place the target of challenging class dominance out of reach of socialist movements.

One response of intellectuals, both cause and consequence of these new types of movements, is withdrawal from the idea of universal human progress. Intellectuals themselves deny that any large patterns are discernible; all that exist are interactions and discourses. History is not the story of progress in institutions, technologies, and ideas, but a series of shifts in *epistemes* or *discursive formations* (Foucault, 1973). New ways of thinking, speaking, and classifying are not necessarily better or more progressive than older ones.

These discursive formations create *collective identities* such as gender, nationality, sexual orientation, social class, religion, ethnicity, and race. As feminists have pointed out in the analysis of gender, these identities can be forced on a population as well as assumed voluntarily. Women have been constituted as a category in a gender system. Identities are not only imposed but also can be embraced as "imagined communities" (Anderson, 1991). Rather than seeing movements as appealing to and recruiting from support bases defined by certain preexisting and relatively stable demographic characteristics, observers now see movements as engaged in discourses and practices that create or constitute such support bases. To a large extent, the movement as discourse and practice predates the emergence of support bases and constitutes its own support bases. For example, in the former Yugoslavia, the actions of political leaders and ethnic militias have forced a religious-ethnic identity on populations that can no longer act outside these collective identities; the movements have forcibly created their own Croat, Serb, and Muslim support bases (Denitch, 1994). Violence and terrorism are practices that are designed primarily to polarize populations and impose collective identities.

Another important concept of the new intellectual currents is the *culture of resistance*. Resistance is always present in interactions, but it hardly can be said to have a particular overall pattern or momentum. Nor does it make much sense to ask whether the elements of any given culture of resistance are progressive or not. Resistance increasingly is seen as an ongoing playful attitude toward hegemonic culture, not as an organized movement that challenges specific concentrations of wealth and power and proposes to replace them with new, purportedly better structures. The clash of hegemonic culture and cultures of resistance is an ongoing process, not a forward movement toward a better society. Emancipation lies in the resistance itself and the disintegration of institutions, rather than in outcomes defined by building new structures and institutions. Language, music, performance, the visual arts, and the breaching of sexual conventions all have a role in this play of resistance (Willis, 1990; Gaines, 1992; Handler, 1992; Hebdige, 1982; Weinstein, 1991; Weinstein & Weinstein, 1993).

The Impact on Social Movement Theory

These changes in movements themselves and in the larger intellectual currents of the times are producing changes in social movement theory. Because these changes are under way now, it is not easy to analyze their outcome. In many ways, the shifts seem more subtle and gradual than the shift from the first to the second period around 1960. The current shift began more as a shift of emphasis, a subtle and incremental reevaluation, than as a qualitative break from existing paradigms.

For example, in her 1991 essay, Margit Mayer was not yet completely ready to assess changes in the field as a qualitative shift. Instead, she tended to see them as new efforts to bring together the classic paradigm (with its social psychological and individual-level analysis) and the resource mobilization paradigm. To this new synthesis, she added the interest in New Social Movements and populism and some shifts within the Marxist/class analysis paradigm. Her assessment is accurate but falls short of recognizing a qualitative change that makes the third period distinct in value orientation as well as in the use of deconstructionist concepts that resonate with broader intellectual currents. There is indeed considerable overlap in the key terms of the two periods—for example, "countermovement" and "multiorganizational field" have carried over from the second to the third period—but these terms are now being used in new ways, along with new terms such as "discourse," "discursive framing," "collective identities," and "cultures of resistance."

The shift into the third period was in many ways quite gradual. One reason why the shift was gradual was that the community of scholars did not expand or change dramatically, as it had in the emergence of the second period in the 1960's, when a new and very large cohort of graduate students suddenly appeared in sociology departments. This time, there was far more continuity in the "cast of characters" in social movement theory; for example, William Gamson, Bert Klandermans, Herbert Kitschelt, Clarence Lo, Doug McAdam, John McCarthy, Aldon Morris, Carol Mueller, Sidney Tarrow, and Mayer Zald continue to be active in the field and were joined, rather than replaced, by new theorists. Among Marxist and Marxist-influenced writers, Stanley Aronowitz (1988), Roberta Garner (1996), and Paul Willis (1990) have assimilated themes of postmodern thought.

Some observers might argue that the negative tone to third period analysis already was present in the organizational-entrepreneurial model of many second period resource mobilization theorists (Mayer, 1991). Resource mobilization theory's initial positive emphasis on rational action easily could be given a negative spin—"too much rationality," as it were, embodied in the position that movements were often manipulative and more the creation of self-interested professionals than a genuine response of the masses to intolerable conditions. These themes came to the fore when research focused on the increased professionalization of movements, the deliberate creation of collective behavior incidents, movements' reliance on elite support, and the lack of spontaneity, authenticity, and indigenous roots in many mobilizations. The characteristic of means-rationality was not questioned when the liberal values of the scholars resonated with those of movements such as the Civil Rights movement, farmworker union drives, and liberal feminism or when Marxist scholars analyzed revolutionary socialist movements. The means-rationality of social movement organizations became the subject of more negative evaluation when it appeared in movements such as ethnonationalism

(Denitch, 1994), pronuclear mobilizations (Zald & Useem, 1987), religious fundamentalism or integralism across several faiths, single-issue constituencies such as the gun lobby, identity politics on campus, and the resurgence of the extreme right.

Despite continuity in the community of social movement theorists, new topics and approaches appeared, as well as a more questioning and less positive value orientation toward the movements of the 1980's and 1990's. In part, the shift had to do with unsolved puzzles and gaps in the two leading second period paradigms. Resource mobilization theory, as noted by Freeman, had given insufficient attention to the ideas and ideologies of movements; these concerns now resurfaced, often associated with *discourse* as a key theoretical term.

Marxist studies faced the unsolved and perhaps insoluble puzzle that although advanced capitalism seems to match Marx's analysis of capitalism in objective terms (such as continuing expansion of markets, penetration of capital into subsistence and semifeudal economies, globalization of cultural and capital markets), the global structure generates few class-conscious movements of the proletariat. Resource mobilization theorists have had to make major modifications in their paradigm, but Marxist theorists have been hit harder. They are able to theorize the transformation in capitalism that is taking place (globalization, post-Fordism, and so on) but have difficulties in conceptualizing how this transformation generates distinct types of movements, such as the rise of identity politics, right-wing activism, and religious fundamentalism. For a while, it appeared that Marxists could analyze cogently how class conflict can shift from the workplace to new sites such as communities and educational institutions, but a perspective focused primarily on overt class conflict is limited in its explanatory power. It is clear that in order to survive as theory, Marxism will have to develop and refine its conceptualization of how advanced capitalist society generates movements without distinct class bases. Some Marxists, most notably Paul Willis (1990), analyze the way in which cultures of resistance playfully deconstruct and reassemble hegemonic culture in music, clothing, and style, in cultural currents such as punk, Rasta, metal, and so on. From an orthodox Marxist perspective, this cultural resistance can be seen at most as a holding action.

The analysis of decentralized, antistatist, and polycephalous movements forms a bridge from the second to the third periods. These movements took different forms in Europe and the United States. In Europe, they were the New Social Movements; in the United States, they appeared as local populist activism and single-issue constituencies. For a while, it appeared that New Social Movement theory was the key to understanding movements in high modern or advanced capitalist societies, but this paradigm was only of limited validity. Even in Europe, it provided a satisfactory analysis of only one part of the spectrum of movements. In the United States, the assumptions made by New Social Movement theorists about the left-libertarian character of new movements were not valid; activists' orientations were more likely to be right-wing or ambiguous. The antistatist discourses can spin to the Right as well as the Left. Some Marxist theories attempt to link developments such as New Social Movements and identity politics to post-Fordist accumulation regimes (Mayer, 1991); this explanation requires further conceptualization.

Despite the difficulties encountered by Marxist theory and the resource mobilization paradigm, the field of social movement theory is responding to internal and external turmoil with resilience. The new and as yet unsolved puzzles have generated scholarly enthusiasm, not discouragement. Social movement theory promises to be one of the most active areas of the social sciences in the opening years of the twenty-first century. It is a prime site for bringing mainstream academic sociology and Marxist theory together with each other and with new developments in cultural studies, feminism, and postmodern thought. The synthesis that is emerging preserves the advances of the second period, returns to important themes of the first period, and opens up new perspectives.

Emerging Themes of the Third Period

Several themes have emerged from the third period, including the following.

1. Movements must be understood not only in terms of organizational behavior but also in terms of belief systems, ideologies, and discourses. Different versions of third period paradigms use different terms here, but the substance is the same: Coherent belief systems, as well as underlying, less coherent, and more fragmentary cultures of resistance, form key elements of movements and must be the object of theory.

2. Although the 1960's represents a wave of movements that had ideologies compatible with liberal-pluralism or democratic socialism, these belief systems constitute only a small part of the ideological spectrum. Social movement theory must concern itself with the formation and dissemination of a wider range of belief systems.

3. Anti- and nonliberal ideologies are especially important in the growing number of countermovements that seek to undo reforms accomplished by movements of the 1960's and 1970's. Indeed, some countermovements would like to roll back large parts of "the modern" altogether, especially its secularism. Analysis of the movement/countermovement dynamic must include attention to ideologies as well as organizational strategies and mobilizations.

4. Movement processes involve much longer time frames than many resource mobilization theorists are prepared to examine in their research (Mayer, 1991). The dynamic of movement and countermovement may take decades or even centuries to play itself out. Identifying the "success" or "failure" of a movement has to involve analysis of these longer time periods. For example, in the United States, under pressure from the Christian Right and conservative ideologues, the Republican Congress of the mid-1990's may be undoing not only Great Society programs and movement-initiated reforms of the 1960's and 1970's but also some New Deal policies that long had been assumed to be permanent "successes" of the liberal reform wave of the 1930's. The structure of the European welfare state, assumed to be a permanent reform feature, was weakened considerably in the 1980's. Religious fundamentalists in the United States are challenging the liberal separation of church and state that has been elaborated since the eighteenth century. Although the term "cycle" may of some value here, it suggests a recurrence of patterns, or at least of the formal properties of movement activities, when what is in place is more an open-ended historical process.

In the analysis of historical outcomes, attention also must be given to unintended and unanticipated consequences of movement "successes." For example, the New Left and New Social Movements' attack on the capitalist state may have contributed (inadvertently) to the spread and popularity of the antigovernment discursive framing used by the New Right. In short, social movement theory needs to consider historical processes and outcomes over much longer time frames (Mayer, 1991). An expansion of the time horizon will in turn require new research methods, probably closer to those of historians than those of sociological field research. At the same time that social movement theorists are examining historical processes, they also are eschewing any simple equation of change and progress.

5. Social movement theory needs to look more carefully not only at movement ideologies but also at the way these belief systems match or fail to match belief systems that already exist in the society. *Frame alignment* and *frame transformation* are concepts that refer to the extent to which movement belief systems match or challenge prevailing beliefs (Snow & Benford, 1988, 1992).

The revival of the term "mentalities" (stripped of its original racist undertones) points to the long-term persistence of cultural forms. Mentalities are habits of mind, transmitted from generation to generation through all the practices of everyday life. Other theorists prefer the term "cultural frameworks" (Goldstone, 1991). They form what members of a cultural community believe to be "common sense" (Tarrow, 1992). For example, individualism is part of the mentality of the United States, and movements as different as the New Left and the New Right both appealed to it. The concept of mentalities links the study of long-term historical processes to the examination of cultural forces in the formation of movements and ideologies. The mentalities or frameworks of a culture limit and shape the ideologies of social movements. The mentalities of a culture make it difficult to transplant ideologies from one culture to another, even in the age of global interconnections. If transplanted, ideologies may be forced into forms that match the mentalities or frameworks of the new host culture, as happened to Marxism in China. Mentalities and cultural frameworks change slowly, an additional reason for a long time frame in movement research.

6. More attention needs to be given to the way in which movement ideologies resonate (or align with), emerge from, and create popular *cultures of resistance* (Mayer, 1991). Movements often are merely the organized and visible tip of an iceberg of alienation, disaffiliation, and opposition that is expressed in interactions, organizations, habits and practices, and cultural forms. Movements have complicated relationships to these inchoate traditions of resistance. They can grow out of the cultures of resistance; for example, the Civil Rights movement drew on centuries of unorganized resistance to racial oppression expressed in virtually every aspect of the everyday life of African Americans (Genovese, 1974).

As Hobsbawm (1959) suggested in his study of banditry, the lines between movements, cultures of resistance, and criminal organizations are fluid. Individuals slip from one to another of these as the situation permits or demands. For example, Elaine Brown's (1994) memoir of life in the Black Panther Party provides some vivid illustrations that update Hobsbawm's argument. Movement ideologues and social control agents vie in applying labels—"partisan" or "bandit," "freedom fighter" or "criminal element."

Movements leave traces in cultures of resistance, even after the movement has "failed" or "disappeared." For example, New Left imagery of rebellion continues to be a theme in the culture of heavy metal (Gaines, 1992; Weinstein, 1991).

Many of these cultures of resistance are informed not by liberal or socialist values but by older, even "premodern," traditions. Many cultures of resistance, both among subaltern groups within the developed nations and in postcolonial societies, represent resistance to some sides of the Enlightenment (its techno-expertise, means-rationality, Eurocentrism, racism, and masculinism). Especially when movements and cultures of resistance emerge among groups that have been marginalized and exploited in the global system, the ideologies may be explicitly in opposition to Enlightenment claims of universalism, rationality, and progress (Foucault, 1973, 1977; Handler, 1992; Hebdige, 1982; Sawicki, 1991; Scott, 1990; Spivak, 1994; Wallerstein, 1990; Williams & Chrisman, 1994). Other cultures of resistance are more completely formed out of deconstructed and reassembled elements of hegemonic culture, like many of the youth cultures of advanced capitalist societies (Gaines, 1992; Hebdige, 1982; Weinstein, 1991; Willis, 1990).

7. The formation of identity is an important component of movements. This process is by no means a given of the social structure. Support bases are not "naturally" present for movement mobilization but are themselves social constructs. Support bases may bring forth movements to become the agents of those groups who feel a structural strain, but movements also create their own support bases. The analysis of social movements has to pay attention to deconstructionist perspectives on how identity, the subject, and a sense of agency are socially constructed (Foucault, 1973; Handler, 1992). The constitution of a subject with a specific identity—for example, an ethnic identity rather than a class or gender identity—necessarily involves the suppression of alternative identities. Whereas the social psychological theorists of the first period thought of individual identity (and the motivations associated with such an identity) as a cause of social movements, third period theorists think of movements as causing identity. In third period theory, movement discourses constitute individuals as acting subjects and define and construct a collective identity for them. This deconstructionist perspective finally realizes some of the substance (if not the exact wording) of Herbert Blumer's call for a symbolic interactionist paradigm of social movements, a paradigm that would take into account the formation of movements through interaction and communication. (There are major differences between interactionist and deconstructionist theories, however, so these two approaches can be seen as dealing with similar issues but are not identical in their concepts and underlying assumptions. See, for example, Weinstein & Weinstein, 1993.)

8. Social movement theory has to give more attention to current transformations in the global economy and political structure. Although observers use a multiplicity of terms such as "high modern," "advanced capitalist," "postmodern," "late capitalist," "postindustrial" (most unsatisfactory), and so on, they usually are pointing to a single cluster of interrelated new developments: Post-Fordism in the economy; the erosion or recomposition of the nation-state with sub- and supernational processes becoming more important, as nation-states lose some of their control over the national economy, for example in the European Union and the North American Free Trade Agreement (Camilleri & Falk, 1993); transnational flows of people, capital, technology, and culture (Appadurai, 1990);

deterritorialized communities and their role in movements, especially nationalist movements (Appadurai, 1990; Hannerz, 1992); and transnational arms flows (Klare, 1994). Technological problems and prospects, like nuclear accidents, also have become transnational and are focal points for cross-boundary movements and mobilizations (Flavin, 1987). Transnational media have speeded up diffusion of movement ideas across national boundaries (McAdam & Rucht, 1993). These global processes have to become a more integral part of social movement theory.

9. It is important to retain the theoretical concepts of the second period and to integrate them with the emerging concerns. Concepts such as social movement organization, resource mobilization, and political opportunity structure are of continuing value. The more individually focused theories of the first period also can make valuable contributions, for example in understanding micromobilization processes (Snow, Rochford, Worden, & Benford, 1986). A revival of social psychological perspectives is under way and is now focused more on the formation of collective identities than on individual predispositions (Gamson, 1992; Taylor & Whittier, 1992). A revived interest in belief systems suggests that social movement theorists are returning to some of the themes of the first period, although with less focus on individual attitudes and psychological aspects of beliefs.

Finally, many theorists are integrating the academic subfield of social movements with macro sociological theory, a tradition of social thought that goes back to both Marx and Weber. The work of Goldstone, Riesebrodt, Skocpol, Wallerstein, and Tarrow (among others) integrates contemporary movement theory with the classical concerns of sociology, the analysis of long-term and large-scale causes and consequences of movements. Thus, the third period is not to be seen as a rejection of the earlier work in both the first and second periods but rather as an expansion, a synthesis, and an embedding of smaller-scale theories in historical analysis. Many of the "either/or" positions expressed in earlier social movement theory are being rejected, and the field is opening to the integration of perspectives previously believed to be incompatible (Zald, 1992). Micro and macro approaches, social psychology and organizational studies, and discourse analysis and structural theories all can find room in this emerging synthesis.

All these emerging themes imply closer attention to history and ideology, as well as the realization that purposive change is a much slower and more conflictual process than one might think. Movements are not only pragmatic attempts to solve structural strains through organizational strategies but also parts of long-term ideological transformations.

Continuities Across Periods: The Unity of the Field

Despite these shifts, there are important similarities across periods—continuities throughout the fifty-year span. Two elements are central to the field throughout the half century under consideration. One of these elements lies in the definition of the field and its underlying assumptions. These assumptions are threefold and have persisted across the three periods. First, there is a continuing consensus on the definition of movements; movements consistently are defined as processes of change, as purposive action (whether rational or irrational), and as noninstitutionalized challenges to institutions. Second, all movement theory plays with the tension between agency and structure. Movements are always in part voluntary, an expression of human agency, but their formation and their outcomes also are determined, a result of structures and constituting processes that limit what is possible. The tension between agency and limits underlies all the human sciences, but it is felt most strongly and explicitly in the study of movements. Third, the field of social movements always has been characterized by the need to expand beyond the boundaries of sociology. Social movement theory has been less constrained by the conventional boundaries of sociology than any other subfield of the discipline. It always has overlapped psychology, political science, history, journalism, and the humanities; academic social movement theorists long have been in a productive dialogue with theorists and activists outside the academic mainstream, especially Marxists and, more recently, feminists. In this respect, the field shows the way for a new integration of the social sciences with cultural studies, an integration that is accelerating in the third period.

The second element of continuity in the field is the commitment among movement theorists to an open and self-reflective society. Most theorists are committed to liberal democracy and pluralism or democratic socialism. Throughout the fifty-year period, movement scholars have evaluated movements in terms of these values. They recognize that specific movements may constitute a challenge to these values, because the new order for which movements call often is a closed and perfected society. Movements often articulate a totalizing vision of society that precludes openness and the possibility of further change. Scholars thus have been critical of the phenomena they study, especially in the first and third periods. At the same time, they recognize that the sum total of movements—the movement sector of a society—is a mechanism for sustaining the values of pluralism, democracy, and openness. The existence of movements in a society allows the correction of injustices, the righting of wrongs, and the pursuit of new possibilities. Thus, a vibrant movement sector, regardless of the closed or dogmatic nature of any one of its movements, is a sine qua non of a democratic society. Although any one movement might call for closure, perfection, or totalization, movements taken together—the sector of movements—function to promote pluralism; movements act in countervailing ways, and thus the society remains open, fluid, self-reflective, and self-correcting. This double vision (that movements embody both openness and closure) contributes to dynamic tensions in the field's value orientations.

Works Cited

Adorno, Theodor, E. Frenkel-Brunswick, D. Levinson, and R. Sanford. (1993). *The Authoritarian Personality*. New York: Norton. (originally published 1950)

Almond, Gabriel. (1954). *The Appeals of Communism*. Princeton, NJ: Princeton University Press.

Almond, Gabriel, and Sidney Verba. (1963). *The Civic Culture: Political Attitudes and Democracy in Five Nations*. Princeton, NJ: Princeton University Press.

Anderson, Benedict. (1991). *Imagined Communities*. London: Verso.

Anderson, Perry. (1976). *Considerations on Western Marxism*. London: New Left Books.

Appadurai, Arjun. (1990). "Disjuncture and Difference in the Global Cultural Economy." In Mike Featherstone (ed.), *Global Culture*. Newbury Park, CA: Sage.

Aptheker, Herbert. (1943). *American Negro Slave Revolts*. New York: International Publishers.

Arendt, Hannah. (1951). *The Origins of Totalitarianism*. New York: Harcourt Brace.

Arjomand, Said A. (1988a). *Authority and Political Culture in Shi'ism*. Albany: State University of New York Press.

_____. (1988b). *The Turban for the Crown*. New York: Oxford University Press.

Aronowitz, Stanley. (1973). *False Promises*. New York: McGraw-Hill.

_____. (1988). "Postmodernism and Politics." In Andrew Ross (ed.), *Universal Abandon: The Politics of Postmodernism*. Minneapolis: University of Minnesota Press.

Beccalli, Bianca. (1994). "The modern women's movement in Italy." *New Left Review* 204 (March/April), 86-112.

Bell, Daniel, ed. (1964). *The Radical Right*. New York: Doubleday.

Bettelheim, Bruno, and Morris Janowitz. (1964). *Social Change and Prejudice*. Glencoe, IL: Free Press.

Blackmer, Donald, and Sidney Tarrow, eds. (1975). *Communism in Italy and France*. Princeton, NJ: Princeton University Press.

Blumer, Herbert. (1946). "Collective Behavior." In Alfred McClung Lee (ed.), *A New Outline of the Principles of Sociology*. New York: Barnes and Noble.

Brecher, Jeremy. (1974). *Strike*. Greenwich, CT: Fawcett World Library.

Brown, Elaine. (1994). *A Taste of Power*. New York: Anchor/Doubleday.

Camilleri, Joseph, and Jim Falk. (1993). *The End of Sovereignty: The Politics of a Shrinking and Fragmenting World*. Brookfield, VT: Edward Elgar.

Cantril, Hadley. (1941). *The Psychology of Social Movements*. New York: J. Wiley and Sons.

Castells, Manuel. (1983). *The City and the Grassroots*. Berkeley: University of California Press.

Christie, Richard, and Marie Jahoda, eds. (1954). *Studies in the Scope and Method of "The Authoritarian Personality."* New York: Free Press.

Cohen, Norman J., ed. (1990). *The Fundamentalist Phenomenon: A View from Within, a Response from Without*. Grand Rapids, MI: Eerdmans.

Curtis, Russell, and Louis Zurcher. (1974). "Social Movements: An Analytical Exploration of Organizational Forms." *Social Problems* 21, no. 3, 356-370.

Dalton, Russell, ed. (1993). *Symposium on Citizens, Protest, and Democracy. Annals of the American Academy of Political and Social Science* 528 (July).

Davies, James. (1962). "Toward a Theory of Revolution." *American Sociological Review* 27, no. 1 (February), 5-19.

Davis, Mike. (1981). "The New Right's Road to Power." *New Left Review* 128 (July/August), 28-49.

Denitch, Bogdan. (1994). *Ethnic Nationalism: The Tragic Death of Yugoslavia*. Minneapolis: University of Minnesota Press.

Eisinger, P. K. (1973). "The Conditions of Protest Behavior in American cities." *American Political Science Review* 67, no. 1, 11-28.

Festinger, Leon, Henry Riecken, and Stanley Schachter. (1956). *When Prophecy Fails*. Minneapolis: University of Minnesota Press.

Flavin, Christopher. (1987). *Reassessing Nuclear Power: The Fallout from Chernobyl*. Washington, DC: Worldwatch Institute.

Foucault, Michel. (1973). *The Order of Things: An Archaeology of the Human Sciences*. New York: Vintage.

_____. (1977). *Discipline and Punish: The Birth of the Prison*. New York: Pantheon.

Freeman, Jo. (1973). "The Tyranny of Structurelessness." In Anne Koedt, Ellen Levine, and Anita Rapone (eds.), *Radical Feminism*. New York: Quadrangle.

_____. (1975). *The Politics of Women's Liberation: A Case Study of an Emerging Social Movement and Its Relation to the Policy Process*. New York: McKay.

_____. (1979). "Resource Mobilization and Strategy: A Model for Analyzing Social Movement Organization Actions." In Mayer Zald and John McCarthy (eds.), *The Dynamics of Social Movements*. Cambridge, MA: Winthrop.

_____, ed. (1983). *Social Movements of the Sixties and Seventies*. New York: Longman.

Freud, Sigmund. (1959). *Group Psychology and the Analysis of the Ego.* New York: Norton. (originally published 1921)

Gaines, Donna. (1992). *Teenage Wasteland: Suburbia's Deadend Kids.* New York: HarperCollins.

Gamson, William. (1975). *The Strategy of Social Protest.* Homewood, IL: Dorsey.

_____. (1992). "The Social Psychology of Collective Action." In Aldon Morris and Carol Mueller (eds.), *Frontiers in Social Movement Theory.* New Haven, CT: Yale University Press.

Garner, Roberta. (1977). *Social Movements in America.* Chicago, IL: Rand McNally.

_____. (1996). *Contemporary Movements and Ideologies.* New York: McGraw-Hill.

Garner, Roberta, and Mayer Zald. (1985). "The Political Economy of Social Movement Sectors." In Gerald Suttles and Mayer Zald (eds.), *The Challenge of Social Control: Citizenship and Institution Building in Modern Society.* Norwood, NJ: Ablex.

Genovese, Eugene. (1974). *Roll, Jordan, Roll.* New York: Vintage.

Goldstone, Jack. (1991). "Ideology, Cultural Frameworks, and the Process of Revolution." *Theory and Society* 20, no. 4 (August), 405-453.

Gramsci, Antonio. (1971). *Selections from the Prison Notebooks.* New York: International Publishers.

Gurr, T. R. (1970). *Why Men Rebel.* Princeton, NJ: Princeton University Press.

Gusfield, Joseph. (1963). *Symbolic Crusade: Status Politics and the American Temperance Movement.* Urbana: University of Illinois Press.

Hadden, Jeffrey K. (1993). "The Rise and Fall of American Televangelism." In Wade Clark Roof (ed.), *Religion in the Nineties. Annals of the American Academy of Political and Social Science* 527 (May), 113-130.

Halliday, Fred. (1989). *From Kabul to Managua.* New York: Pantheon.

Handler, Joel. (1992). "Postmodernism, Protest and the New Social Movements." *Law and Society Review* 26, no. 4, 697-731.

Hannerz, Ulf. (1992). *Cultural Complexity*. New York: Columbia University Press.

Hebdige, Dick. (1982). *Subculture*. London: Methuen.

Hobsbawm, Eric. (1959). *Primitive Rebels*. New York: Norton.

Hockenos, Paul. (1994). *Free to Hate: The Rise of the Right in Postcommunist Eastern Europe*. New York: Routledge.

Hofstadter, Richard. (1955). *The Age of Reform*. New York: Knopf.

Jacoby, Russell. (1983). *The Repression of Psychoanalysis: Otto Fenichel and the Political Freudians*. New York: Basic Books.

Jelen, Ted. (1992). "Political Christianity: A Contextual Analysis." *American Journal of Political Science* 36 (August), 692-714.

Jenkins, J. Craig, and Charles Perrow. (1977). "Insurgency of the Powerless: Farm Worker Movements (1946-1972)." *American Sociological Review* 42, 249-268.

Katznelson, Ira. (1981). *City Trenches: Urban Politics and the Patterning of Class in the United States*. Chicago: University of Chicago Press.

Kitschelt, Herbert. (1986). "Political Opportunity Structures and Political Protest: Anti-Nuclear Movements in Four Democracies." *British Journal of Political Science* 16, 57-85.

Klandermans, Bert. (1991). "New Social Movements and Resource Mobilization: The European and the American Approach Revisited." In Dieter Rucht (ed.), *Research on Social Movements*. Boulder, CO: Westview Press.

Klare, Michael. (1994). "Armed and Dangerous." *These Times* 18 (June 13), 14-19.

Kornhauser, William. (1959). *The Politics of Mass Society*. New York: Free Press.

Kuhn, Thomas. (1962). *The Structure of Scientific Revolutions*. Chicago: University of Chicago Press.

Lane, Robert. (1962). *Political Ideology.* New York: Free Press of Glencoe.

Lang, Kurt, and Gladys Lang. (1961). *Collective Dynamics.* New York: Cromwell.

Laqueur, Walter. (1993). *Black Hundred: The Rise of the Extreme Right in Russia.* New York: HarperCollins.

Lasswell, Harold, and Daniel Lerner. (1966). *World Revolutionary Elites: Studies in Coercive Ideological Movements.* Boston: Massachusetts Institute of Technology Press.

LeBon, Gustave. (1897). *The Crowd.* London: Unwin.

Lens, Sidney. (1966). *Radicalism in America.* New York: Thomas Crowell.

Levitas, Ruth, ed. (1986). *The Ideology of the New Right.* Cambridge, England: Polity Press.

Lipset, Seymour Martin. (1960). *Political Man.* New York: Anchor/Doubleday.

Lo, Clarence. (1990). *Small Property vs. Big Government: Social Origins of the Property Tax Revolt.* Berkeley: University of California Press.

Lynd, Alice, and Staughton Lynd. (1973). *Rank and File: Personal Histories by Working Class Organizers.* Boston: Beacon Press.

McAdam, Doug, and Dieter Rucht. (1993). "The Cross-National Diffusion of Movement Ideas." In Russell Dalton (ed.), *Symposium on Citizens, Protest, and Democracy. Annals of the American Academy of Political and Social Science* 528 (July), 56-74.

McCarthy, John, and Mayer Zald. (1987). "Social Movement Industries: Competition and Conflict Among SMOs." In Mayer Zald and John McCarthy (eds.), *Social Movements in an Organizational Society.* New Brunswick, NJ: Transaction.

Mansbridge, Jane. (1986). *Why We Lost the ERA.* Chicago: University of Chicago Press.

Marty, Martin, and R. Scott Appleby. (1992). *The Glory and the Power: The Fundamentalist Challenge to the Modern World*. Boston: Beacon Press.

Mayer, Margit. (1991). "Social Movement Research and Social Movement Practice: The U.S. Pattern." In Dieter Rucht (ed.), *Research on Social Movements*. Boulder, CO: Westview Press.

Melucci, Alberto. (1989). *Nomads of the Present: Social Movements and Individual Needs in Contemporary Society*. London: Hutchinson Radius.

Mills, C. Wright. (1959). *The Sociological Imagination*. New York: Oxford University Press.

Moaddel, Mansoor. (1993). *Class, Politics, and Ideology in the Iranian Revolution*. New York: Columbia University Press.

Mollenkopf, John. (1983). *The Contested City*. Princeton, NJ: Princeton University Press.

Moore, Barrington. (1965). *The Social Origins of Dictatorship and Democracy*. Boston: Beacon Press.

Morris, Aldon. (1981). "Black Southern Student Sit-in Movement: An Analysis of Internal Organization." *American Sociological Review* 46 (December), 744-767.

_____. (1984). *The Origins of the Civil Rights Movement*. New York: Free Press.

Mottl, Tahi. (1980). "The Analysis of Countermovements." *Social Problems* 27 (June), 620-635.

Oberschall, Anthony. (1973). *Social Conflict and Social Movements*. Englewood Cliffs, NJ: Prentice-Hall.

Piven, Frances Fox, and Richard Cloward. (1977). *Poor People's Movements: Why They Succeed, How They Fail*. New York: Pantheon.

Reich, Robert. (1992). *The Work of Nations*. New York: Vintage.

Riesebrodt, Martin. (1993). *Pious Passion: The Emergence of Modern Fundamentalism in the United States and Iran*. Berkeley: University of California Press.

Sawicki, Jana. (1991). *Disciplining Foucault: Feminism, Power and the Body.* New York: Routledge.

Scott, Alan. (1990). *Ideology and the New Social Movements.* London: Unwin Hyman.

Seeley, John. (1967). *The Americanization of the Unconscious.* New York: International Science Press.

Shils, Edward. (1956). *Torment of Secrecy: The Background and Consequences of American Security Policies.* Glencoe, IL: Free Press.

Shils, Edward, and Morris Janowitz. (1948). "Cohesion and Disintegration in the Wehrmacht in World War II." *Public Opinion Quarterly* 12 (Summer), 280-315.

Skocpol, Theda. (1979). *States and Social Revolutions: A Comparative Analysis of France, Russia, and China.* New York: Cambridge University Press.

Smelser, Neil. (1963). *Theory of Collective Behavior.* New York: Free Press.

Snow, David, and Robert Benford. (1988). "Ideology, Frame Resonance and Participant Mobilization." In Bert Klandermans, Hanspeter Kriesi, and Sidney Tarrow (eds.), *From Structure to Action: Comparing Social Movements Across Cultures.* Greenwich, CT: JAI Press.

_____. (1992). "Master Frames and Cycles of Protest." In Aldon Morris and Carol McClurg Mueller (eds.), *Frontiers in Social Movement Theory.* New Haven, CT: Yale University Press.

Snow, David, E. B. Rochford, Steven Worden, and Robert Benford. (1986). "Frame Alignment Process, Micromobilization, and Movement Participation." *American Sociological Review* 51 (August), 464-481.

Spivak, Gayatri Chakravorty. (1994). "Can the Subaltern Speak?" In Patrick Williams and Laura Chrisman (eds.), *Colonial Discourse and Post-Colonial Theory: A Reader.* New York: Columbia University Press.

Stinchcombe, Arthur. (1967). "Agricultural Enterprise and Rural Class Relationships." *American Journal of Sociology* 67, 165-176.

Stouffer, Samuel. (1955). *Communism, Conformity, and Civil Liberties.* New York: Doubleday.

Tarde, G. (1903). *The Laws of Imitation.* New York: Holt.

Tarrow, Sidney. (1988). *Democracy and Disorder: Protest and Politics in Italy, 1965-1975.* New York: Oxford University Press.

_____. (1991). *Struggles, Politics, and Reform: Collective Action, Social Movements and Cycles of Protest.* Ithaca, NY: Cornell University Press.

_____. (1992). "Mentalities, Political Cultures, and Collective Action Frames: Constructing Meanings Through Action." In Aldon Morris and Carol Mueller (eds.), *Frontiers in Social Movement Theory.* New Haven, CT: Yale University Press.

_____. (1994). *Power in Movement: Social Movements, Collective Action and Politics.* New York: Cambridge University Press.

Taylor, Verta, and Nancy Whittier. (1992). "Collective Identity in Social Movement Communities." In Aldon Morris and Carol Mueller (eds.), *Frontiers in Social Movement Theory.* New Haven, CT: Yale University Press.

Thompson, E. P. (1963). *The Making of the English Working Class.* New York: Random House.

Tilly, Charles. (1978). *From Mobilization to Revolution.* Reading, MA: Addison-Wesley.

Touraine, Alain. (1981). *The Voice and the Eye: An Analysis of Social Movements.* New York: Cambridge University Press.

Turner, Ralph, and Lewis Killian. (1987). *Collective Behavior.* Englewood Cliffs, NJ: Prentice-Hall. (originally published 1957)

Useem, Bert. (1984). "Solidarity Model, Breakdown Model, and the Boston Anti-Busing Movement." *American Sociological Review* 45, 357-369.

Wallerstein, Immanuel. (1974). *The Modern World System.* New York: Academic Press.

_____. (1980). *The Modern World System II*. New York: Academic Press.

_____. (1990). "Culture as the Ideological Battleground of the Modern World System." In Mike Featherstone (ed.), *Global Culture*. London: Sage.

Weinstein, Deena. (1991). *Heavy Metal*. New York: Free Press.

Weinstein, Deena, and Michael Weinstein. (1993). *Postmodern(ized) Simmel*. New York: Routledge.

Weinstein, James. (1967). *The Decline of Socialism in America: 1912-1925*. New York: Random House.

Wilcox, Clyde. (1992). *God's Warriors: The Christian Right in the Twentieth Century*. Baltimore, MD: Johns Hopkins University Press.

Williams, Patrick, and Laura Chrisman, eds. (1994). *Colonial Discourse and Post-Colonial Theory: A Reader*. New York: Columbia University Press.

Willis, Paul. (1990). *Common Culture*. San Francisco: Westview Press.

Wills, Garry. (1990). *Under God: Religion and American Politics*. New York: Simon and Schuster.

Wolf, Eric. (1969). *Peasant Wars of the Twentieth Century*. New York: Harper and Row.

Woodward, C. Vann. (1963). *Tom Watson: Agrarian Rebel*. New York: Oxford University Press.

Zald, Mayer. (1992). "Looking Backward to Look Forward: Reflections on the Past and Future of the Resource Mobilization Research Program." In Aldon Morris and Carol Mueller (eds.), *Frontiers in Social Movement Theory*. New Haven, CT: Yale University Press.

Zald, Mayer, and Roberta Ash. (1966). "Social Movement Organizations." *Social Forces* 44 (March), 327-341.

Zald, Mayer, and Michael Berger. (1971). "Social Movements in Organizations: Coup d'Etat, Insurgency, and Mass Movements." *American Journal of Sociology* 83 (January), 823-861.

Zald, Mayer, and John McCarthy, eds. (1979). *The Dynamics of Social Movements: Resource Mobilization, Social Control and Tactics.* Cambridge, MA: Winthrop.

_____. (1987). *Social Movements in an Organizational Society.* New Brunswick, NJ: Transaction Books.

Zald, Mayer, and Bert Useem. (1987). "From Pressure Group to Social Movement: Organizational Dilemmas of the Effort to Promote Nuclear Power." In Mayer Zald and John McCarthy (eds.), *Social Movements in an Organizational Society.* New Brunswick, NJ: Transaction Books.

A GUIDE TO THE BIBLIOGRAPHY

The bibliography is organized into two parts with a total of thirteen chapters. Part I, consisting of the first three chapters, covers three analytic approaches to the study of social movements. The first chapter of Part I is dedicated to social movement theory and to a wide variety of explanatory frameworks used by researchers in the field of social movements. The second chapter explores the temporal context of movements, or the characteristics of the time periods in which they emerge. It lists works that analyze the historical and economic conditions in which movements arise. Chapter 3 focuses on the spatial dimension of the analysis of movements, based on an area case study approach to social movements. It offers a sample of empirical studies and research monographs that analyze the interaction of movements in a specific country or region.

Part II, comprising chapters 4 through 12, covers studies of specific transnational movements. Chapters in this part contain separate listings for books (including book chapters) and articles in periodicals. Articles were selected to meet three criteria: Lasting theoretical interest, recent publication, and reader accessibility. All articles selected had to meet the standard of providing in-depth analysis rather than reportage or narrative accounts of specific movements or instances of activism. Most periodical articles selected for the bibliography were published after 1985, although articles of major and lasting theoretical importance published before that date are included. Articles were included only if they are in periodicals that typically are available in university libraries in the United States. The chapters are organized according to movements. Each chapter in this part ends with a brief subsection titled "Also of Interest," which lists related works, without annotations. The bibliography ends with chapter 13, an essay on films and novels that feature social movements.

The reader should be aware that no bibliographical guide is complete and that it is especially difficult to establish a comprehensive and definitive listing of periodical articles. Many of the books in the bibliography contain reference sections, and these may be useful sources for identifying additional materials.

For further periodical materials, readers may wish to consult several types of sources. *International Social Movement Research* and *Research in Social Movements, Conflicts, and Change* are two specialized journals that publish research and theory for scholars in the field. Articles about social movements also appear frequently in major journals of sociology such as the *American Sociological Review*, *American Journal of Sociology*, *Social Forces*, *Social Problems*, *Sociological Forum*, and *British*

Journal of Sociology, as well as in political science journals, especially *Politics and Society* and the *Annals of the American Academy of Political and Social Science*. Coverage of feminism, women's movements, and movements of sexual orientation can be found in journals such as *Signs*, *Gender and Society*, and *Feminist Review*. Analysis of the rhetoric of social movements and their impact on public opinion appears in journals in the fields of communications and political science.

A number of periodicals on the left end of the political spectrum offer thought-provoking perspectives. The leading publication in this respect probably is the *New Left Review*, with its wide-ranging theoretical articles as well as analytic overviews of movements, parties, and collective action in specific nations and at the global level. In its pages, readers will find ongoing discussions between a sophisticated Marxist perspective and other theoretical points of view. Also of interest are *Monthly Review*, *Socialist Review*, and *Dissent*.

Finally, readers can consult several computerized databases to update and expand their reading lists. The most useful of these for purposes of finding articles about social movements and collective action probably is Sociofile, which indexes hundreds of journals, including international listings, as far back as the 1970's and provides an abstract for each article. The Wilson Social Science Index also is valuable. It includes a larger range of popular publications as well as scholarly ones. Newspaper Abstracts and The Reader's Guide provide constantly updated journalistic accounts.

Readers will also find much of interest on the Internet, both as an aid to research and as a locus of social activism.

PART I

ANALYTICAL APPROACHES

Chapter 1
SOCIAL MOVEMENT THEORY

This chapter includes overviews of theory; essays on specific theoretical problems and issues; books and articles with a broad, inclusive, and analytic scope in their coverage of movements (rather than a descriptive focus on a specific movement); studies that have a comparative framework; and studies that focus on a specific case study in order to build theory or develop concepts.

Aberle, David. (1991). *The Peyote Religion Among the Navaho*. Norman: University of Oklahoma Press.
This is a new edition of a classic study of a revitalization movement. One of its contributions to theory is the classification of movements into alterative, redemptive, reformative, and transformative types. Includes an appendix on Navaho population and education by Denis F. Johnston.

Adorno, Theodor, E. Frenkel-Brunswick, D. Levinson, and R. Sanford. (1993). *The Authoritarian Personality*. New York: Norton. (abridged version of 1950 first edition)
A social psychological study of predispositions toward fascism and related political ideologies. The authors propose an inventory—the F-scale—to measure these predispositions, with emphasis on ethnocentrism, deference to authority, and rigidity in thought and attitudes. The analysis draws on Adorno's interest in psychoanalysis, culture, and Marxist theory, so that despite its apparently empirical approach and psychological orientation, it is really an essay on the sources of fascism, ethnocentrism, and right-wing authoritarianism in modern societies. Despite some dated aspects of the data, it remains a theoretical milestone.

Anderson, Benedict. (1991). *Imagined Communities*. London: Verso.
An essay on the nature and origins of nationalism. The book defines nationalism, traces its connection to print media and nation-state formation, and examines different phases of nationalism from origins in the Americas to decolonization after World War II. The detailed and complex theoretical argument takes a social constructionist view that nationalism is not a primordial form of identity but a sentiment that is experienced and elaborated only under certain conditions that are characteristic of modern, capitalist societies. The study is important for

social movement theory in general as well as the theory of nationalism because of its exemplary documentation of the process by which identity is socially constructed.

Arendt, Hannah. (1965). *On Revolution*. New York: Viking.
This essay is a reflection on the concept of revolution. It contrasts the American and French revolutions, arguing that the former was a successful political revolution whereas the latter was an effort to change social relationships and eliminate social inequality, an inherently more difficult project than change in the political system. The continuing importance of Arendt's analysis is in the definition of revolution and the distinctions she makes between political and societal goals.

Aronowitz, Stanley. (1973). *False Promises*. New York: McGraw-Hill.
An essay about the Left in the United States in the post-World War II period. The author uses his own experience to discuss American culture, political ideology, and the role of movements and unions. He suggests that unions became mechanisms for integrating the working class into capitalism and that increasingly, the media and popular culture also are serving this function. The book provides a valuable overview, from a Marxist perspective, of American culture in the postwar period. Its theoretical conclusions about changes within capitalist societies can be applied to most of the developed market democracies in this period.

Berman, Marshall. (1982). *All That Is Solid Melts into Air*. London: Verso.
Discussion of the modern as a form of society and culture, as well as a movement in literature and the arts. The chapters are organized as essays on works that define the modern age—Goethe's *Faust*, Marx's *Communist Manifesto*, and so on. The author brings together change in the arts (modernism) and change in social structure (modernity), arguing that these changes are part of the same process of movement into a volatile, innovative, and unpredictable form of culture.

Blumer, Herbert. (1951). "Collective Behavior." In Alfred McClung Lee (ed.), *New Outline of the Principles of Sociology*. New York: Barnes and Noble.
A major work of theory, in which Blumer places the study of social movements within a symbolic interactionist framework. He views social movements (like all human action) as ongoing processes of communication among social actors. The essay was widely read and cited at the time of its publication but did not have a proportionate

influence on the empirical research agenda of its day. The essay bears rereading in the light of renewed attention to interaction and discourse in cultural studies in the 1990's.

Buechler, Steven. (1993). "Beyond Resource Mobilization? Emerging Trends in Social Movement Theory." *Sociological Quarterly* 34, 217-235.
The author argues that the two-decades-long dominance of resource mobilization theory in the field may be waning and suggests that women's movements in the United States pose challenges to this theoretical paradigm.

Burbach, Roger. (1994). "Roots of Postmodern Rebellion in Chiapas." *New Left Review* 205 (May/June), 113-123.
The author defines the movement of the Zapatistas in Mexico as postmodern because of its post-Cold War context, its effort to reform civil society from the bottom up, and its fluid structure. He contrasts the wealth of resources and production in Chiapas to the abject poverty of the people. After the 1970's, capitalism penetrated deeply into the region, disrupting traditional communities and old forms of clientelistic political control by the PRI (Institutional Revolutionary Party). The social upheaval involved the uprooting of peasants, new labor markets, a cattle and petroleum boom, and increasing class inequality within indigenous villages. As the Salinas government's agrarian policies gutted the institution of communal farming (the *ejido*), the sum total of these changes set the stage for collective action. Although focused on a specific national instance, the analysis has implications for a general theoretical understanding of postmodern social strains and the movements they spark.

Cardoza, Anthony L. (1982). *Agrarian Elites and Italian Fascism: The Province of Bologna 1901-26*. Princeton, NJ: Princeton University Press.
A carefully researched scholarly study of the origins of fascism in central Italy, with a focus on fascist connections to agribusiness. The study is a major contribution to the understanding of fascism and of general interest to theorists in its analysis of the social base of the fascist movement, including adherents, constituents, and beneficiaries of the movement.

Chaliand, Gerard. (1989). *Revolution in the Third World*. New York: Penguin.

A critical analysis of Third World independence movements. In the author's view, in spite of their socialist rhetoric, they brought into power an "administrative bourgeoisie" that failed to transform social structure or reduce social inequalities. The analysis offers a broadly comparative contribution to understanding decolonization, social revolution, and national liberation movements in the post-World War II period.

Cohen, Stanley. (1987). *Folk Devils and Moral Panics: The Creation of the Mods and Rockers.* Oxford, England: Basil Blackwell.
This study of British youth movements introduced the terms "folk devils" and "moral panics" as key concepts for the analysis of public opinion and media coverage of movements.

Converse, Philip E. (1964). "Ideology in Mass Publics." In David Apter (ed.), *Ideology and Discontent.* New York: Free Press.
A valuable contribution to the study of ideology and belief systems. The author argues that most people do not have coherent, internally consistent ideological views of politics and society (such as socialism or conservatism). Rather, their belief systems are partial and fragmentary. The implications are that people with these fragmentary belief systems can be mobilized in different directions and that perhaps a certain share of them may be difficult to mobilize at all, because their ideas are so sketchy and inconsistent. Contemporary concepts for understanding the organization and influence of political discourses, such as "frames" and "spin," will lend a new depth to a reading of this article.

Curtis, Russell L., and Benigno Aguirre, eds. (1993). *Collective Behavior and Social Movements.* Boston: Allyn and Bacon.
A collection of current and classic scholarly articles that includes theoretical essays and empirical studies of specific movements. It contains a number of valuable essays in the social movement field and covers a wide spectrum of theories and empirical approaches, with emphasis on case studies within the U.S. context. A useful overview of organizational theory in the social movement field is provided by Russell and Zurcher, in "Social Movements: An Analytical Exploration of Organizational Forms." Another selection of note is J. Craig Jenkins and Charles Perrow, "Insurgency of the Powerless: Farmworker Movements 1946-72," which develops theoretical issues in resource mobilization theory and the analysis of the relationship between movements

of the powerless and societal elites. The collection does not have a comprehensive bibliography or index.

Dalton, Russell, ed. (1993). *Symposium on Citizens, Protest, and Democracy. Annals of the American Academy of Political and Social Science* 528 (July).

The symposium is a collection of research articles and scholarly essays on new forms of movements, especially in Western Europe and North America. It emphasizes processes of citizen mobilization, the impact of movements on public policy, cross-boundary movements, relationships between parties and movements, and the interconnection of movements with media. The volume as a whole is of vital importance to social movement theory and the comparative study of political behavior. The volume contains the following articles: Jeffrey Berry, "Citizen Groups and the Changing Nature of Interest Group Politics in America"; William Gamson and G. Wolfsfeld, "Movements and Media as Interacting Systems"; Carol Hagen, "Citizen Movements and Technological Policymaking in Germany"; Marjorie Hershey, "Citizens' Groups and Political Parties in the United States"; Herbert Kitschelt, "Social Movements, Political Parties, and Democratic Theory"; Diarmuid Maguire, "Protesters, Counterprotesters, and the Authorities"; Doug McAdam and Dieter Rucht, "The Cross-National Diffusion of Movement Ideas"; Thomas Rochon and Daniel Mazmanian, "Social Movements and the Policy Process"; and Ronald Shaiko, "Greenpeace USA: Something Old, New, Borrowed."

Davies, James. (1962). "Toward a Theory of Revolution." *American Sociological Review* 27, no. 1 (February), 5-19.

This article is a theoretical discussion of the conditions that are likely to precipitate revolutions. The author suggests that these movements often emerge after a period during which elites have carried out reforms designed to preempt, coopt, or defuse opposition; these reforms lead to rising expectations for continued social change, and if the rate of reform slows, a sense of disappointment ensues that contributes to incidents of rebellion and increasing radicalization of opposition movements.

Donald, James, and Stuart Hall, eds. (1986). *Politics and Ideology: A Reader*. Philadelphia: Milton Keynes.

The editors pull together a number of essays that explore the establishment of hegemony in societies, a process of class rule that depends on the creation of popular consent, often by incorporating some ele-

ments of popular opinion and condensing contradictory discourses into
a new prevailing "common sense." Much of this perspective is informed by the thought of Antonio Gramsci, an Italian Marxist who
wrote in the pre-World War II period. These ideological processes are
in turn linked to more specifically political ones in order to consolidate
class rule in democratic systems.

Eyerman, Ron, and Andrew Jamison. (1991). *Social Movements.* University Park: Pennsylvania State University Press.
The authors view movements as voices of new cognitive praxis. Each
movement represents a new cognitive understanding of social reality.
In this perspective, emphasis is on what other theorists call movement
ideologies, on the ideas of movements, and especially on innovations
in ideas that may sooner or later alter the mainstream cognitive praxis
of a society.

Fagen, Richard, Carmen Deere, and José Luis Coraggio. (1986). *Transition and Development.* New York: Monthly Review Press.
An important collection of essays about the problems faced by Third
World revolutionary regimes. Several of the essays focus on Nicaragua, and others provide cross-national comparisons. Given global
developments since the mid-1980's, the volume offers a post mortem
on many of the states that succumbed to the problems diagnosed by
the authors: counterinsurgency, external pressures including economic
and military support for counterrevolutionary movements, economic
dislocations caused by the regimes' efforts to equalize opportunities
and/or to break with the logic of producing low-wage goods and
agricultural exports for global markets, difficulties in obtaining loans
in international credit markets, and domestic cultural tensions. Although uniformly sympathetic to the socialist regimes about which
they write, the authors are objective and unsentimental in their analysis
of these problems.

Fendrich, James Max, and Kenneth Lovoy. (1988). "Back to the Future:
Adult Political Behavior of Former Student Activists." *American Sociological Review* 53, 780-784.
The authors examine the adult political behavior of a sample of student
activists of the 1960's and find continuity in values and orientations.
The former student activists continued to hold views on the left side of
the political spectrum and became participants in movements that were
consistent with the value positions of their earlier activism. There was

no support for the notion of a "Big Chill" that led former activists to withdraw from politics or to shift to more conservative orientations.

Fernandez, R., and Doug McAdam. (1989). "Multiorganizational Fields and Recruitment to Social Movements." In P. G. Klandermans (ed.), *Organizing for Change: Social Movement Organizations Across Cultures.* Greenwich, Conn: JAI Press.
Working within the resource mobilization framework, the authors look at patterns of competition in recruitment and mobilization of potential supporters.

Freeman, Jo, ed. (1983). *Social Movements of the Sixties and Seventies.* New York: Longman.
This collection is composed of essays by social scientists analyzing the emergence, ideologies, and mobilization strategies of a variety of movements in the United States, including the women's movement, the Civil Rights movement, and movements on behalf of disabled people. Many of the essays make theoretical contributions to an understanding of the period, and most are readable for novices in the field. The position of the authors combines scholarly objectivity, a measure of historical distance from the events, and a dispassionate tone with some degree of sympathy for the movements. This is one of the best collections available for understanding movements of the period.

Gamson, William. (1975). *The Strategy of Social Protest.* Homewood, Il: Dorsey Press.
Empirical tests of the effectiveness of various movement strategies and organizational forms, focusing on variables such as size, incentive structure, use of violence, bureaucratization, factionalism, and centralization of movements. The author provides interesting comparisons of movements within the United States from 1800 to after World War II and offers conclusions about which types of movements produce which types of outcomes in terms of gaining advantages for the challenging group or the acceptance, cooptation, preemption, or collapse of the group. Methodologically sophisticated and of great importance to theory construction. A revised edition was published in 1991.

_____. (1992). "The Social Psychology of Collective Action." In Aldon Morris and Carol Mueller (eds.), *Frontiers in Social Movement Theory.* New Haven, CT: Yale University Press.
This article revisits the topic of social psychological factors in movement participation and suggests a need for renewed emphasis on

individual predispositions, informed by current research on the formation of collective identities.

Garner, Larry, and Roberta Garner. (1981). "Problems of the Hegemonic
Party: The PCI and the Structural Limits of Reform." *Science and
Society* 45, no. 3 (Fall), 257-273.
The article uses the concept of hegemony to analyze dilemmas faced
by the Italian Communists as the party reached beyond its working-
class base and participated in the Italian political process in the 1970's.
Reforms that were important to its industrial working class core
constituency created economic pressures that alienated a larger cross-
class potential support base. The article uses the Italian case to discuss
dilemmas that faced Euro-Communist parties and socialist parties in
general as they contended for a leading role in market societies and
thereby offers predictive insight into the rightward shift that took place
in the 1980's in many of these nations. The article also provides a short
summary of the concept of hegemony as it appeared in the work of
Antonio Gramsci and subsequent Marxist theorists.

Garner, Roberta. (1977). *Social Movements in America.* Chicago: Rand
McNally.
A historical treatment of the emergence and consequences of major
movements in the United States from a Marxist-influenced perspective. The rise of movements is explained in terms of changes in the
capitalist political economy in successive periods of U.S. history, from
the decline of the mercantilist economy through the growth of large
corporations in the late nineteenth century to the Great Depression and
the post-World War II military-industrial boom. Transformations of the
mode of production generated class movements but also brought to the
fore other types of activism along lines of ethnicity, cultural difference,
and gender; though not class based, these types of movements can be
explained by a structural analysis focused on changes in the capitalist
mode of production. The analysis points to the way in which the
reforms proposed by movements frequently were incorporated into
U.S. political and social institutions in forms that had been unintended
by their proponents. In addition to the specific case study of movements in the United States, the book provides a theoretical framework
focused on historical change and the mode of production that could be
extended to any society.

_____. (1996). *Contemporary Movements and Ideologies.* New
York: McGraw-Hill.

This book offers an introduction to transnational movements and ideologies. The first part provides a basic vocabulary of the social movement field and covers a wide range of theoretical approaches. Emphasis is placed on movements within the context of modern social history. The second part of the book gives brief summaries of the ideology, structure, and historical circumstances of eight major types of movements: conservatism, liberalism (in the broadest sense), socialism and the Left, religious movements, nationalism, fascism and Nazism, movements of gender and sexual orientation, and environmental movements. The concept of the postmodern is used to discuss emerging characteristics of movements. The book is aimed at giving the beginner a basic vocabulary, a theoretical overview, and background information.

Garner, Roberta, and Mayer Zald. (1985). "The Political Economy of Social Movement Sectors." In Gerald Suttles and Mayer Zald (eds.), *The Challenge of Social Control: Citizenship and Institution Building in Modern Society.* Norwood, NJ: Ablex.
This essay defines the concept of the "social movement sector" as a sphere of activity and proposes a research agenda of comparative analysis of its structure and its relationship to political institutions. The examples are drawn from the United States and Western Europe, most notably Italy. The analysis of political opportunity structures and multiorganizational fields is enhanced by the concept of the social movement sector.

Gerlach, Luther. (1983). "Movements of Revolutionary Change: Some Structural Characteristics." In Jo Freeman (ed.), *Social Movements of the Sixties and Seventies.* New York: Longman.
This essay emphasizes variations in movement structure, including decentralized ("acephalous" and "polycephalous") and segmented forms. It marks a break with theoretical analysis that emphasized centralization and bureaucracy in movements and provides the foundation for contemporary analysis of movement networks. The Pentecostal movement is one of the examples that furthers the theoretical analysis.

Gitlin, Todd. (1980). *The Whole World Is Watching.* Berkeley: University of California Press.
The author analyzes how the media promoted the movement of opposition to the war in Vietnam but ultimately misrepresented it to the public and distorted its structure. The promotion of individuals to the

role of "media stars" who spoke for the movement and the pressure on the movement to create attention-grabbing events to gain media coverage are examples of the way in which media-movement interaction proved disruptive for the movement. This book is a classic in analyzing media-movement interaction. Gitlin brings to his work both a strong theoretical approach and movement participant experience. A must for the student of media, movements, and contemporary political life.

——————. (1993). "The Rise of 'Identity Politics': An Examination and a Critique." *Dissent* 40, no. 2 (Spring), 172-177.
The author analyzes the shift in politics from commonality and aspirations for inclusion on universalistic terms to a new politics that is defensive and celebrates a victimization stance. This shift represents a challenge to progressive liberal and Marxist ideologies. Offers thought-provoking theoretical analysis of recent trends in collective identity and action.

Goldstone, Jack. (1991a). "Ideology, Cultural Frameworks, and the Process of Revolution." *Theory and Society* 20, no. 4 (August), 405-453.
The author contrasts the role of ideology in several revolutions: the English revolution of 1640, the French Revolution, the Ming-Quing transition in seventeenth century China, and rebellions in the Ottoman Empire. The author discusses various forms of ideology (popular and elite) and the difference between ideologies as distinct programs of change and the larger cultural matrix that provides the vocabulary from which ideological discourses are built. These cultural frameworks shape the limits of how transformations are envisioned, even in radical ideologies. In the West, the Judeo-Christian framework, with its apocalyptic imagery, "set the stage" for more radical views of revolutionary transformation, while in the East, cyclical cultural frameworks channeled revolutionary ideology toward the reestablishment of "purer virtue," a more conservative formulation. A good example of the renewed theoretical interest in the cultural context of social movements and the formation of ideologies.

——————. (1991b). *Revolution and Rebellion in the Early Modern World*. Berkeley: University of California Press.
The author looks at revolutions in terms of state crises in the middle of the seventeenth, eighteenth, and nineteenth centuries and interprets these crises as the results of long-term cyclical processes involving demographic changes as well as social, economic, and political transformations.

Goodwin, Jeff, and Theda Skocpol. (1989). "Explaining Revolutions in the Contemporary Third World." *Politics and Society* 17 (December), 489-509.

This article explains revolutions in terms of state structure. It uses a neo-Weberian perspective that highlights the form of a regime and its relationship to social structure as a key variable in explaining the outcome of revolutionary movements. The article suggests that patrimonial regimes, such as those of the Somoza family in Nicaragua and Haile Selassie in Ethiopia, are the ones most likely to fall to revolutionary movements. The article is of both theoretical and empirical significance because it examines a number of actual political situations and proposes a coherent theoretical framework to explain the outcomes.

Gorz, Andre. (1985). *Paths to Paradise: On the Liberation from Work.* Boston: South End.

The author offers a vision of a society of advanced technology and democratic socialism. Values of egalitarianism, cooperation, freedom from want, reduction of onerous work, and creative opportunities are enhanced. The text does not purport to provide a realistic strategy for establishing such a society but serves as an engaging political fantasy.

Gould, James A., and William Truitt. (1973). *Political Ideologies.* New York: Macmillan.

Covers liberalism, fascism, conservatism, the radical right, Marxism and Marxism-Leninism, democratic socialists, the New Left, Third World movements, and anarchism and counterculture through selected documents and position statements. Dated, but some materials are still of interest.

Gramsci, Antonio. (1971). *Selections from the Prison Notebooks.* New York: International Publishers.

These collected essays are the contributions of a leading Italian Marxist to the theoretical understanding of the relationship between culture and class structure. The extensive use of Italian historical examples may create some problems for initial reading, and these problems are compounded by the fact that Gramsci wrote under conditions of prison censorship as a political prisoner of Fascism. This volume develops and applies Gramsci's concepts of "hegemony" and "organic intellectuals" (those intellectuals who emerge out of and speak for the experience of a social class). It is a classic of Marxist analysis that now has wide influence in the social sciences and cultural studies.

Greene, Thomas. (1990). *Comparative Revolutionary Movements: Search for Theory and Justice*. Englewood Cliffs, NJ: Prentice-Hall.
An introduction to basic terms and concepts for the discussion of political movements, applied to a number of twentieth century revolutions. The definition of terms is clear and useful for the beginning student of social movements. The selected terms can be used within several different theoretical frameworks and thus provide a useful general background vocabulary. The chronologies and discussions of several twentieth century revolutions form a good starting point for further reading and analysis.

Gurr, Ted. (1970). *Why Men Rebel*. Princeton, NJ: Princeton University Press.
The author uses a social psychological framework to explain social movements as a response to societal strain. A condition of relative deprivation is experienced when people perceive a gap between their aspirations and their actual opportunities, especially as they compare themselves to various reference situations such as their past situation or the situation of comparable groups. When existing cultural practices permit an expression of anger against political targets, various forms of turmoil, political violence, and internal war may emerge. The analysis continues to be of value to social movement theory.

Gusfield, Joseph. (1963). *Symbolic Crusade: Status Politics and the American Temperance Movement*. Urbana: University of Illinois Press.
Analyzes the U.S. temperance movement in terms of status politics, as a response of the Protestant middle strata to what they perceived to be threats to their social and cultural position at the turn of the century, in the context of massive Southern and Eastern European immigration. The author provides a historical case study of the translation of cultural conflicts into movement activism and moral crusades, an example that continues to be relevant for an understanding of U.S. politics, the "war on drugs," and reactions to renewed immigration.

Hadden, Jeffrey K. (1993). "The Rise and Fall of American Televangelism." In Wade Clark Roof (ed.), *Religion in the Nineties*. Special issue of *The Annals of the American Academy of Political and Social Science* 527 (May), 113-130.
The author gives an insightful explanation of the political and economic reasons why televangelists came to dominate religious broadcasting in the United States in the 1980's and also points to some factors in the decline of televangelism later in the decade. Historical depth is

added by a discussion of the consistent rightward tilt of evangelism throughout the century. This article is a valuable contribution to several overlapping areas of inquiry: the role of religion in U.S. politics, the relation between media economic structure and political ideologies, the interaction between movement ideologues and mass constituencies in the era of electronic media, and the formation of the religious right.

Handler, Joel. (1992). "Postmodernism, Protest and the New Social Movements." *Law and Society Review* 26, no. 4, 697-731.
The author uses ideas from Derrida and deconstructionist philosophy to focus on the diffusely subversive character of new social movements. These movements purport to be everywhere, taking the form of cultural resistance within virtually all institutions and interactions. The author raises the question whether resistance that is neither organized nor focused on specific institutional goals can really accomplish lasting social change; being everywhere, these movements may turn out to be nowhere, that is, not to create any lasting structural changes. This stimulating think piece is followed by several replies.

Hebdige, Dick. (1982). *Subculture*. London: Methuen.
Analysis of youth culture and oppositional cultural movements in Britain in the postwar period: Mods, rockers, Rastafarians, and punks. The book discusses the interplay of English and West Indian culture and the political meaning of cultural movements. It uses concepts from structural theory, especially the work of French structuralist anthropologist Claude Lévi-Strauss, to explain the elements of youth cultures and how these elements are assembled. The work is useful for insight into the relationship between cultures of resistance and more explicitly political movements. Some chapters present rather difficult points of theory and require some background in structural theory.

Hobsbawm, Eric. (1959). *Primitive Rebels: Studies in Archaic Forms of Social Movements*. New York: Norton.
Mobs, banditry, secret societies, and forms of anarchism are interpreted as oppositional movements and mobilizations in the context of European history. Many of them can be identified as primitive types of movements that arose as a first line of response to the impact of capitalism on agrarian societies. The analysis points to areas of overlap between movements and criminal activity, especially in social contexts that lack elaborated modern political ideologies.

_____. (1981). *Bandits*. New York: Pantheon.
Examines banditry as a primitive form of oppositional mobilization triggered by the impact of capitalism in rural areas, especially in Southern Europe and Latin America.

Hoffman, Louise. (1984). "Psychoanalytic Interpretations of Political Movements." *Psychohistory Review* 13, no. 1 (Fall), 16-29.
An overview of the history of psychoanalytic theories of movements, beginning with Freud and ranging through the legacy of the Frankfurt School, which combined Hegelian, Marxian, and psychoanalytical approaches and related modern movements such as fascism to the dislocations inherent in modern mass society.

Johnson, Chalmers. (1964). *Revolution and the Social System*. Stanford, CA: Stanford University Press.
The author draws on the work of Talcott Parsons and other structural-functional theorists to suggest that revolutions occur when there is a crisis of legitimacy, when values and environment are dis-synchronized. As this occurs, existing authorities either undertake reforms to restore the integration of values and environment or turn to coercion. The latter strategy often is only a stopgap measure that exacerbates the crisis of legitimacy and brings on violent, revolutionary forms of systemic change. Thus, value orientations, political legitimacy, and system coherence are the major concepts of this theoretical approach. The book is a contribution to the theory of revolution that continues to be of interest.

Kitschelt, Herbert. (1990). "New Social Movements and the Decline of Party Organizations." In Russell Dalton and Manfred Kuechler (eds.), *Challenging the Political Order*. New York: Oxford University Press.
Looking especially at Western European examples, the author connects the rise of the New Social Movements (such as the peace movement, environmentalist movements, urban squatter movements, and movements that challenge the gender system) in the post-1960's period to weakening coherence of party structure. Political parties became less able to contain and coopt ideological challengers. The article is a contribution to understanding the relationship between social movements and more institutionalized political actors.

Klandermans, Bert. (1989). Various articles in *International Social Movement Research*, vol. 2.
This volume of the journal *International Social Movement Research* contains a series of articles by Bert Klandermans and others that

address topics of multiorganizational fields, alliances and conflicts between movements, interorganizational networks, leadership and management in social movement organizations, exit behavior in social movement organizations, and the relationship between movement organization and effectiveness. The author argues for the complementarity of several theoretical approaches: traditional breakdown or social strain theories, resource mobilization theory, New Social Movement theory, and theories that focus on the construction of meaning.

_____. (1991). "The Peace Movement and Social Movement Theory." *International Social Movement Research* 3, no. 1, 1-39.
This is the introduction to an issue of the journal that compares the peace movement and the anti-cruise missile campaign of the late 1970's in six countries—the United States, Great Britain, The Netherlands, West Germany, Belgium, and Italy. The author emphasizes that this situation forms a natural experiment in which movements within different national political systems and cultures pursued the same goal. The peace movement also illustrates the internationalization of protest.

_____. (1993). "A Theoretical Framework for Comparisons of Social Movement Participation." *Sociological Forum* 8, no. 3 (September), 383-402.
The theoretical framework includes mobilization potentials, multiorganizational fields, organizational characteristics, and action orientation as characteristics of movement organizations within their environments. The framework is used to compare three movements in The Netherlands: a labor union's strike campaign, a local peace movement campaign, and campaigns of women's groups. Differences in levels of participation and motivation are explained in terms of organizational characteristics. A contribution that relates movement structure to participation and support base mobilization.

Koopmans, Ruud. (1993). "The Dynamics of Protest Waves: West Germany, 1965-1989." *American Sociological Review* 58, 637-658.
The author examines similarities in protest waves in West Germany, Italy, The Netherlands, and the United States using newspaper accounts from the mid-1960's to the late 1980's. The dynamics of protest waves are shaped by the interplay of external factors (facilitation, repression, and the chance of success) and internal factors associated with activists' choices among strategic options. The article contributes to a growing body of theory concerned with the dynamics of movement

organizations and forms of collective action over a medium-range time period.

Kornhauser, William. (1959). *The Politics of Mass Society*. New York: Free Press.

The author explains social movements and other forms of social unrest in terms of mass society, a conceptualization of modern society that emphasizes its characteristic social strains arising from rapid social change, the disruption of stable traditional communities, and an increasingly anomic normative order.

Kuhn, Thomas. (1962). *The Structure of Scientific Revolutions*. Chicago: University of Chicago Press.

Using a history of science perspective, the author analyzes how change takes place within fields of scientific inquiry. Fields develop not only through the routine accumulation of empirical knowledge but also, and more important, through paradigm shifts—sudden and total reformulations of theory, methods, and basic questions. Although most of the examples are drawn from the natural sciences, anyone interested in how disciplines, bodies of theory, and fields of inquiry develop will benefit from reading this work, now an academic classic.

Laraña, Enrique, Hank Johnston, and Joseph R. Gusfield, eds. (1994). *New Social Movements: From Ideology to Identity*. Philadelphia, PA: Temple University Press.

A collection of articles by leading scholars in social movement theory attempts to answer the question, "What are New Social Movements?" They are characterized by dislocation from class structure, diversified ideologies that are both democratic and antipolitical, and a strong emphasis on new dimensions of identity, especially concern with the self and the circumstances of everyday life. The articles include analyses of collective action as diverse as the anti-drunk driving movement, the Dutch peace movement, the Greens, women's movements, and new forms of nationalist movements. The volume ends on a hopeful but not completely convincing note in Richard Flacks' "The Party's Over—So What Is to Be Done?," which expresses the view that despite—or perhaps because of—the collapse of party structures, the decline of the Left, the weakening of the nation-state, the dismantling of the welfare state, and the globalization of the economy, it will be possible to create democratic and decentralized forms of collective action and community empowerment. The volume as a whole is thought provoking and readable, as well as of theoretical significance.

Lasswell, Harold, and Daniel Lerner. (1966). *World Revolutionary Elites: Studies in Coercive Ideological Movements*. Boston: MIT Press.
A comparative study of the formation and specialization of leaders in Communist, nationalist, and Fascist/Nazi movements, in terms of their administrative, ideological, and coercive roles and social origins. Though dated in some of the analysis, the collection of essays still provides insights into the roles and social origins of leaders of these historical movements.

Luker, Kristin. (1984). *Abortion and the Politics of Motherhood*. Berkeley: University of California Press.
A major empirical study that situates activists' ideology and movement commitments within a larger set of experiences and concerns, on both sides of the abortion issue. Activism is associated (on both sides) with ideas about the nature of women and personal commitments to one or another way of being a woman. The study provides theoretical insights into the ideological and social underpinnings of movements and countermovements.

McAdam, Doug, John McCarthy, and Mayer Zald. (1988). "Social Movements." In Neil Smelser (ed.), *Handbook of Sociology*. Beverly Hills, CA: Sage.
An excellent overview of the field as it had developed by the end of the 1980's. The authors are associated with resource mobilization theory, and their emphasis is on the organization, strategies, and instrumental rationality of movements.

McClellan, David. (1971). *The Thought of Karl Marx*. New York: Harper and Row.
The author explains the basic ideas both in chronological order and by major concepts, accompanied by excerpts from the writings. Excellent organization for the reader who wants an introductory overview or is looking for key illustrative passages.

_____, ed. (1977). *Karl Marx: Selected Writings*. Oxford, England: Oxford University Press.
A major one-volume selection of the works of Karl Marx. This is a valuable collection because the editor has provided long text selections rather than engaging in a scissors-and-paste assembly of key passages. Marx's thinking continues to influence sociology and social movement theory in forms that have been revised to fit the realities of contemporary capitalism.

McCoy, Charles Allan. (1982). *Contemporary Isms: A Political Economy Perspective*. New York: Franklin Watts.

An overview of liberalism, communism, market socialism, and fascism. Good exposition of ideologies, a bit dated in the descriptive data.

Melucci, Alberto. (1989). *Nomads of the Present: Social Movements and Individual Needs in Contemporary Society*. London: Hutchinson Radius.

Written in a rather abstract style, this book-length essay identifies three levels of explanation for collective action—social sectors, mobilization processes, and individual commitment. Movements are seen as an essential element of contemporary society, which is always in a state of self-reflective reconstruction.

Miliband, Ralph. (1969). *The State in Capitalist Society*. London: Weidenfeld and Nicolson.

This analysis remains valuable for its discussion of why it is difficult for socialist parties (and movements) to accomplish their goals within the structure of capitalist society. It provides an explanation of why socialist parties, once voted into office, remain limited in their effect on society.

Moore, Barrington. (1965). *Social Origins of Dictatorship and Democracy*. Boston: Beacon Press.

A modern classic. The author offers a coherent comparative explanation of modern political systems in terms of underlying class structures and interaction among classes. In societies in which modernization involved the formation of a bloc of peasants, workers, and the middle class against landed elites, the outcome was liberal democratic political systems, as in England, France, and the United States. Where modernization was a project of landed elites attempting to transform themselves into industrial capitalist ruling classes, fascism appeared, most notably in Germany and Japan. Where the project of modernization and rural transformation failed, as in China and Russia, socialist revolution was the outcome. Moore illustrates the use of a relatively small number of cases to develop a sophisticated general theoretical model of the outcomes of collective action within determining structures.

Morris, Aldon. (1981). "Black Southern Student Sit-In Movement: An Analysis of Internal Organization." *American Sociological Review* 46, 744-767.

A milestone in development of contemporary movement theory, emphasizing the role of organization in civil rights mobilization.

_____. (1984). *The Origins of the Civil Rights Movement.* New York: Free Press.
In a leading study of the Civil Rights movement, the author develops a framework that links movement organization and collective action to the structure of the support base, for example in discussing the relationship of the movement organizations to other, preexisting organizations in the African American community such as the black churches. His work is associated with resource mobilization theory in a broad sense of the term, although he places somewhat less emphasis on purely strategic organizational processes than do other theorists within this perspective.

_____. (1993). "Birmingham Confrontation Revisited: An Analysis of the Dynamics and Tactics of Mobilization." *American Sociological Review* 58, no. 5 (October), 621-636.
The author considers the tactics of the 1963 confrontation in Birmingham, Alabama, arguing against the proposition that the movement succeeded by deliberately provoking violence. The case study is used to discuss the relationships of movement organization, mobilization, and tactics and their contribution to movement outcomes.

Morris, Aldon D., and Carol McClurg Mueller, eds. (1992). *Frontiers in Social Movement Theory.* New Haven, CT: Yale University Press.
This is a major recent collection of essays in social movement theory. Many of the essays reaffirm some variant of resource mobilization theory but expand the possibilities toward more cultural and social-psychological approaches, such as frame analysis. Most of the essays presuppose familiarity with the field and its issues. The volume includes articles on social movement theory and rational choice theories of behavior, the social psychology of collective action, social movements within multiorganizational fields, the formation of collective identity, the analysis of networks, cycles of protest, mentalities and political culture, frame analysis, and the relationship between movements and state and civic infrastructures. The contributors are theorists who are in the forefront of social movement theory, including Robert Benford, Richard Cloward, Myra Marx Ferree, Debra Friedman, William Gamson, Clarence Lo, Bert Klandermans, Gerald Marwell, Doug McAdam, John McCarthy, Aldon Morris, Carol Mueller, Pamela Oliver, Frances Fox Piven, Michael Schwartz, Paul Shuva, David

Snow, Verta Taylor, Sidney Tarrow, Nancy Whittier, Mark Wolfson, and Mayer Zald. In terms of the scope of the contributions and the strength of the new syntheses, this volume probably is the definitive current collection in the social movement theory field. It sets a research agenda that will be pursued, discussed, and challenged for years.

Mottl, Tahi. (1980). "The Analysis of Counter Movements." *Social Problems* 27 (June), 620-635.
One of the first articles to define the concept of countermovement.

Oberschall, Anthony. (1973). *Social Conflict and Social Movements.* Englewood Cliffs, NJ: Prentice-Hall.
An introduction to the concept of resource mobilization. Emphasizes the rational, organizational side of movements. Though not recent, some of the examples (like the Biafran war) continue to be of theoretical and historical interest.

_____. (1993). *Social Movements: Ideologies, Interests, and Identities.* New Brunswick, NJ: Transaction.
Like many contemporary social movement theorists, the author looks at a wide range of collective action and collective conflict, rather than movements in a stricter sense. He emphasizes that the phenomena conventionally referred to as movements must be understood in terms of loose structures, ill-defined boundaries, and a tendency to form networks of loose coalitions engaged in shifting and long-term types of conflict. He explores these themes by examining several of these open-ended processes as they constituted the European witch craze, the 1965 Los Angeles riot, the 1960's sit-ins, the decline of the movements of the 1960's, the upheaval or failed revolt of 1968 in historical perspective, the women's movement, and the New Christian Right. The book is a good example of how social movement theory has returned to some themes of collective behavior theory but in refined and more historically grounded forms.

Oegema, Dirk, and Bert Klandermans. (1994). "Why Social Movement Sympathizers Don't Participate: Erosion and Non-Conversion of Support." *American Sociological Review* 59, no. 5 (October), 703-722.
The authors address a key question for social movements: Why do potential supporters often fail to participate actively (nonconversion) or drop out (erosion)? Interviews with 224 sympathizers with the Dutch peace movement before and after its anti-cruise missile campaign shed light on the individual perceptions of the social environment that contribute to nonconversion and erosion.

Olson, Mancur. (1965). *The Logic of Collective Action.* Cambridge, MA: Harvard University Press.
The author focuses on the linkage among individual motivations and choices, movement strategies, and outcomes. He draws on a rational choice model of human action and devotes attention to the problem of the "free rider," the individual (or group or category of individuals) who plans to benefit from successful outcomes of collective action without taking the risks associated with it. These types of problems for social movements are then linked to a discussion of internal social control mechanisms that movements use to sustain commitment.

Opp, Karl Dieter. (1991). "Party Identification and Participation in Collective Political Action." *Journal of Politics* 53, no. 2 (May), 339-371.
Previous research had suggested a positive relation between party identification and conventional political activism. This study, based on a sample of twelve hundred residents of the German Federal Republic, suggests that the relationship between party identification and collective action can be explained largely by their mutual relationship with variables related to participatory incentives operating at the individual level, such as political dissatisfaction, moral incentives, and conformity to the expectations of others. Only for the Greens does there appear to be a direct effect of party identification on protest participation apart from these underlying participatory incentives. The article is a contribution to the understanding of the relationship between organizations, collective action, and individual-level perceptions of incentives.

_____. (1994). "Repression and Revolutionary Action: East Germany in 1989." *Rationality and Society* 6, no. 1 (January), 101-138.
The author proposes a rational choice model of behavior in which potential participants in collective action weigh repression against positive incentives or benefits of taking action, such as public goods, social incentives, and moral values. An inverted U-curve describes the relationship, in that increasing repression instigates positive incentives up to a point, beyond which positive incentives decrease. A survey study of residents of Leipzig generally supports the model. The severe repression characteristic of East Germany did not deter collective action because political events had increased positive incentives. The rational choice model is stated and discussed in relation to the collapse of Communist regimes in Eastern Europe in an introductory article in the same periodical issue, by Karl Dieter Opp and Jack Goldstone, "Rationality, Revolution, and 1989 in Eastern Europe."

Opp, Karl Dieter, and Christiane Gern. (1993). "Dissident Groups, Personal Networks, and Spontaneous Co-operation: The East German Revolution of 1989." *American Sociological Review* 58, no. 5 (October), 659-680.

A survey of Leipzig residents suggests support for the theory that microprocesses of personal networks and individual incentives are crucial factors in explaining collective action. Political discontent, positive incentives emerging out of the changing political context, and mobilization through personal networks explain participation in demonstrations. The research fits into micro-mobilization and rational choice perspectives on collective action.

Rucht, Dieter. (1991). *Research on Social Movements*. Boulder, CO: Westview Press.

This collection provides an outstanding comparative overview of social movement theory and research in recent decades. The essays are devoted to social movement scholarship in specific countries of North America and Western Europe. Considerable attention is devoted to the emergence of and recent challenges to "New Social Movement theory," sociological theories about the form and goals of left-wing, antistatist movements in the developed market democracies. Of particular interest to U.S. readers is Margit Mayer's "Social Movement Research and Social Movement Practice: The U.S. Pattern." In this review essay, the author considers change in the field and identifies classical theory, resource mobilization theory, and several additional approaches. She also criticizes the assumption in New Social Movement theory that such movements are usually on the left of the political spectrum and represent progressive rather than conservative ideologies, because antistatist, grassroots movements in the United States have tilted toward the right as much as toward the left. This is probably the single best overview of what has been written in the field of social movements since World War II, but it is not an essay for the beginning reader; it assumes some familiarity with the field. Also of interest is Bert Klandermans' "New Social Movements and Resource Mobilization: The European and the American Approach Revisited," as well as Mayer Zald's "The Continuing Vitality of Resource Mobilization Theory: Response to Herbert Kitschelt's Critique."

Ryan, Charlotte. (1991). *Prime Time Activism*. Boston: South End Press.

The author uses case studies of the media strategies of grassroots organizations, including the Central America solidarity movement, to understand how movements attempt to influence or counteract media framing of issues.

Sawicki, Jana. (1991). *Disciplining Foucault: Feminism, Power and the Body*. New York: Routledge.

An essay on Michel Foucault's approach to power and the body. The author provides an exposition of Foucault's ideas about the constitution of bodies through disciplinary knowledge and practice (for example, in psychology and psychotherapy) as well as resistance to such processes of power. The author then appropriates this type of analysis for feminist theory. The book is useful in two ways for the student of social movements and anti-institutional action, as a clear statement of Foucault's perspective and as an application of this perspective to the development of feminist theories of power and resistance.

Scheper-Hughes, Nancy. (1992). *Death Without Weeping*. Berkeley: University of California Press.

The author provides a detailed ethnography and analysis of life and death—especially infant mortality—in a poor sugar-growing community in the Brazilian Northeast. The theoretical importance of the study for the analysis of social movements lies in showing how the lived experience of poor Brazilian women generally works against community organizing and political activism. Immediate survival pressures, as well as negative sanctions exercised by local elites, prevent collective action, forcing the women into individual coping strategies and high levels of fatalism. Community organizing based on liberation theology has made some positive inroads, but in certain ways it reinforces traditional arrangements, especially in the construction of gender.

Scott, Alan. (1990). *Ideology and the New Social Movements*. London: Unwin Hyman.

An effort to define the ideologies of movements that usually are considered to be on the Left but are more decentralized, less structured, less involved in electoral politics, and more antistatist than historical movements on the Left. The term is especially useful for discussing European movements, such as feminism, the peace movement, urban squatter movements, and environmental movements in the 1970's and 1980's; it is somewhat less applicable to movements in this period in the United States, which were less clearly "on the left" and less clearly the result of a breakdown of some preceding status quo of disciplined party and trade union structures. Good background for understanding theoretical disagreements in the analysis of these movements.

Sibley, Mulford Q. (1970). *Political Ideas and Ideologies: A History of Political Thought*. New York: Harper and Row.
This volume or any other standard history of political thought may be useful as background for the understanding of movement ideologies. The final chapters on ideologies of the early modern and modern periods are the most relevant, although contemporary movements such as Catholic integralism draw on earlier belief systems, such as that of Thomas Aquinas.

Skocpol, Theda. (1979). *States and Social Revolutions: A Comparative Analysis of France, Russia, and China*. New York: Cambridge University Press.
A contemporary classic, offering an analysis of the relationship between state and society in the causes and outcomes of three major revolutions. By looking at revolutions in terms of the relationship between social structure and the state, the author develops a synthesis of the perspectives based on the work of Karl Marx and Max Weber. Three principles guide her analysis and contribute to the synthesis. First, she insists on a structural explanation of revolutions that deemphasizes the role of agency, of voluntarist elements in the formation and outcome of revolutions. The social movement theorist must focus on characteristics of the society, not on the ideas, goals, or motivations of individuals or organized groups. Second, revolutions must be studied in terms of international structures and world historical development, not only in terms of the political and class structures of a single society or nation-state. Third, the state must be defined as a relatively autonomous coercive organization, not as a simple product or reflection of class forces, as some Marxists see it. She applies this structural perspective to the French Revolution in the eighteenth century, the Russian revolution, and the Chinese revolution. The work is essential reading for the theory of social movements and revolutions.

_____. (1988). "Social Revolutions and Mass Military Mobilization." *World Politics* 40 (January), 147-168.
The author looks at military mobilization as part of the process of postrevolutionary regime consolidation. Civil wars and/or invasions that typically follow revolutions provide opportunities for the new regimes to penetrate the life of the masses and alter their behavior in ways that sustain the revolutionary state and its societal goals.

_____. (1989). "Reconsidering the French Revolution in World-Historical Perspective." *Social Research* 56 (Spring), 53-70.
The author reinforces her perspective on revolutions in a critique of an "internalist" interpretation of the French Revolution that emphasizes political and cultural processes within French society. The author defends the "externalist" interpretation that views the revolution within an international context and explains revolutions in general in terms of a structural analysis focused on the state and its relationship to society. The specific case of the French Revolution forms the basis for a discussion of the general theory of revolutions.

Smelser, Neil. (1963). *Theory of Collective Behavior*. New York: Free Press of Glencoe.
A pioneering work of sociological theory explaining movements in terms of social structure and beliefs rather than psychological factors. The author develops a value-added model of social movements. The author identifies six factors, all characteristics of societies rather than individuals, that impinge on social movement formation and outcomes: structural conduciveness (societal opportunity structures), structural strain (perceived problems), generalized beliefs (ideology), leadership and communication (organization), precipitating incidents, and the action of social control agents.

Snow, David, and Robert Benford. (1988). "Ideology, Frame Resonance and Participant Mobilization." In Bert Klandermans, Hanspeter Kriesi, and Sidney Tarrow (eds.), *From Structure to Action: Comparing Social Movements Across Cultures*. Greenwich, CT: JAI.
The authors explore the ways in which movement belief systems or ideologies have to "resonate" or match with existing frames their potential support bases use to organize the understanding of social reality. If alignment or resonance is not accomplished, movement ideologies fail to "make sense" to potential participants, and they cannot be mobilized.

Snow, David, E. B. Rochford, Steven Worden, and Robert Benford. (1986). "Frame Alignment Process, Micromobilization, and Movement Participation." *American Sociological Review* 51, 464-481.
The authors emphasize the importance for a movement of aligning its frames—its conceptualizations and representations—with the frames held by potential supporters. These frame alignment processes take place through media as well as through smaller-scale interpersonal contacts that lead to mobilization and participation.

Tarrow, Sidney. (1991). *Struggles, Politics, and Reform: Collective Action, Social Movements and Cycles of Protest.* Ithaca, NY: Cornell University Press.

_____. (1994). *Power in Movement: Social Movements, Collective Action, and Politics.* New York: Cambridge University Press.
In these two volumes, the author offers a new synthesis of social movement theory by pulling together the analysis of cycles, the insertion of social movements within a larger field of collective action, and the effort to understand collective action in relation to political systems. This approach is an effort to capture the processual and open-ended nature of movements and their interaction with changing but usually more stable political institutions. He discusses the relationships between movements and electoral politics as well as between movements and support groups and allies. He looks at outcomes, especially the extent to which reform is a product of protest and the ways in which it may condition a subsequent cycle of collective action. Examples are drawn from the author's work in Western Europe, especially Italy. These volumes underline the way in which contemporary social movement theory is giving attention to the larger, looser field of collective action, synthesizing this perspective with the analysis of political opportunity structures, and developing ways to conceptualize change over medium-range time periods.

_____. (1992). "Costumes of Revolt: The Symbolic Politics of Social Movements." *Sisyphus* 8, no. 2, 53-71.
The author emphasizes the importance of symbols and discourse in movements and their role in mobilizing adherents. Several theoretical approaches to the analysis of symbols and discourse are discussed (the concept of mentalities, the political culture perspective, and the concept of collective action frames). Poland's Solidarity movement and the U.S. Civil Rights movement are used to illustrate the use of symbols.

Taylor, Verta. (1989). "Social Movement Continuity: The Women's Movement in Abeyance." *American Sociological Review* 54, no. 5 (October), 761-775.
Examines continuity in movements, specifically the women's movement in the United States, emphasizing that activists find ways of sustaining movements, even during periods of reduced mobilization or support, such as the women's movement experienced in the 1940's and 1950's. The ideas of the movement are preserved by small communi-

ties of the committed, and networks of interest and identity are preserved even if the participants in the networks are not involved in
activism or expanded mobilization.

Tilly, Charles. (1978). *From Mobilization to Revolution.* Reading, MA:
Addison-Wesley.
Collective action is the key concept in the author's theoretical approach. It is defined as "people's acting together in pursuit of common
interests" and can take many forms, ranging from routine group
competition to revolution in which the object of group conflict is
control of the polity, the entire apparatus of the state. Violence is not
an exceptional strategy but often a part of routine collective action,
although governments attempt to retain their monopoly of coercion. In
contrast to more social psychological theories, the author emphasizes
the formation of organized groups and access to resources. Tilly's work
has been influential in defining social movements as one form of
collective action, in turning attention to resource mobilization, and in
developing empirical methods for studying collective action during
relatively long historical periods.

Touraine, Alain. (1971). *The Post-Industrial Society: Tomorrow's Social
History: Classes, Conflicts and Culture in the Programmed Society.*
New York: Random House.
As the outlines of a "postindustrial" society became visible in the
economically developed countries of Western Europe, the author considers what types of conflicts and movements may become characteristic of societies without the industrial working classes or rural strata
of the past. A precursor to the work of the author and other European
theorists on the New Social Movements.

_____. (1981). *The Voice and the Eye: An Analysis of Social
Movements.* New York: Cambridge University Press.
The author looks at the role of social movements in transforming
societies. He emphasizes their historicity (their association with modern societies), their rational objectives, their interaction with other
movements and institutions, and their contextualization in and ability
to change fields of action (such as labor relations or the family).
Movements also have an impact on sociology itself and change ways
in which social scientists understand and interpret social reality.

Turner, Ralph H., and Lewis Killian. (1987). *Collective Behavior.* Englewood Cliffs, NJ: Prentice-Hall.

A classic theoretical statement and textbook that connects the social movements field to other noninstitutionalized and emergent behavior, such as crowds, fashions, and panics. Although the connection between social movements and other forms of collective behavior is a major theoretical theme of the book, it also includes a large range of perspectives and excellent overviews of the field.

Walton, John. (1983). *Reluctant Rebels.* New York: Columbia University Press.

The author offers a comparative perspective on national revolts and protracted conflicts in the Third World, such as the Huks (Philippines), La Violencia (Colombia), and the Mau-Mau (Kenya). These large-scale mobilizations altered the structure of the state and/or achieved independence but fell short of being revolutions.

Weber, Max. (1958). *From Max Weber.* Edited by Hans Gerth and C. Wright Mills. New York: Oxford University Press.

This selection from the work of the great German sociological theorist serves two purposes. First, it introduces the reader to Max Weber's perspectives, which continue to influence social movement theory, especially his ideas about the role of the state, forms of organization, the mutual influence of culture and economy, and the interplay of class, status, and political power as elements of social inequality. More specifically, it includes his definition and discussion of charismatic authority, which continues to be an important concept in the analysis of authority and leadership in movements.

Weinstein, Deena, and Michael Weinstein. (1993). *Postmodern(ized) Simmel.* New York: Routledge.

Although not in the mainstream of social movement theory, this book is of interest in emphasizing playful and individualized forms of resistance to power. It offers a reading of the great turn-of-the-century theorist, Georg Simmel, as a precursor of postmodern theorists of interactive and discursive processes of contention and resistance.

Wickham-Crowley, Timothy. (1992). *Guerrillas and Revolutions in Latin America: A Comparative Study of Insurgents and Regimes Since 1956.* Princeton, NJ: Princeton University Press.

The comparative analysis looks at factors associated with the success (or failure) of guerrilla insurgencies, such as the presence of a patrimonial praetorian regime (like that of Anastasio Somoza in Nicaragua), the withdrawal of U.S. support from regimes, the military organization of the insurgency, and the relationship between the guerrillas and the peasants. Well argued and an excellent example of comparative analysis. The emphasis is on guerrilla insurgencies more than on the revolutionary project in general, and thus the analysis must be understood in a historical context, the period of commitment to guerrilla movements.

Willis, Paul. (1990). *Common Culture*. Boulder, CO: Westview Press.
An essay on emerging forms of youth culture and resistance to political and social control. The author locates resistance to the cultural and political forms of Thatcherite England in youth culture and practices of everyday life, for example, homemade clothing and flea market shopping as a way of rejecting the values of "good taste," consumption, and compulsive shopping. The author's argument is engaging and forces the reader to consider new forms of opposition to hegemony, forms that lie outside the more traditional structures of unions, shop floor practices, and political parties.

Wolf, Eric. (1969). *Peasant Wars of the Twentieth Century*. New York: Harper and Row.
A contemporary classic that explains six major revolutions—in Mexico, Russia, China, Cuba, Vietnam, and Algeria—in terms of the penetration of capitalism into rural social structure. As agriculture tilted toward production for national and international markets, peasant-landlord relationships became more openly exploitive, and peasants were less able to meet subsistence needs. These types of dislocations of the local economy and the village community created conditions for revolutionary movements. The author skillfully identifies common patterns of all the revolutions without losing attention to the specificity of each case.

Zald, Mayer, and Roberta Ash. (1966). "Social Movement Organizations." *Social Forces* 44, 327-341.
A milestone article that relates movement outcomes to the behavior and transformations of organizations. An early statement of resource mobilization theory, it presents an organizational perspective on movements, challenges the "iron law of oligarchy" (Robert Michels' claim that movements inevitably take on a bureaucratized form with control lodged in a small elite), and suggests that social movement organizations have to be understood as actors in specific situations.

Zald, Mayer, and John McCarthy. (1979). *The Dynamics of Social Movements: Resource Mobilization, Social Control and Tactics*. Cambridge, MA: Winthrop.

An excellent collection of articles illustrating the mature phase of resource mobilization theory. The contributions focus on social movement organizations, strategies that movement organizations use to mobilize potential supporters and obtain other types of resources such as funds and media coverage, and processes of social control and professionalization that are internal to movement organizations. Although some of the specific case studies may be of historical rather than contemporary interest, the volume remains an important contribution to social movement theory.

_____, eds. (1987). *Social Movements in an Organizational Society*. New Brunswick, NJ: Transaction.

An important collection of essays that expands and consolidates resource mobilization and organizational perspectives on movements. The contributions deal with the internal structure of movements, the formation of countermovements, the professionalization of movement activism, and the role of religion in movement formation.

Chapter 2
MOVEMENTS IN TEMPORAL CONTEXT

This chapter includes books and articles that examine the historical context of social and political movements. They connect social movement theory to historical analysis by analyzing the historical circumstances that gave rise to movements. A number of the works explore the concept of the "postmodern." Several books also provide a background in economic trends and modern economic history. The analysis in most of the works in this section is explicitly or implicitly cross-national and/or global rather than focused on a single state or region, even in those instances in which a single nation or city is used as the initial point of the discussion.

Althusser, Louis. (1969). *For Marx*. London: Allen Lane.
Essays in structural Marxism. The analysis emphasizes the structural determination of historical change rather than agency, consciousness, and movements as social actors.

Appadurai, Arjun. (1990). "Disjuncture and Difference in the Global Cultural Economy." In Mike Featherstone (ed.), *Global Culture*. Newbury Park, CA: Sage.
The present global political climate is shaped by flows of people, capital, technology, media, and ideas. The deterritorialization of population contributes to movement formation, especially the formation of nationalist movements within exile communities.

Aries, Philippe. (1965). *Centuries of Childhood*. New York: Random House.
A richly detailed classic that traces the emergence of an ideology of childhood between the European Middle Ages and the nineteenth century; this ideology is the notion that children are innocent beings whose character must be formed into the mold of responsible adulthood. The ideology, argues Aries, is a relatively recent development in Western history and succeeded an earlier stage in which children were seen as small adults to be reared in an unplanned, matter-of-fact, and unsheltered manner. With the rise of the ideology of childhood, parents—especially mothers—replaced wet nurses, servants, and casual bystanders as socializing agents. The ideology of childhood is linked closely to the ideology of domesticity and the ideal of the nuclear, neotraditional family. The book offers insight into current ideological

debates over "family values" as well as a classic discussion of the basis of Western socialization and character structure.

Bell, Daniel. (1976). *The Coming of Post-Industrial Society: A Venture in Social Forecasting*. New York: Basic Books.

Discussion of the new form of society, based on information and services rather than manufacturing, that seemed to be emerging by the 1970's. Although some elements of the analysis are dated, the book is valuable as one of the earliest efforts to analyze the types of society that are emerging at the end of the twentieth century. It is of interest to social movement studies because it examines the societal conditions within which movements arise and suggests that movements reflecting the class structure of industrial society may be coming to an end.

Bluestone, Barry and Bennett Harrison. (1982). *The De-Industrialization of America*. New York: Harper & Row.

This book provides a useful background for understanding how declines in union strength and in the vitality and size of the industrial working-class support base affected movements and political behavior in the United States. Although the focus is on the United States, similar deindustrialization processes took place in other developed industrialized market economies in the 1970's and early 1980's as the result of new technologies, new areas of enterprise, and the shift of industrial plants to the Third World.

Callinicos, Alex. (1990). *Against Post-Modernism: A Marxist Critique*. New York: St. Martin's Press.

The author argues that the fundamental concepts and analytic perspectives of Marxist theory are still valid, given that capitalism remains the prevailing global economic and social system. The new categories introduced by postmodern social thinkers obfuscate an understanding of the basic structure of contemporary societies.

Castells, Manuel. (1983.) *The City and the Grassroots*. Berkeley: University of California Press.

In the framework of an updated Marxist theory, the author examines the formation of new social movements in response to shifts in urban structure. The city is the site of struggles in capitalist society. Local government represents the lowest level of state organization, and at least in the 1970's, it was often also the fiscally weakest level. An interesting effort to integrate theories of spatial form with Marxist theories of capitalist development and social movements.

Coontz, Stephanie. (1988). *The Social Origins of Private Life: A History of American Families 1600-1900*. New York: Routledge.
The author's history of family life in colonial North America and the United States provides background information for understanding the emergence of women's movements as well as the general social climate. The perspective emphasizes the genderized nature of institutions that shaped what was conventionally defined to be "private" and "natural."

_____. (1993). *The Way We Never Were*. New York: Basic Books.
In a readable and lively book, a social historian documents the falseness of many current nostalgic images of family life, gender roles, and sex in the 1950's. *Leave It to Beaver* was not reality. The more accurate data show why a variety of movements began to emerge in the period, while the false, nostalgic images remain an essential part of the discursive framing of many contemporary conservative movements.

Davis, Mike. (1990). *City of Quartz*. London: Verso.
A detailed examination of Los Angeles' urban social and economic structure, political process, and law enforcement policies from a Marxist perspective. The discussion of changes in urban form, urban demographic composition, real estate markets and the movement of capital, city culture and politics, and law enforcement has implications for understanding recent restructuring in many world cities, not only Los Angeles. These structural changes in turn create a new context for social movements, both movements and mobilizations of dispossessed populations and those of middle-class and wealthy property owners.

Fairchilds, Cissie. (1984). "Women and Family." In Samia Spencer (ed.), *French Women and the Age of Enlightenment*. Bloomington: Indiana University Press.
This article discusses the emergence of modern family structure and family ideology in Western Europe. Sections of the French aristocracy, as well as the bourgeoisie, began to elaborate and live out an "ideology of domesticity" that called for parental, especially maternal, commitment to child rearing and a strong affective bond between husband and wife. This ideology and its associated family structure contrasted sharply with earlier attitudes of indifference toward spouses and children, expressed through practices such as marriages of convenience, adultery, and use of wet nurses. The new ideology of domesticity set the stage for twentieth century political debates and movement activism over the role of women in modern society and the meaning of "family values."

Foucault, Michel. (1979). *Discipline and Punish*. New York: Random House.

This book is probably the most accessible of the poststructuralist philosopher's work. It charts a transformation in the exercise of power from prerevolutionary imposition of brutal corporal punishments to a modern practice of surveillance and, ideally, self-monitoring of the body, intentions, gestures, and actions. These new, pervasive, and largely self-administered practices of control are associated particularly with new fields of knowledge such as psychology and psychiatry. The implication of this view for social movements is that liberation lies not in a political revolution against elites that dominate economic and political structures but in a pervasive challenge to power in discourses and interactions.

Frank, Andre Gunder. (1981). *Crisis in the Third World*. New York: Monthly Review.

Analysis of growing global inequalities in the 1970's, from a dependency theory perspective. The book provides useful information on the decline of wages and living standards in this period, associated with growing indebtedness and unfavorable terms of trade in the world economy.

Fukuyama, Francis. (1992). *The End of History and the Last Man*. New York: Free Press.

Emphasizes the global preeminence of liberal democracy and market economies. Some sections of the book apply philosophical perspectives based on Hegel's philosophy of history to current prospects. The most interesting element of the argument for social science readers is probably the notion that there appear to be few attractive alternatives to market democracy as a viable form of societies, states, and economies.

Gorz, Andre. (1982). *Farewell to the Working Class*. Boston: South End Press.

Analysis of changing class structure in advanced industrial-capitalist societies with a shrinking industrial proletariat, and implications of these changes for movements.

Halliday, Fred. (1989). *From Kabul to Managua*. New York: Pantheon.

Insightful discussion of the relationship between the Cold War and outcomes of Third World revolutions. This book is a must for the political scientist who wants to understand what happened globally in the 1980's; it dissects the relationship between the superpowers, bringing together the arms race and the struggle for spheres of influence in the Third World. The growing assertiveness of the United States in supporting counterinsurgencies against Third World revolutionary socialist regimes, coupled with U.S. escalation of the arms race, led to major problems in Soviet policy. The book gives insights into the logic of global policy in Washington and Moscow, showing the reader the essence of the Reagan Doctrine and the process by which Soviet decision makers revised their views of the Third World from a vanguard region of socialist revolution to a burden that required disengagement. Though sympathetic to socialist movements, Halliday is unflinching in his discussion of their problems in this period.

Harrison, Bennett, and Barry Bluestone. (1988). *The Great U-Turn*. New York: Basic Books.
Analysis of patterns of social inequality and political process in the United States during the Reagan period. Good background for understanding changing forms of political movements. Although the analysis is focused on the United States, the general framework is useful for understanding the rightward shift in many developed market democracies in the 1980's.

Heilbroner, Robert. (1989). *The Making of Economic Society*. Englewood Cliffs, NJ: Prentice-Hall.
This is an excellent introductory level book in economic history. It offers useful background for the student of social movements who feels a need to understand major economic trends. For example, reforms proposed by movements during the Progressive Era, the New Deal, and the formation of post-World War II welfare states are covered here in terms of their translation into government economic policies. The instructor looking for a supplementary text to provide historical background on economic change will find this book concise and equipped with pedagogic aids such as glossaries of key concepts.

Hobsbawm, Eric. (1962). *The Age of Revolution*. New York: NAL.

_____. (1979). *The Age of Capital*. New York: NAL.

_____. (1989). *The Age of Empire*. New York: Random House.

_____. (1994). *The Age of Extremes*. New York: Random House.
These four volumes constitute a major effort to analyze the origins and characteristics of what we call the "modern world"—the sources of the global social, political, and economic conditions in which we live

today. They provide an outstanding background for the student of social movements. In fact, Hobsbawm devotes attention specifically to the role of movements in creating our world—especially liberal-democratic movements, fascism, socialism, and nationalism. The framework might be described as a contemporary Marxism that gives emphasis to the changing nature of capitalism and class structure as a decisive element of historical change, without ever descending into mechanical economic determinism. This is not a mere narrative history, moving from event to event; it is more concerned with social, cultural, political, and economic trends. Unlike conventional history, it focuses on the lives of ordinary men and women of all social classes, not primarily on political elites or "men who make history." The final volume is particularly important for understanding social movements of our own times.

Hounshell, David. (1984). *From the American System to Mass Production, 1800-1932*. Baltimore: Johns Hopkins University Press.
The author provides insight into the formation of modern mass production systems, especially the Fordist model of standardized production of cheap consumer durables for an expanding domestic market. Useful for understanding the changing structure of the industrial working class and consequently the kinds of movements it developed.

Jameson, Fredric. (1984). "Postmodernism or the Cultural Logic of Late Capitalism." *New Left Review* 146 (July/August), 53-92.
A definitive theoretical essay that identifies key features of postmodern culture. Good background reading for understanding contemporary culture and forms of consciousness. The author conducts a two-pronged argument, on one hand concurring with Marxists that our culture is still shaped by capitalism but on the other hand contending that late capitalism has a logic that is distinct from capitalism in earlier periods. Late capitalist culture is characterized by a turn away from modernism; it has ceased to be preoccupied with an anxious search for truth or authenticity and instead revels in surface intensities exemplified by video images, the obliteration of the high/pop culture distinction, postmodern architecture, and pastiche as a dominant style of expression. The search for a true past is given up in favor of nostalgia, a shamelessly false pastiche of past representations. Jameson's essay is dense and difficult, with many references to cultural landmarks, but has become a classic in defining late twentieth century culture.

Kaplan, Robert. (1994). "The Coming Anarchy." *Atlantic Monthly* (February), 44-76.
A pessimistic essay emphasizing growing regional conflicts, population pressures, and destructive movements. Although not a scholarly article, its gloomy vision may be of interest to students of social change and social movements.

Klare, Michael. (1994). "Armed and Dangerous." *In These Times* 18, no. 15 (June 15), 14-19.
A summary of the author's work on the international arms market, the easy access of movements to weapons, and the consequent tendency for conflicts to become violent and protracted.

Laslett, Peter. (1984). *The World We Have Lost: England Before the Industrial Age.* New York: Macmillan.
A description of culture, social structure, and everyday life in England in the Renaissance and early modern period. It is useful for understanding the type of society from which modern movements emerged, not only in England but also in Western Europe and North America.

Lerner, Daniel. (1958). *The Passing of Traditional Society.* New York: Free Press.
Discusses the impact of modernization, focused on western Asia at mid-century. Useful as a theoretical view of modernization and its possible impact on ideologies and mobilizations. Now dated, but still of value in understanding the long-term historical process of modernization.

Lipset, Seymour Martin. (1960). *Political Man.* New York: Anchor/Doubleday.
Essays in political sociology. The examples are dated, but useful concepts are introduced, especially the notion that societies with cross-cutting social divisions are more politically stable than those in which lines of cleavage such as class, race, religion, and so on are superimposed. Also interesting, though controversial, is Lipset's contention that although the working class may be on the egalitarian left on economic issues, it can be authoritarian in its social and cultural stands and styles.

Mandel, Ernest. (1975). *Late Capitalism.* London: New Left Books.
A Marxist analysis of capitalism that takes up the challenge of seeing how capitalism has evolved in an age of automation. Mandel offers an incisive dismissal of the "postindustrial" concept: Far from being

postindustrial, capitalism in the later part of the twentieth century is characterized by the penetration of industrialization into every sphere of production, including areas such as agriculture and information processing.

Newman, Katherine. (1988). *Falling from Grace*. New York: Vintage.
The author, an anthropologist, gives the reader a brilliant ethnographic account of the subjective experience of downward mobility in the 1980's and the impact of this experience on identity and family structure. She is insightful into the gender dimensions of downward mobility. Two of her best chapters deal with the "downsized" executive and his family and with downward mobility of divorced middle-class homemakers. The author does not explore direct links to movement formation (indeed, there may not be any), but the book is valuable as a portrait of strain in U.S. society.

Payer, Cheryl. (1982). *The World Bank: A Critical Analysis*. New York: Monthly Review Press.
A negative view of the policies of the World Bank, one of the major international financial institutions, especially with regard to its lending practices in the developing nations during the crucial period of the 1970's. Its emphasis on austerity in government budgets and its reluctance to lend to socialist-oriented states created difficulties for movement-initiated regimes that sought to implement egalitarian economic reforms, expand the public sector, and/or move away from export promotion.

Polanyi, Karl. (1957). *The Great Transformation: The Political and Economic Origins of Our Time*. Boston: Beacon Press.
Classic analysis of the onset of capitalism in Western Europe, with a focus on England. Polanyi discusses how a household economy was transformed into a market economy in the period between 1500 and the middle of the nineteenth century. These economic transformations were accompanied by sweeping changes in the legal and political framework, especially in the areas of property rights and poor law.

Przeworski, Adam. (1991). *Democracy and the Market*. New York: Cambridge University Press.
The author surveys the situation at the end of the Cold War, with a focus on two types of nations that "returned to democracy" in the 1980's: the former Communist states in Eastern Europe and the former right-wing military dictatorships in Latin America. The return to democracy also was a return to a system of free markets. He argues that this transfor-

mation has a negative as well as a positive side and that substantial parts of the "Second World" of the former Communist states will not achieve First World standards of living and viable political and market institutions, in part because the transformation took place without suitable mechanisms for integrating the working class into the system through some form of social contract. Important comparative analysis.

Reich, Robert. (1992). *The Work of Nations*. New York: Vintage.
Observations on the transformation of nationally based corporations into a global web in which production processes and management are subcontracted or carried out in widely dispersed locations. As corporations lose their national character, they can no longer be counted on a secure source of employment for a nation's labor force, as they had been during the 1950's. The workforce is splitting into three strata: Routine production workers, in transnational locations; in-person servers, usually in a low-wage sector of local employment; and a privileged directing stratum of symbolic analysts with declining national loyalties. Reich identifies but does not solve the political problem that symbolic analysts have come to have a low stake in the education and upgrading of their nation's labor force at the precise moment that training for high-value-added work is the only way in which a nation as a whole can remain competitive and prosperous in the world economy. The book provides a perspective on the problems of adjustment to a post-Fordist and post-Keynesian restructuring of work, labor markets, corporate enterprise, class structures, and the global economy.

Ross, Andrew, ed. (1988). *Universal Abandon: The Politics of Postmodernism*. Minneapolis: University of Minnesota Press.
Authors in the collection address the question of what radical politics might look like in a postmodern and post-Communist age, as capitalism mutates, parties decline, identities proliferate, and culture explodes. Thought provoking and lively.

Sahlins, Peter. (1995). *Forest Rites*. Cambridge, MA: Harvard University Press.
The author looks at a peasant rebellion in southwestern France in 1829-1830, in which men dressed as women attacked forest guards and charcoal makers in an effort to assert collective rights to the use of the forest against claims of "rational" management of forest resources. The festive character and playful gender inversion of this local "war" requires more than a utilitarian explanation focused on economic issues. The author uses the incident to comment on the need for a

complex understanding of collective action in its cultural construction as well as economic origins and calls for a reassessment of the traditional/modern dichotomy in historical research.

Sassen, Saskia. (1994). *Cities in a World Economy*. Thousand Oaks, CA: Pine Forge Press/Sage.
An excellent and clearly written introduction to the study of urban form in a period of globalizing markets. Sassen covers the impact of the global economy on urban economies and looks carefully at inequalities among regions, cities, and classes. Most of her examples are drawn from the developed market economies, but there are also comparative data on cities in peripheral regions. Students of social movements can use the information to understand social inequality as well as processes of immigration and deterritorialization as bases of social movement activity.

Starr, Peter. (1995). *Logics of Failed Revolt: French Theory After May '68*. Stanford, CA: Stanford University Press.
How were left-wing French intellectuals to interpret the failed revolt of 1968? Was this instance of collective action to be seen as an abortive revolution or perhaps, as Regis Debray suggested, as a homeostatic mechanism of advanced capitalism in which young revolutionaries unintentionally helped to sweep away old European social institutions that blocked the path to freer markets, a regionalized and globalized economy, and educational institutions better matched to new economic forces? Starr does not directly address these political questions, but his examination of French intellectual life after 1968 is provocative and valuable to the reader who wants to understand this most abstract and contentious of milieus. Developments such as Lacanian psychoanalytic theory and its feminist challengers, the structural Marxism of Louis Althusser, and the vociferous New Philosopher anticommunism of former left-wing militants are seen as responses to the failures of the May uprising. A clear, witty, and challenging overview of theories that were advanced to explain the failed rebellion.

Tarrow, Sidney. (1993). "Modular Collective Action and the Rise of the Social Movement: Why the French Revolution Was Not Enough." *Politics and Society* 21 (March), 69-90.
The author examines the rise of early modern social movements based on modular collective action that went beyond traditional forms of social protest such as grain seizures or mob riots. These collective actions were flexible, adaptable, and more sustainable than the tradi-

tional protests; they were associated with the rise of print, a medium that helped to carry the form across national boundaries. Although the French Revolution is associated with modular collective action and the rise of the social movement, it was not the cause of these new forms; the new forms appeared in many countries and thus reflect a more complicated underlying set of causes than a single revolution.

Therborn, Goran. (1977). "The Rule of Capital and the Rise of Democracy." *New Left Review* 103 (May/June), 3-42.
An important analysis of the conditions under which democracy, in the sense of universal suffrage, was established in developed capitalist nations. The author uses seventeen OECD nations as his sample and conducts a case-by-case analysis of popular movements for democracy, ruling class strategies to deal with these mass pressures, and external interventions—especially international war—as factors in the outcome. He concludes that the extension of the franchise was not usually a steady process accompanying economic development, literacy, and urbanization, but a periodized and discontinuous one associated with upheavals, such as World War I. He also concludes that targeted political prohibitions (for example, the illegality of certain parties) came to replace across-the-board class exclusion as a mechanism for sustaining class dominance in the face of popular pressures for democracy.

Wallerstein, Immanuel. (1974). *The Modern World System*. New York: Academic Press.

_____. (1980). *The Modern World System II*. New York: Academic Press.
These two volumes address the formation of the global system of markets, states, and societies in which we live. The author examines how, beginning at the end of the European Middle Ages, global markets came into being at the same time that political systems generally were molded into the nation-state structure. The analysis is dense and complex, and it is not for the novice in the social sciences. Wallerstein's work has been influential, and although not all researchers would adopt all aspects of it, it remains a major framework for understanding long-term, large-scale social change, including the structural causes of movements.

_____. (1990). "Culture as the Ideological Battleground of the Modern World System." In Mike Featherstone (ed.), *Global Culture*. Newbury Park, CA: Sage.

The modern world system involves the uneven layering of political forms (largely nation-states), the global capitalist market economy, and culture. The dislocations created by this structure currently are being experienced and expressed as particularistic cultural resistances against the Western/Enlightenment culture that had become the dominant strand of world system culture. The culture of the Enlightenment made universalistic and scientific claims for itself, but these claims often became the basis for racist (and to some extent, sexist) assessments of other cultures. These "other" cultures are now reasserting themselves in a variety of forms. Such cultural conflicts are the terrain of resistance to the world system as a whole; its economic dimensions are not forefronted in this challenge. The essay is a provocative but rather abstract analysis of the challenge of the local and particularistic cultures against the universal claims of Western culture.

Wolf, Eric. (1982). *Europe and the People Without History*. Berkeley: University of California Press.

The author shows how relatively early in modern history, by the sixteenth century, non-European populations were drawn into European-initiated trading spheres, such as the slave trade and the fur trade. These processes led to the transformation of the societies, with profound consequences for their class structures, political systems, economies, and cultures. Wolf explicitly rejects the idea that non-European societies were relatively unchanging until the era of colonialism as well as the notion that they were passive victims of the European impact. Wolf places his analysis in the perspective of the transformations of the capitalist system as a system of global markets in products and labor.

Wood, Ellen Meiksins. (1994). "Identity Crisis." *In These Times* 18, no. 15 (June 13), 28-29.

The author deplores the contemporary tendency toward mobilization along the lines of ethnicity, religion, culture, gender, and/or sexual orientation instead of class. Contrary to some postmodern theorists, the author does not believe that all these identities are fundamentally arbitrary. Class identity corresponds to the structure of capitalism, which is not merely a system of oppression but also a system with a logic of transformation. Only class consciousness and class organization can transcend the existing situation, leading to a new set of possibilities rather than mere renegotiation of old conflicts.

Zeitlin, Irving. (1994). *Ideology and the Development of Sociological Theory.* 5th ed. Englewood Cliffs, NJ: Prentice-Hall.

An excellent review of the historical interplay between ideologies and the social sciences. Because there is a sizable overlap between social movement ideologies and social science frameworks, this historical essay illuminates both, tracing the impact of Enlightenment thought on the social sciences, the legacy of the conservative reaction, the emergence of Marxist theories and ideologies, and twentieth century currents in ideology. The exposition is indispensable for the student of social thought and the history of ideologies. The material is demanding, but the writing is clear and readable.

Chapter 3
MOVEMENTS IN SPATIAL CONTEXT

These books and articles are about a variety of movements in a single country or region. They examine more than one movement and, in many cases, address the interplay of movements, the relationships between movements and institutionalized political actors, and the dynamics of the social movement sector. For example, they may cover movements and countermovements. Accounts by movement participants also are included.

The reader should take this chapter as a sampling of such regional and national case studies, not as a complete inventory. Many of the works are classics of social movement literature that offer historical background rather than contemporary analysis. Some additional works may be found in the index under the country or region.

Anderson, Benedict. (1988). "Cacique Democracy and the Philippines: Origins and Dreams." *New Left Review* 169 (May/June), 3-31.
An overview of Philippine history and politics. Points to continuity between the Aquino-led democracy movement and existing elites.

Black, George, with Milton Jamail and Norma Stoltz Chinchilla. (1984). *Garrison Guatemala*. New York: Monthly Review Press.
A history and analysis of conflict in Guatemala, covering the overthrow of the reformist regime of Jacobo Arbenz, the rise of guerrilla movements and a popular opposition, and the counterinsurgency strategies of the military in the 1980's. An important work for understanding the history of the Left, especially the armed left, in Central America.

Brenan, Gerald. (1969). *The Spanish Labyrinth: An Account of the Social and Political Background of the Spanish Civil War*. Cambridge, England: Cambridge University Press.
A detailed analysis that remains one of the most comprehensive studies of the conflict in the 1930's.

Brown, Elaine. (1994). *A Taste of Power: A Black Woman's Story*. New York: Anchor/Doubleday.
A memoir of one woman's involvement with the Black Panther Party in the United States. It is critical of Black Panther leadership and policies as well as of law enforcement agencies, and it contains revealing personal accounts of sexism and violence within the move-

ment. Although not formulated as a work of theory, it contains material that is of interest to the theorist, especially in terms of gender issues, social movement organization, multiorganizational fields of competing and conflicting social movements, and social control by law enforcement agencies. It gives a vivid portrait of movements on the left and Black Power movements in the United States in the 1960's and 1970's.

Cruse, Harold. (1984). *The Crisis of the Negro Intellectual: A Historical Analysis of the Failure of Black Leadership.* New York: Morrow.
A controversial history of African American social and political thought. Cruse identifies three major themes in black intellectual history: The black nationalist current that was first clearly articulated by Marcus Garvey, the self-help black enterprise theme associated with Booker T. Washington, and the theme of integration pursued by W. E. B. Du Bois (though Cruse recognizes that the genius of Du Bois was able to encompass all three positions and that he was not exclusively integrationist). Cruse traces the development of these ideological currents from the early part of the century to the 1960's, arguing that a major problem in the black community has been the discontinuity of ideological organizations. Organizations of activist intellectuals have not become stable, viable entities able to build on accomplishments of the past. In addition to this critique of black intellectual institutions, Cruse takes a hard look at the relationship of black and Jewish intellectuals and activists, arguing that the former must develop a greater degree of independence from the latter. The argument may strike some as dated or pointless, others as cogent. Although not entirely up to date, Cruse's book contains a thought-provoking discussion of the formation of the organic intellectuals of an ethnic community, and his three major traditions are visible today.

Davis, Mike. (1986). *Prisoners of the American Dream.* London: Verso.
A Marxist analysis of political processes in the United States. It includes an essay about why the labor movement failed to generate a mass socialist movement in the United States as well as discussion of the relationship between the Left and the Democratic Party. One of the best essays in the book covers the political response to the crisis of the Fordist/Keynesian accumulation regime in the 1970's. Dense and difficult writing, but a rewardingly high-level analysis for the reader who devotes the necessary attention.

Denitch, Bogdan. (1994). *Ethnic Nationalism: The Tragic Death of Yugo-slavia*. Minneapolis: University of Minnesota Press.
An excellent discussion of the background of ethnic warfare in the former Yugoslavia. The author focuses less on traditional animosities (which he believes could have been overcome) and more on the recent process of breakdown associated with the precipitous transition out of socialism and intervention by foreign powers and exile communities. Important for understanding how ethnic difference can deteriorate into ethnonationalism and ethnic violence.

Flacks, Richard. (1988). *Making History: The Radical Tradition in American Life*. New York: Columbia University Press.
The author reviews the history of radical movements in the United States and focuses on the New Left. He suggests that the cultural context of the United States emphasizes pragmatism and the concerns of everyday life, an outlook that works against radical ideas and collective action.

Gaines, Donna. (1992). *Teenage Wasteland: Suburbia's Deadend Kids*. New York: HarperCollins.
An impressionistic study of "burnouts" in a U.S. suburban community provides insight into youth subcultures of resistance and opposition to mainstream culture. The youth in question are white, of lower-middle-class and working-class background, and alienated from the college-oriented culture of the high school. Heavy metal rock music, use of alcohol and drugs, and a nostalgic affiliation to the countercultures of the 1960's are the materials from which the dead-end culture is composed. The social movement theorist can look for linkages between these currents of opposition and social movements in a narrower sense.

Geoghegan, Thomas. (1991). *Which Side Are You On?* New York: Farrar, Straus, & Giroux.
A spirited defense of the labor movement in the United States, charting its rise, successes, and decline, and arguing that it needs to be revived. The style blends analysis with personal reflections.

Goldberg, Robert. (1991). *Grassroots Resistance: Social Movements in Twentieth Century America*. Belmont, CA: Wadsworth.
A brief introduction contrasts resource mobilization theories to classi-cal theories that are identified largely as mass society and anomie theories, such as those of Hannah Arendt and William Kornhauser. Most of the book is not heavily theorized but offers accounts of the historical situations, activist motivations, leadership, and outcomes of

eight grassroots movement organizations that are extremely different in their ideology: the Anti-Saloon League, the Industrial Workers of the World, the Ku Klux Klan, the Communist Party, the John Birch Society, the Student Nonviolent Coordinating Committee, the Berkeley Free Speech Movement, and the National Organization for Women. Although the examples are thought provoking, there are conceptual problems inherent in grouping these diverse movements together and then treating them largely in terms of specific movement organizations rather than broader fields of collective action; the theoretical implications of these choices are not fully explored, probably because the volume is designed for the undergraduate reader.

Halliday, Fred, and Maxine Molyneux. (1982). *The Ethiopian Revolution.* London: Verso.
Analysis of the causes and consequences of the revolution. Though limited in time frame because it was written before the overthrow of the revolutionary regime by regional/ethnonationalist counterinsurgencies, the analysis is excellent for the period covered. Prerevolutionary Ethiopia had been marked by extreme class differences, deep ethnic divisions, and a remarkably archaic patrimonial regime. Though in general sympathetic to social revolution, the authors are not timid about discussing the theoretical weaknesses, practical mistakes, and violent actions of the revolutionaries. The book provides useful insights into the process and problems of Third World revolutionary movements.

Hanlon, Joseph. (1990). *Mozambique: The Revolution Under Fire.* London: Zed Books.
Discussion of the problems faced by a socialist-oriented revolutionary regime in eastern Africa that faced economic problems as well as a South African-supported insurgency against the central government. A case study of the difficulties encountered by revolutionary movements when they came to power in Third World nations.

Harris, David. (1983). *Dreams Die Hard.* New York: St. Martin's Press.
A fascinating account of the mobilizations and the climate in the United States that set the backdrop for the murder of Congressman Al Lowenstein by a desperate former student whom he had drawn into the movements of the 1960's. Harris offers a brilliant portrait of recruitment of student cadres at Stanford, the intensity of the civil rights struggle in the early 1960's, and the unresolved hopes for a just society that activists continued to feel after the southern phase of the movement

came to a successful conclusion. These tensions were brought forward into the movements of the later 1960's, and during the war in Vietnam they were transmuted into an increasingly isolated and paranoid style. The author was an activist himself and is sympathetic to the movements but also cognizant of their powerful psychological impact on people who were predisposed to emotional instability.

Hyden, Goran. (1980). *Beyond Ujamaa in Tanzania*. Berkeley: University of California Press.
An analysis of the difficulties that confronted efforts to build an African form of socialism with rural communal development.

Katsiaficas, George. (1993). "Alternative Forms of Organization in German Social Movements." *New Political Science* 24-25 (Spring/Summer), 129-143.
The author points to the instability and divisions in Germany's left, including the Greens who are further split into realists and fundamentalists, the Autonomen (committed to direct action that has a potential for fascism), and various radical social movements.

King, Deborah. (1988). "Multiple Jeopardy, Multiple Consciousness: The Context of a Black Feminist Ideology." *Signs* 14, no. 1 (Autumn).
The author traces three overlapping movement histories in the United States—those of women's movements, African American movements, and class-based movements. The way each movement defined its issues, goals, and core constituency led to a triple marginalization of black women (almost all of whom were also workers). What is needed is an ideology and a movement that addresses these historically excluded concerns and brings together these three bases of collective action.

LaFeber, Walter. (1984). *Inevitable Revolutions*. New York: Norton.
Although dated, the book contains some useful analyses of the social strains in Central America that contributed to the formation of insurgencies and civil wars. The author emphasizes the impact of U.S. foreign policy and its support for the perpetuation of large social inequalities.

Landau, Saul. (1994). *The Guerrilla Wars of Central America: Nicaragua, El Salvador, and Guatemala*. New York: St. Martin's Press.
The author surveys the conflicts that gripped these nations as revolutionary nationalists attempted to establish new directions in development that would move them out of the U.S. orbit and counterrevolu-

tionaries opposed the movements. The perspective is sympathetic to the revolutionary movements.

Laurell, Cristina. (1992). "Democracy in Mexico: Will the First be the Last?" *New Left Review* 194 (July/August), 33-54.
The author focuses on new pressures for democracy in Mexico and the counterstrategies of the PRI (the ruling party), which is intent on preserving its power. After briefly reviewing the history of Mexican politics and the "frozen revolution," she discusses the economic restructuring and transformation of society that began in the 1960's and continues to accelerate. The PRI is forced to develop new mechanisms of control that are more refined than the old ones of clientelism and corruption, though vote fraud and thuggery still thrive. During the Salinas presidency, the PRI attempted to reduce the power of the independent labor movement, to create support from the poor by the use of public funds, and to develop new alliances (including a shaky one with some forces within the PAN), but its neo-liberal policies of deregulation and privatization unintentionally swelled new challenges. An excellent analytic summary of recent changes.

Leys, Colin. (1994). "Confronting the African Tragedy." *New Left Review* 204 (March/April), 33-47.
The author analyzes the generally dismal conditions of the region, which include widespread absolute poverty, corrupt and undemocratic regimes, and ethnic conflict and collapsing public order. He disagrees with Basil Davidson that this situation is the outcome of the colonial imposition of the nation-state as the basic political unit. Instead, Leys argues that it was the colonial failure to transform the mode of production that created the conditions for political and economic disaster. Colonial regimes exploited natural resources and cheap labor but did not transform agriculture, develop industry, and reorganize the kinship-based system of production. Consequently, many African countries lack the economic base for democratic political modernization and cannot compete in the global economy. An important perspective for understanding regional issues and movements.

Manz, Beatrice. (1988). *Refugees of a Hidden War: The Aftermath of Counterinsurgency in Guatemala.* Albany: State University Press of New York.
The author looks at the effects of counterinsurgency in Guatemala during the 1980's, a campaign of large-scale military attacks on Mayan villages in the highlands as well as death squad activity and the

concentration of population in controlled resettlement communities. Counterinsurgency was carried out to eliminate insurgent movements among the indigenous population. In addition to tens of thousands of deaths, it resulted in the internal exile or flight into Mexico of more than 100,000 refugees. The return and resettlement of the refugees is a source of concern; many may not be able to get their land back and face risk of reprisals. The author, an anthropologist, provides a careful accounting of the numbers and the circumstances of flight, exile, and return.

Menchu, Rigoberta. (1984). *I, Rigoberta Menchu: An Indian Woman in Guatemala*. London: Verso.
A moving life narrative of a woman who continues to struggle for indigenous rights and improved conditions for Guatemala's peasants, even though most of her family was murdered by the military regime. The book depicts the life of Maya communities, efforts to organize a peasant movement and Christian base communities, and relentless repression carried out by the military.

North, Liisa. (1985). *Bitter Grounds*. Toronto: Between the Lines Press.
A review of recent Salvadoran history with emphasis on class divisions, the hold of an oligarchy on land and the economy, and the formation of the insurgency as well as countermobilizations and death squad activity. It is sympathetic to the FMLN and provides background for more recent developments.

Orwell, George. (1952). *Homage to Catalonia*. Boston: Beacon Press.
A bitter narrative of the author's experiences in the Spanish Civil War, in which the forces defending the Republic were deeply divided. He is very critical of the role of the Communist Party and the Soviet Union.

Perera, Victor. (1993). *Unfinished Conquest: The Guatemalan Tragedy*. Berkeley: University of California Press.
The author covers thirty years of conflict in Guatemala, presenting a perspective on the origins of the conflict, guerrilla warfare, ethnic and economic cleavages, religious change associated with evangelical movements, environmental issues, and the scale of human rights abuses. A good overview written in a readable style with close-ups focusing on individuals and families caught up in the ongoing upheaval.

Saul, John. (1991). "South Africa: Between 'Barbarism' and Structural Reform." *New Left Review* 188 (July/August), 3-44.

A useful interim report on South Africa shortly before the end of apartheid. Although it does not cover these developments, it gives the reader a picture of the major social forces and their associated movement and party organizations.

Schlesinger, Arthur, Jr. (1988). *The Age of Jackson*. Boston: Little.
A historical study of an early wave of laissez-faire, anti-elitist activism, designed to remove the vestiges of mercantile and Federalist dominance and government economic regulation, thereby opening opportunities for new entrepreneurs and speculators. The analysis is interesting in showing the early intertwining of populist themes with entrepreneurial values and antistatist mobilizations, ambiguous ideological "packages" that continue to play a role in U.S. politics and social movements.

Schlesinger, Stephen, and Stephen Kinzer. (1983). *Bitter Fruit*. Garden City, NY: Anchor/Doubleday.
Two U.S. journalists provide a detailed and definitive account of the 1954 U.S.-supported coup against the reformist government of Jacobo Arbenz in Guatemala.

Sharpe, Kenneth. (1977). *Peasant Politics: Struggle in a Dominican Village*. Baltimore, MD: Johns Hopkins University Press.
An excellent microlevel study of politics in a village in a coffee-growing area of the Dominican Republic. The author charts the efforts of peasants and Catholic activists to create new grassroots economic, political, and social institutions, especially by forming cooperatives, and gives insight into the ideological and practical limits of these projects.

Smith-Ayala, Emilie. (1991). *The Granddaughters of Ixmucané*. Toronto: Women's Press.
The author has compiled life narratives from women in the popular movement in Guatemala. Though different in ethnic origin (indigenas and ladinas), social class, and ideology, the women are united in their opposition to the forms of military control and repressive regimes that have dominated Guatemala since 1954. The narratives reflect on experiences of repression, reasons for joining the movement, and the goals of the movement. The book concludes with a moving essay by Rigoberta Menchu about her mother and the traditions of the Maya. An excellent choice for classroom use, including women's studies.

Tocqueville, Alexis de. (1990). *Democracy in America*. New York: Random House.

Tocqueville was a French aristocrat who traveled through the United States in the nineteenth century, then wrote a classic analysis of American culture and politics. Despite a century and a half of immigration and technological and cultural transformations, many of his observations remain valid. He was struck by the egalitarian spirit of the United States, the absence of a feudal and aristocratic tradition, the dominance of a commercial and entrepreneurial culture, and the organizational activism of ordinary citizens. This portrait continues to give us insight into the political culture within which social movements emerge in the United States.

Van Wolferen, Karel. (1989). *The Enigma of Japanese Power*. New York: Vintage.

The author analyzes Japanese society as a closed cultural system in which a high degree of congruence and overlap of elites ensures stability and continuity. Although a liberal-democratic political system was established after World War II, Japanese society does not exhibit the political openness and separation of functions that define liberal society. For the student of social movements, this study provides insights into the outcomes of movements in Japan such as the labor movement, the Left, and movements of *burakumin* (an outcast group). Movements frequently are coopted into the structures of power.

Wiarda, Howard, and Harvey F. Kline, eds. (1990). *Latin American Politics and Development*. Boulder, CO: Westview Press.

Each article in this excellent collection is devoted to the political history and twentieth century political systems of a Latin American nation, so that the volume as a whole provides complete coverage of the region. The articles are written at a high level of analysis but in a form that is accessible for the beginning student of comparative politics. Outstanding as concise background material for understanding the context of social movements in each nation.

Womack, John. (1971). Zapata and the Mexican Revolution. New York: Knopf.

An important and comprehensive study of the Mexican Revolution in the early twentieth century and the role of Emiliano Zapata in leading the revolution. The author presents valuable material on the social structure of prerevolutionary Mexico, on the social origins of Zapata and his followers, and on the course of the revolution as—in part—a radical movement of landless peasants and poor farmers. He gives the reader a close-up of how this wing of the revolution was able to seize land, hold the capital, and influence social policy, but was unable to establish a viable revolutionary regime that managed state power to accomplish long-term goals of changing Mexican social structure. The book is readable and embeds the analysis in a detailed, well-written narrative account of Zapata's life.

Wood, James, and Maurice Jackson. (1982). *Social Movements: Development, Participation and Dynamics*. Belmont, CA: Wadsworth.
Covers theories of cause and process and includes case studies of various movements in the United States such as the New Left, the Chicano movement, Vietnam veterans, Moonies, and anticultists.

Zeitlin, Maurice. (1967). *Revolutionary Politics and the Cuban Working Class*. Princeton, NJ: Princeton University Press.
The author describes the class structure and how it facilitated the revolutionary process. The working class was concentrated in urban service occupations, light manufacturing, and the sugar industry. The Cuban working class was relatively large in comparison to those of other Latin American countries at the time of the revolution. The author looks at several movement organizations, including the Communist Party, that tried to mobilize these strata.

PART II

MOVEMENTS AND IDEOLOGIES

This part of the bibliographical guide covers distinct types of movements. These types are distinguished largely by their ideologies. They have distinct goals, values, and visions of a good society. Within each movement type, a wide range of organizational forms and strategies may appear. Finer shadings of ideology may emerge. Often, these differences in organization, strategy, and ideological nuance fall along national lines, as a transnational movement develops distinct national variants that match national political cultures and political institutions. Nine such categories are identified: Conservatives, including the New Right; liberals, including civil rights and human rights movements; socialism in both its revolutionary and social-democratic variants, as well as the New Left; populism, an ambiguous category of anti-elitist movements; movements based on religious faith; nationalism; the far right, including fascism, Nazism, neo-Nazism, and ethnoracism; movements focused on issues of gender inequality and sexual orientation; and environmental movements.

Chapter 4
CONSERVATIVE IDEOLOGIES AND MOVEMENTS

This chapter covers a highly heterogeneous cluster of ideologies. Their common origin is opposition to the egalitarian vision of the French Revolution, but from this point on they rapidly changed, diverged, and recombined as their original support base—landed elites—declined in political power and new social bases in the business community and the middle class emerged. Burkean conservatism (named for its first and foremost theorist, Edmund Burke) accepts change as long as the pace is slow, the state is relatively uninvolved in change, no radical intellectual projects are implemented, and existing institutions are largely preserved even though they may be modified. These themes persist in conservative thought. Another abiding theme is respect for property, but this theme has shifted toward enthusiasm for the free market (not one of its original precepts). In many respects, free market or laissez-faire ideology has become identified as the leading form of contemporary conservative thought, especially in North America, where earlier variants based on feudal thought essentially did not exist. In Europe and Latin America, a free market position often is termed "neo-liberalism." In recent years, cultural conservatism and even religious fundamentalism have added themes to conservative thought. The New Right is a term associated with the effort to recombine cultural conservatism and free market ideology into a single politically efficacious movement, especially in North America and Great Britain. Themes of neotraditional family and religious values do not always square with free market themes, leading to tensions within the New Right that are explored in several of the listed works.

Books and Book Chapters

Abraham, David. (1986). *The Collapse of the Weimar Republic*. New York: Holmes and Meier.

The author uses the concept of hegemony to analyze the inability of the Weimar Republic to withstand the growing power of the Nazis. The absence of unity within the capitalist class and its weak ideological cohesion combined with the persistence of an agrarian elite (the Junkers, or Prussian estate owners) with antidemocratic orientations produced a political system that could not sustain liberal democracy in the face of a growing right that operated both within and outside the

parliamentary process. The book is relevant to the study of conservative ideology because it links processes within conservative right-wing
elites to the formation of extreme right-wing movements with a mass
base.

Bell, Daniel, ed. (1964). *The Radical Right.* Garden City, NY: Anchor
Books.
Written after McCarthyism, during the rise of the John Birch Society,
and before the New Right, this series of essays contains a historical
analysis and themes that may still be of interest to the contemporary
reader seeking to understand the Right in the United States. The authors
largely represent the liberal mainstream and moderate conservative
thought in the social sciences and rely heavily on the concepts of
"status politics" and "status anxiety" to explain the rise of the postwar
right. These concepts could be adapted to an analysis of the role of the
Right in contemporary "culture wars."

Blumenthal, Sidney. (1986). *The Rise of the Counter-Establishment:
From Conservative Ideology to Political Power.* New York: Times
Books.
An interim report on the growing strength of conservatives. The author
conceptualizes them as a counterestablishment challenging a liberal
establishment that defined the national agenda and preserved welfare
state reforms of the 1930's and the postwar period. The steps taken
during the Reagan Administration to undo these structures and the
more radical dismantling undertaken by the congressional Republicans
after 1994 suggest that the counterestablishment is on the way to
becoming the new establishment.

Burke, Edmund. (1961). *Reflections on the Revolution in France.* Garden
City, NY: Doubleday.
A classic of conservative thought. Burke, an Anglo-Irish politician and
ideologue, had supported the American Revolution but excoriated the
French Revolution for its violent discontinuity and its visionary goals.
His analysis contains the core of modern conservative thought: Social
change should only take place slowly and with little planning, permit-
ting a gradual mutual adaptation of institutions and individuals to new
conditions. Change that is instituted by the state under the guidance of
intellectuals is almost certain to be disruptive, detached from the values
and goals of ordinary people, and ultimately unsuccessful. It is almost
always better to allow traditional institutions, no matter how oppressive they may seem, to change gradually rather than to put an end to

them. These criticisms of planning, intellectual blueprints, social revolution, and state initiatives form major themes of modern conservatism with its distrust of the state, its defense of traditional institutions, its opposition to radically egalitarian projects, and its attack on ideological, theoretical, and abstract thought (though it too, of course, constitutes an ideology, and a theoretically sophisticated one at that).

Chalmers, Douglas, Maria do Carmo Campello de Souza, and Atilio Boron, eds. (1992). *The Right and Democracy in Latin America*. New York: Praeger.
The authors of the articles in the collection examine the direction of the Right in the region in the post-Cold War, post-military dictatorship period. They discuss differences in the definitions of the term "Right," some of them based on ideological criteria and others focusing on the social bases of a right-wing position. They emphasize the general shift in the Right from military regimes to electoral politics and its support for neo-liberal economic policies of privatization and deregulation. There continue to be, however, sectors of the Right that are ambivalent toward antistatist rhetoric and free market policies. The Catholic and Protestant religious right are discussed. Some authors suggest that the Right as a whole continues to be a potential threat to democracy in the region, despite current involvement in electoral politics. Articles focus on the Right in several countries, among them Argentina, Mexico, and Brazil.

Conover, P. J., and V. Gray. (1983). *Feminism and the New Right: Conflict Over the American Family*. New York: Praeger.
The authors examine conflicting ideas held by feminists and cultural conservatives about family structure, women's roles, parental authority, and the place of public policy and government initiatives on the family.

Deutsch, Sandra McGee, and Ronald Dolkart, eds. (1993). *The Argentine Right: Its History and Intellectual Origins, 1910 to the Present*. Wilmington, DE: Scholarly Resources.
A historical rather than sociological treatment of the material, with fairly detailed accounts of movements, movement and party organizations, ideologies, and movement impact on the political system.

Diamond, Sara. (1995). *Roads to Dominion*. New York: Guilford.
Using primary sources, the author traces four right-wing movements in the United States since World War II—the anticommunist movement, the racist right, the religious right, and neo-conservatives. She

examines their ideologies, organizations, and relationships with one another and with administrations in power. She identifies the processes that have made the Right as a whole a resurgent force in U.S. politics.

Dorrien, Gary. (1993). *The Neo-Conservative Mind. Philadelphia, PA: Temple University Press.*

The author makes clear that although he does not consider himself a proponent of neo-conservative ideology (as the term is used in the United States), it is an intellectual position that must be respected and understood. He critically examines the history of neo-conservatism in the United States, noting its roots in breakaway positions of the Old Left. He then summarizes and discusses the thought of several leading neo-conservatives, including Irving Kristol, Norman Podhoretz, Michael Novak, and Peter Berger. A good introduction, from a critical but not hostile perspective.

Edsall, Thomas. (1984). The New Politics of Inequality. New York: Norton.

The author connects a number of shifts in the American political scene of the late 1970's and early 1980's: the decline in union strength, the drop in voting, and the subsequent shift of policy in a less egalitarian and more rightward direction—a shift that then fueled a self-fulfilling prophecy of alienation from government and politics as institutions. The analysis is highly readable. While paralleling more theoretical discussions of post-Fordism, it remains at a less technical level and gives insight into the origins of disillusion with government.

Friedman, Milton and Rose Friedman. (1980). Free to Choose: A Personal Statement. New York: Harcourt Brace Jovanovich.

A clear and engaging statement of faith in the free market as the foundation of freedom in general. A leading monetarist economist and his wife elaborate the position that a relatively unregulated capitalist economy forms the major safeguard of individual liberties.

Genovese, Eugene. (1969). The World the Slaveholders Made. New York: Pantheon.

Drawing on Antonio Gramsci's concept of hegemony as the process in which a ruling class commands allegiance through consent rather than coercion, the author discusses the formation and content of the southern plantation owners' ideology. A useful work for understanding a particular type of reactionary, anti-egalitarian ideology.

Gilder, George. (1981). *Wealth and Poverty*. New York: Basic Books.
A rather standard conservative argument for the beneficial effects and irremediable causes of social inequality.

Goldwater, Barry. (1960). *The Conscience of a Conservative*. Shepardsville, KY: Victor.
A classic statement of personal philosophy by a former U.S. senator and presidential candidate. In his view, conservatism is associated with the free market and individual rights to life, liberty, and property. Recently, he has distanced himself explicitly from various forms of cultural conservatism and religious fundamentalism.

Gusfield, Joseph. (1963). *Symbolic Crusade: Status Politics and the American Temperance Movement*. Urbana: University of Illinois Press.
This study is relevant for understanding conservative movements. It relates their emergence to status politics, activism of strata that feel under cultural (rather than economic) strain. In some ways, the temperance movement provides a template for later conservative movements of opposition to immigration, cultural diversity, and deviation from puritanical norms.

Hall, Stuart, and Martin Jacques, eds. (1983). *The Politics of Thatcherism*. London: Lawrence and Wishart.
Thatcherism is analyzed from a Marxist perspective informed by the concept of hegemony and the thought of Antonio Gramsci. Thatcherism was an attempt to create popular consent for a particular form of class rule within a specific period of capitalism by a manipulation of antistatist themes and promises to dismantle the welfare state, combined with actual centralization of power—themes of authoritarian populism. Its contradictory ideological appeals included the formulation of "free market, strong state." The volume is a contribution to understanding contemporary conservative ideology.

Hayek, F. A. von (1944). *The Road to Serfdom*. London: Routledge.
A classic defense of the market against socialism and expanding government involvement in the economy.

Hertsgaard, Mark. (1989). *On Bended Knee*. New York: Schocken.
The author analyzes the role of the media in the Reagan era, emphasizing their uncritical and rather unreflective support for much of the conservative agenda. This book is a thought-provoking contribution to the discussion of whether the media support liberal or conservative ideologies and practices in the United States.

Kirk, Russell. (1953). *The Conservative Mind*. Chicago: Regnery.
A classic statement of mainstream conservative thought in the United States, before the emergence of the New Right. A slow pace of change, the political value of property, tradition, and institutional continuity appear as central themes in this sympathetic discussion.

Klatch, Rebecca. (1987). *Women of the New Right*. Philadelphia: Temple University Press.
Using empirical data, the author explores some of the tensions between social conservatives and laissez-faire conservatives, with attention to differences in gender ideology. The social (or cultural) conservatives see themselves as defending the interests of traditional women and as protecting their claims against the individualistic, market-oriented policies favored by many feminists and laissez-faire conservatives.

Kristol, Irving. (1995). *Neoconservatism: The Autobiography of an Idea*. New York: Free Press.
The author develops his ideas in a collection of essays. These ideas include critiques of the welfare state and multiculturalism. Reflections on being Jewish in America give a provocative twist to his apparent eschewal of the politics of cultural diversity. His perspective is developed in a particularly interesting way in the essay on "the stupid party," a term John Stuart Mill applied to conservatives. Dogged loyalties to institutions (often highly inegalitarian ones, one might add), opposition to innovation, and a fiduciary relationship to the whole nation (and hence, a tendency to espouse patriotism and voice intolerant opposition to difference) give an appearance of stupidity to the conservative intellectual enterprise; Kristol, like Edmund Burke, strives to reveal the political and social wisdom inherent in these positions. Very thought provoking.

Lasch, Christopher. (1979). *Haven in a Heartless World*. New York: Basic Books.
The author looks at families in nineteenth century America to understand the origins of a privatized view of personal life, one that contrasts the security and warmth of the family to a negative image of the public and collective spheres of activity. These themes continue to inform American discourse, contributing both to the ideology of "family values" and to a privatized view of individual happiness.

Levitas, Ruth, ed. (1986). *The Ideology of the New Right*. Cambridge, England: Polity Press.

An excellent set of critical essays about various aspects of the belief system of the Right. The focus is on England during the Thatcher period, but the analysis has broad implications for an understanding of the Right in many developed market democracies. A number of the essays address the intertwining of free market economic ideology with cultural conservatism and the contradictions inherent in this combination; for example, see David Edgar, "The Free or the Good."

Lipset, Seymour Martin, and Earl Raab. (1978). *The Politics of Unreason: Right-Wing Extremism in America, 1790-1977.* Chicago: University of Chicago Press.
A historical overview of the cultural sources and political agendas of the far right in the United States, with attention to the themes of ethnocentrism, anti-Semitism, right-wing populism, and cultural anxieties.

Lo, Clarence. (1982). "Countermovements and Conservative Movements in the Contemporary United States." In Ralph Turner and J. F. Short (eds.), *Annual Review of Sociology* (vol. 8). Palo Alto, CA: Annual Reviews.
An overview of movements on the right in the United States in the 1970's, with emphasis on the concept of "countermovement." A good historical baseline essay for an understanding of the emergence of the New Right, tax revolts, and property owners' movements.

_____. (1990). *Small Property vs. Big Government: Social Origins of the Property Tax Revolt.* Berkeley: University of California Press.
A landmark study for understanding recent conservative mobilizations in the United States (and for that matter, in any developed market democracy). The author uses a variety of empirical methods (interviews, archival data, observation of political processes) to understand how middle-class communities in California were drawn into an anti-tax bloc whose leaders and primary beneficiaries were business owners, especially in real estate development. The constituency of homeowners and small property owners came to define its interests as coinciding with large business through a shared identity as "taxpayers" and not with poor or working-class people who were believed to benefit disproportionately from government programs. The author discusses the unfolding of this hegemonic process, including the formation of grassroots movements and citizens' mobilizations. The data are impressive, and the analysis is masterful; it is pointed without being

polemical. A must read for understanding contemporary American politics.

Mansbridge, Jane. (1986). *Why We Lost the ERA*. Chicago: University of Chicago Press.

The author is both an advocate and an empirical researcher. This study offers an in-depth discussion that will be of interest to students of conservative movements as well as feminist researchers and activists for women's rights. Mansbridge presents data and analysis supporting the view that a combination of factors led to the eventual defeat of the Equal Rights Amendment by negative votes in a small number of key state legislatures, despite considerable public opinion in favor of it. One of the most important reasons was that anti-ERA forces on the cultural right were able to reach legislators in these states, at the same time convincing sizable numbers of women that the legislation would have far-reaching negative consequences for their status and security.

Mayer, Arno. (1971). *Dynamics of Counterrevolution in Europe, 1870-1956*. New York: Harper and Row.

The author groups together a range of ideologies and movements on the right, ranging from the more traditional conservative forces to the fascist and Nazi movements. He analyzes the dynamic within this broad spectrum of the Right, especially the way traditional conservatives turned to more extreme movements as a way of countering the perceived threat from the socialist and communist left. What unites the right end of the spectrum is its position (and self-definition) as a countermovement to an expanding left. The treatment is rather abstract, rather than being a concrete analysis of specific cases, and assumes some familiarity with the outlines of modern European history.

Moore, Barrington. (1965). *Social Origins of Dictatorship and Democracy*. Boston: Beacon Press.

This book's value in the analysis of conservative movements is its insight into the linkage between conservative regimes engaged in elite-initiated modernization and fascist forms of the state, with the former constituting a precondition for the latter. For a more complete discussion of this book, see the entry in Chapter 1.

Murray, Charles. (1984). *Losing Ground*. New York: Basic Books.

The author argues that the expansion of the welfare system in the 1960's and 1970's promoted dependence on the state and interfered with poor people's capacity to meet the demands of a modern market economy. As flaws in the original design of the system grew instead of being corrected, it became dysfunctional to the nation as a whole as well as to the poor. A controversial book that contributed to the conservative initiative to formulate radically redesigned and reduced welfare policies.

Phillips, Kevin. (1970). *The Emerging Republican Majority*. New York: Anchor Books.
The author argues that the New Deal coalition that supported thirty years of Democratic administrations and liberal policy agendas came to an end in the late 1960's, unraveling over issues of race and social mores in the context of a slowing economy. Of most importance is the defection of white, blue-collar constituencies and white Southerners. These disenchanted Democrats can be attracted into a voting bloc with more traditional Republicans who represent business interests if the Republican Party offers support for culturally conservative positions. Although Phillips' predictions have not all been fulfilled—especially because the blue-collar base has been less reliably socially conservative than he believed—there are enough insights in this book to make it worth a look for those who want to understand some of the odd twists and turns of U.S. politics in recent decades. In many ways, this is also a reflection on how populism can turn to the Right as well as to the Left.

Piven, Frances Fox, and Richard Cloward. (1982). *The New Class War: Reagan's Attack on the Welfare State and Its Consequences*. New York: Pantheon.
The authors argue that cutbacks in welfare state policies and programs in the United States not only directly affected the immediate beneficiaries of these policies but also contributed to a shift in class forces. Cutbacks in the safety net had an indirect but powerful effect on wage rates, the ability of labor to organize, and the general political power of working-class people. These cutbacks signaled and initiated a conservative shift away from even the low level of welfare state or social democratic social policies that prevailed in the United States.

Rieder, Jonathan. (1985). *Canarsie: The Jews and Italians of Brooklyn Against Liberalism*. Cambridge, MA: Harvard University Press.
The author explores the orientations and political activities of a middle-income white ethnic community, tracing the increasing feelings of danger and dispossession, racial hostility, and rejection of a liberal agenda that previously had a strong support base. A growing self-defi-

nition as conservative, support for Reagan and conservative policies, and local mobilizations against busing mark a change in the identity of white middle- and working-class communities. The book provides insight into shifts in ideology as well as into the microdynamics of local countermovement mobilizations.

Roberts, Paul Craig. (1984). *The Supply Side Revolution: An Insider's Account of Policymaking in Washington.* Cambridge, MA: Harvard University Press.
One of the most important pieces of conservative ideology was the need to shift government initiatives from Keynesian demand-side policies that stimulate the economy through spending programs that increase mass purchasing power to supply-side policies that stimulate the economy by reducing taxes on investors. In other words, in this view, tax breaks for the wealthy can have the same job-creating effects as government spending on defense or on social programs. These policies were begun in the first Reagan Administration but were not applied consistently, and in many respects they were abandoned in the later 1980's. The author gives some insight into the political process of implementing these ideas.

Robinson, Michael. (1981). "Television and American Politics 1956-1976." In Morris Janowitz and Paul Hirsch (eds.), *Reader in Public Opinion and Mass Communication.* New York: Free Press.
A key essay for understanding the political effects of television. Robinson provides insight into how television undermined an older structure of opinion leadership, allowing stands on issues to become far more individualized, volatile, and detached from anchoring in social institutions and groups. He shows how it contributed to a sense of disillusionment with political institutions. Although often liberal in the manifest content of the programs, television had a largely unintended effect, promoting conservatism by eroding faith in political institutions and government. For a similar but more contemporary argument, the reader may want to look at James Fallows (1996), "Why Americans Hate the Media," *Atlantic Monthly* 277, no. 2 (February), 45-64.

Rossiter, Clinton. (1955). *Conservatism in America: The Thankless Persuasion.* New York: Random House.
The viewpoint is sympathetic to conservatism as a variant of classical liberalism, one that emphasizes the free market, property rights, national loyalties, and individualism. The viewpoint is limited, however, by the norms of European-origin middle-class communities. Historical

organization is from colonial times to the present. The book was written at a time when New Deal enthusiasm for a socially active state was still widespread; hence, conservatism is described as a "thankless persuasion." The book may be of interest now, in a post-Reagan period of conservative revitalization.

Schlafly, Phyllis. (1964). *A Choice Not an Echo*. Alton, IL: Pere Marquette Press.
An angry little book in which the author attacks the "kingmakers" in the Republican Party, from a position distinctly to the right of the party's leadership at the time. Although the specific issues addressed here are no longer current, the book marks the beginning of a period of intensified ideological struggle within the Republican Party that continues to the present. It is also the first major piece of writing by a leading activist on the right.

Stacey, Judith. (1991). *Brave New Families*. New York: Basic Books.
The author uses ethnographic methods and life narratives to analyze the formation of new cultural values and family forms. She traces the lives of several members of families that define themselves as fundamentalist and postfeminist. What is intellectually engaging in this account is the portrait of families that are able to encompass ways of life previously believed to be contradictory. For example, considerable marital instability, female autonomy, and female labor force participation coexist with traditional ideologies of male authority. Stacey provides a micro study of how neotraditional family values are actualized within a volatile market economy and an unstable cultural milieu, thereby helping readers to understand how the fundamentalist utopia of the free market economy and Christian conservatism might be realized on Earth—or, at any rate, in California.

Stockman, David. (1986). *The Triumph of Politics: How the Reagan Revolution Failed*. New York: Harper and Row.
The supply-side "revolution" was designed to be a radical restructuring of government fiscal policies, based on the premise that major cuts in taxes imposed on the owners of capital (and commensurate cuts in government spending) would provide incentives for investment, which would act as the mechanism of stimulating the economy. It was a supply-side policy, in contrast to the Keynesian demand-side policies that used government spending to increase aggregate demand (mass purchasing power) to stimulate investment and the economy in general. The architect of the supply-side revolution argues that it was not fully

implemented because of political pressure against radical cuts, especially spending cuts. Many powerful constituencies—or "special interests"—had reasons for limiting change. The analysis is of value as an example of how larger ideological visions are often only partially and imperfectly implemented in practical reforms.

Trimberger, Ellen K. (1978). *Revolution from Above: Military Bureaucrats in Japan, Turkey, Egypt and Peru.* New Brunswick, NJ: Transaction.

The author examines the role of military elites in modernizing societies. The regimes differ in the level of social change and egalitarian policies that they pursued and accomplished, but they shared a common vision of the military as a force in society that can reduce the power of traditional landed oligarchies in favor of more dynamic, modern elites. In this sense, the military regimes carried out the "revolution from above," paralleling but also preempting mass revolutions "from below" that seek to achieve similar projects of social structural transformation. The revolutions from above also share a nationalist ideology and the establishment of strong central state bureaucracies, modeled after or directly linked to the military establishments.

Viereck, Peter. (1956). *Conservatism from John Adams to Churchill.* Princeton, NJ: Van Nostrand.

A historical overview of themes in conservative thought, with an emphasis on upholding traditional institutions and mores. It reflects conservative thought in the period before the New Right and the religious right complicated the texture of conservative ideology. Incidentally, the author fell afoul of some of the more radical forces on the right as he insisted on the conservative ideal of upholding the U.S. Constitution and protecting the executive branch from the zeal of anti-Communist investigators.

Periodical Articles

Davis, Mike. (1981). "The New Right's Road to Power." *New Left Review* 128 (July/August), 28-49.

An important essay for understanding the rise of the New Right in the United States and its role in the Reagan presidency. Davis traces the ability of a national core of right-wing ideologues to aggregate single-issue constituencies and disgruntled business interests into a type of loosely networked front structure that brought resources to the Reagan campaign. The organizations and interest groups that became components of the movement were for the most part far less ideologically coherent than were its core activists. He links these new organizational forms to underlying changes in U.S. social structure, especially the fragmentation of the working class caused by the decline of Fordist models of accumulation and class integration.

Desai, Radhika. (1994). "Second Hand Dealers in Ideas: Think Tanks and Thatcherite Hegemony." *New Left Review* 203 (January/February), 27-64.
The author traces the sources, formulation, and dissemination of Thatcherite ideology, from specific think tanks associated with factions of the Conservative Party to the British media and public opinion. An important essay for students of conservative ideology and the New Right.

Erwin, Lorna. (1993). "Neoconservatism and the Canadian Pro-Family Movement." *The Canadian Review of Sociology and Anthropology* 30 (August), 401-420.
Using survey data, the author traces issues in the ideology of the Canadian cultural conservative right. Moving from direct rhetorical attacks on liberalized sexual and family norms and behaviors, neo-conservative ideologues repositioned themselves with an agenda focused on fiscal issues. Fiscal conservatism could function to reprivatize the family, most specifically by implementing cutbacks in government programs that support women's disengagement from families. The rank and file of the movement were characterized by high religious commitment, fundamentalism, and some experience of financial upward mobility.

Jessop, Bob, Kevin Bonnett, Simon Bromley, and Tom Ling. (1984). "Authoritarian Populism, Two Nations and Thatcherism." *New Left Review* 147 (September/October), 32-60.

_____. (1987). "Popular Capitalism, Flexible Accumulation, and Left Strategy." *New Left Review* 165 (September/October), 104-122.
These articles criticize the concept of "authoritarian populism" used by Stuart Hall to analyze the Thatcherite project of constructing popular consent to policies that simultaneously dismantled the welfare state and strengthened central government control. The authors develop a competing Marxist perspective on Thatcherism that emphasizes the crisis of Fordist production and Keynesian macroeconomic

policy, economic restructuring in England, and the formation of a new ruling bloc that brings together transnational capital with homeowners, shareholders, and beneficiaries of privatized education and health care. This bloc supports deregulation, privatization, and the introduction of commercial criteria in the state sector. A dual labor market of the privileged and the excluded is being formed as this radical neo-liberal agenda evolves.

Klatch, Rebecca. (1994). "The Counterculture, the New Left, and the New Right." *Qualitative Sociology* 17, no. 3 (Fall), 199-214.
The author explores some convergences between the left and right sides of the political spectrum in the United States. The counterculture served to bridge anti-authoritarian and antistatist themes in the libertarian right and the New Left. These themes put the libertarian right at odds with the traditional right, which opposed the counterculture's devaluation of religion and conventional family life. The conclusions are based on interviews with Students for a Democratic Society and Young Americans for Freedom activists as well as archival materials for each organization.

Ladd, Helen F., and Julie Wilson. (1985). "Proposition 2 1/2: Explaining the Vote." *Research in Urban Policy* 1, 199-243.
The authors conducted a telephone survey of 1,586 households in Massachusetts to discover attitudes underlying the tax cap vote. They found relatively little elaborated ideological commitment to shrinking public sector services or altering their financing; rather, voters' goals were to lower taxes and improve government efficiency. This finding supports the theoretical analysis (see the Davis [1981] entry in the periodicals section of this chapter and the Lo [1990] entry in the books section) that New Right ideologues were effective in aggregating and focusing less ideological positions into a coherently antistatist shift in policies.

McRobbie, Angela. (1994). "Folk Devils Fight Back." *New Left Review* 203 (January/February), 107-116.
The author uses the concept of "folk devil," a popular culture image of groups or ideas that embody evil, to describe the rhetorical attacks of Thatcherites on feminism, new social movements, young black people, and the Left in Great Britain. This rhetoric ultimately was unsuccessful in rallying popular opinion against these movements, because many people (especially women) were more inclined to blame Thatcher and the Conservatives for social problems than they were to

see left-oriented movements or racial minorities as the cause of problems they encountered in their everyday life. Furthermore, the demonized groups were able to create their own media and contend in public discourse. The Labour Party has been extremely slow in responding to these issues and in drawing in these new collective actors. The essay is an excellent contribution to the analysis of discourses and "spin" in popular explanations of social problems and views of collective action.

Wolfe, Alan. (1981). "Sociology, Liberalism and the Radical Right." *New Left Review* 128 (July/August), 3-25.
A relatively early analysis of the formation of the New Right, with an astute identification of the many contradictions that the ideology welds together: synthetic naturalism, democratic authoritarianism, centralized localism, globalist isolationism, and conformist individualism. In the author's view, there exists a contradiction in right-wing discourse between an apparent antistatist rhetoric and an agenda of centralizing power, shrinking the space available for competing political actors, and policing personal life. Although dated in some respects, this is still a very insightful discussion of how right-wing ideology derives power from its ability to encompass contradictory positions.

Also of Interest

Gottfried, Paul. (1992). *The Conservative Movement.* New York: Twayne.

Chapter 5
VARIETIES OF LIBERALISM

Liberal movements are joined by the common ideological threads that governments should have carefully limited and defined spheres of action, that individuals have natural human and civil rights, that the state should rule only with the consent of its citizens, and that as many functions of society as possible should be constituted by civil society rather than through the coercive action of the state. Classic liberalism largely has shifted toward liberal democracy, an ideology that continues liberalism's basic precepts but puts more emphasis on institutions of citizen representation in government. Some forms of liberalism overlap laissez-faire conservative thought; others (corresponding to the usage of "liberal" in North American political discourse) envision a larger and more positive role for the state in the society and the economy, converging to some extent with social democratic forms of socialism. Themes in liberal thought currently are associated with transnational movements for civil rights and human rights, as well as with prodemocracy movements.

Books and Book Chapters

Berlin, Isaiah. (1969). *Four Essays on Liberty*. New York: Oxford University Press.
Essays that define the meaning of liberty, classical liberal ideology with its largely negative approach to the state, and later changes in these belief systems.

Carson, Clayborne. (1981). *In Struggle: SNCC and the Black Awakening of the Nineteen Sixties*. Cambridge, MA: Harvard University Press.
A study of the Student Nonviolent Coordinating Committee, one of the most important movement organizations of the Civil Rights movement. The author discusses the formation of the organization, its crucial role in voter registration drives, its relationship to other civil rights groups and to the African American community, and the stresses it experienced as struggles shifted from civil rights to issues of economic equality and cultural autonomy.

_____. (1991). *The Eyes on the Prize Civil Rights Reader*. New York: Viking/Penguin.

One of the best selections of documents and essays on the Civil Rights movement in the United States.

Coser, Lewis. (1965). *Men of Ideas*. New York: Free Press.
An engaging social history of the role of intellectuals in modern European societies, with attention to their changing levels of political activism and commitment to roles of social critic, revolutionary, or ideologue for the status quo. It focuses on intellectuals' part in the formation and propagation of the ideologies of classical liberalism and socialism.

Dahl, Robert. (1963). *Preface to Democratic Theory*. Chicago: University of Chicago Press.

_____. (1983). *Dilemmas of Pluralist Democracy*. New Haven, CT: Yale University Press.

_____. (1990). *After the Revolution: Authority in a Good Society*. New Haven, CT: Yale University Press.
These three books contain theoretical and normative essays on the definition and practice of democracy.

Findlay, James F., Jr. (1993). *Church People in the Struggle: The National Council of Churches and the Black Freedom Movement 1950-1970*. New York: Oxford University Press.
The author documents the role of mainline churches in the Civil Rights movement. They formed a major constituency of the movement, both as participants and as a wider conscience constituency that could make resources available.

Friedman, Milton. (1962). *Capitalism and Freedom*. Chicago: University of Chicago Press.
Although he often is defined as a conservative, the famous monetarist economist in many respects adheres to the tenets of classical liberalism, that is, the call for the withdrawal of the state and its coercive apparatuses from the economic and personal spheres. He argues that capitalism and personal freedom are intimately linked and that it is only capitalism with minimal state intervention that safeguards individual liberty. Freedom is defined by private choices made in the absence of state coercion; markets may indeed constrain these choices, but this constraint is not the same as coercion exercised by the state.

Garrow, David. (1987). *Bearing the Cross: Martin Luther King, Jr. and the Southern Leadership Conference 1955-1968*. New York: Random House.

A detailed and carefully researched biography of the civil rights leader, with emphasis on the crucial years of struggle in the South, his relationship to black churches and civil rights organizations, his beliefs, and his growing commitment to a larger set of goals of justice and socioeconomic equality in the society as a whole, once juridical equality was won.

Graham, Hugh Davis. (1990). *The Civil Rights Era: Origins and Development of National Policy 1960-1972*. New York: Oxford University Press.

Analysis of elite response to civil rights mobilizations, covering the period from the initial reluctance of the Kennedy Administration to become too deeply involved to more supportive and proactive positions by the end of the decade.

Hartz, Louis. (1955). *The Liberal Tradition in America*. New York: Harcourt, Brace and World.

Brilliant analysis of the hegemony of liberal ideology in the United States. A classic work of scholarly interpretation. The author argues that lacking a feudal tradition, the United States never developed a truly conservative ideology. Instead, all disagreements were articulated within the framework of liberalism, with its emphasis on equality, property rights, civil liberties, and restriction of the power of the state. Even slaveholders reinterpreted the liberal tradition to make it their own. Nor did the United States develop a mass-based socialist ideology, despite the presence of a working class. The author's method of argument is to examine major texts of political and social ideology, showing how they remained within the liberal framework.

Hofstadter, Richard. (1948). *The American Political Tradition*. New York: Random House.

A classic portrait of the men who molded the political ideas and practices of the United States. Although the style and perspective are not always in accord with contemporary fashion, there is still much to be learned from this book.

_____. (1955). *The Age of Reform*. New York: Knopf.

A classic discussion of the age of populism and the Progressive Era in the United States at the turn of the century. The author has many insights into the ideology and social origins of these two related movements. He is critical of the populist impulse, and his interpretation of populism is still relevant and debated today.

King, Mary. (1987). *Freedom Song*. New York: William Morrow and Company.
The author tells her story of participation in the Student Nonviolent Coordinating Committee. The organization was integrated, but the leadership was predominantly African American. In the author's view, the SNCC was able to nurture local black grassroots leadership while effectively involving a white student constituency. It had some of the characteristics of an organization of professional revolutionaries but did not fall into Marxist-Leninist-style elitism or sectarianism. The book includes a criticism of the role of the Kennedy Administration as well as of the unsuccessful, pragmatic (some might say duplicitous) effort by Lyndon Johnson and Hubert Humphrey to keep both civil rights and anti-civil rights factions in the Democratic Party. The author also is critical of black nationalist ideology, which she believes contributed to the failure to form a progressive alliance.

McAdam, Doug. (1990). *Freedom Summer*. New York: Oxford University Press.
An excellent sociological study of participation in the Civil Rights movement with attention to internal structure and the mobilization of constituencies.

McMillen, Neil. (1991). *The Citizen's Council: Organized Resistance to the Second Reconstruction*. Urbana: University of Illinois Press.
A study of countermovements and countermobilizations to the Civil Rights movement.

Macpherson, C.B. (1965). *The Political Theory of Possessive Individualism*. London: Oxford University Press.
A political theorist examines the formation of modern thought, as reflected in the works of Hobbes and Locke, and the way in which it links individualism, property rights, the limitation of state power, and a vision of society that corresponds to the worldview of the emerging bourgeoisie. A sophisticated Marxist-influenced interpretation of the origins of modern political thought and ideology.

Malcolm X. (1965). *The Autobiography of Malcolm X*. New York: Grove Press.
The life narrative of a major figure in African American history. His father was a supporter of black nationalist Marcus Garvey. Malcolm

Little spent his youth as a petty criminal and in prison, where he began his activism in the Nation of Islam. After a period as a Black Muslim engaged in an essentially nationalist effort to build the power of black communities, he converted to orthodox Islam and turned to a larger, more inclusive antiracist mission. His autobiography gives the reader a vivid picture of individual motivation to participate in political struggles as well as insight into ideologies and currents of opinion in the African American community.

Marable, Manning. (1985). *Black American Politics: From the Washington Marches to Jesse Jackson*. London: Verso.

_____. (1991). *Race, Reform and Rebellion: The Second Reconstruction, 1945-1960*. Jackson: University Press of Mississippi.
The author traces the role of both class and race in the Civil Rights movement as well as post-civil rights era black politics in the United States. He discusses the difficulties in forming a progressive movement in a racially divided society. Middle-class African Americans are linked strongly to the Democratic Party, whereas working-class and poor whites are difficult to bring into a movement with predominantly black leadership and a large black constituency.

Mill, John Stuart. (1978). *The Collected Works of John Stuart Mill*. Edited by J. M. Robson. Toronto: University of Toronto Press.
A classic statement of liberal ideology.

Morris, Aldon D. (1984). *The Origins of the Civil Rights Movement: Black Communities Organizing for Change*. New York: Free Press.
See chapter 1 for an annotation.

Parks, Rosa. (1992). *Rosa Parks—My Story*. New York: Penguin.
Rosa Parks tells her story in a straightforward way, providing great insight into the formation of an activist and the events that led up to and developed from her historic refusal to give up her seat to a white bus rider in Montgomery, Alabama. This decision was far from a spontaneous gesture by a tired seamstress: Parks's family had resisted white racism, she was active in the NAACP, and she had participated in the programs of the Highlander school. She traces the growing involvement of black churches and the leadership of Dr. King as the bus boycott unfolded, a trend that brought in a mass base beyond NAACP supporters. The style of the book makes it accessible to

readers at all levels, but even the advanced scholar will find details in the account that contribute to the understanding of movements.

Przeworski, Adam. (1991). *Democracy and the Market*. New York: Cambridge University Press.
A difficult but insightful analysis of the transition to market democracies in Eastern Europe and Latin America. The author explores market democracies as political systems reflecting specific distributions of individual preferences and class power. As the state—whether military dictatorship or ruling party—withdraws from the economy, a space is opened up for democratic politics, but at the same time, key economic decisions are removed from political control and resolved by the market. The author is relatively pessimistic about the future of the post-Communist states. Neither they nor the countries of Latin America are likely to enjoy widespread prosperity unless a social and political contract, along social democratic lines, can be established between the working class and new economic elites.

Wills, Garry. (1981). *Explaining America: The Federalist*. New York: Doubleday.
Exposition of the ideas underlying the Constitution. The author notes the influences of David Hume and the Scottish Enlightenment, discusses the thought of James Madison and Alexander Hamilton, and covers both issues of political structure (checks and balances) and representation (party and "interests"). The approach is one of understanding the ideas and intellectual origins of U.S. political ideology.

Zinn, Howard. (1964). *SNCC: The New Abolitionists*. Boston: Beacon Press.
A sympathetic account of the Civil Rights movement organization and its activism in the U.S. South during the period of integration of public facilities and voter registration drives.

Periodical Articles

An-Na'im, Abdullah Ahmed. (1987). "Religious Minorities Under Islamic Law and the Limits of Cultural Relativism." *Human Rights Quarterly* 9, no. 1 (February), 1-18.
The author discusses problems and prospects in reconciling Shari'ah (Islamic law) with international standards for protection of the rights of religious minorities.

Barnett, Bernice McNair. (1993). "Invisible Southern Black Women Leaders in the Civil Rights Movement: The Triple Constraints of Gender, Race, and Class." *Gender and Society* 7, no. 2 (June), 162-182.
The author argues that many female activists remained invisible or were locked into structurally limited roles. Interviews and archival data are used to reconstruct their roles and to explain their exclusion from the recognized leadership cadre.

Blumberg, Rhoda Lois. (1990). "Women in the Civil Rights Movement: Reform or Revolution." *Dialectical Anthropology* 15, no. 2-3, 133-139.
The author suggests that women were more active in the early, noninstitutionalized phases of the movement but later withdrew in favor of male leadership, a thesis that some may find controversial.

Chomsky, Noam. (1980). "Towards a New Cold War: A Critique of Superpower Politics." *Philosophy and Social Action* 6, no. 3-4 (July-December), 5-28.
Interesting as a critique of the uses made of human rights discourses, especially by the government of the United States. U.S. efforts to "protect freedom" often are a cover or an excuse for overt or covert intervention, and in many cases, the United States itself has been a force in creating detrimental conditions for human rights. The author, a longtime critic of U.S. foreign policy, challenges some prevailing notions about the concept of human rights and suggests that it is subject to manipulation.

Clark, Ann Marie, and James McCann. (1991). "Enforcing International Standards of Justice: Amnesty International's Constructive Conflict Expansion." *Peace and Change* 16, no. 4 (October), 379-399.
A discussion of why the organization is effective, focusing on its use of symbols and discourses as well as its pragmatic types of demands.

DuBois, Ellen. (1991). "Woman Suffrage and the Left: An International Socialist-Feminist Perspective." *New Left Review* 186 (March/April), 20-45.
The author surveys a number of countries and concludes that woman suffrage cannot be explained as an inevitable outcome of either economic and social development or the pressures of world war. Independent mobilization was an important factor. The movements and parties of the Left usually supported woman suffrage, but only after initial resistance and often mainly for purposes of competing with the middle-class suffrage movement for a mass support base among

women. The author draws some analogies to class divisions in women's movements today and calls for movements that are both socialist and feminist.

Edwards, Bob, and John D. McCarthy. (1992). "Social Movement Schools." *Sociological Forum* 7, no. 3, (September), 541-550.
A review essay of a number of books on the Highlander folk schools, informal grassroots schools for movement activists that had a crucial role in the formation of civil rights workers from the 1930's to the civil rights era.

Eide, Asbjorn. (1986). "The Human Rights Movement and the Transformation of the International Order." *Alternatives* 11, no. 3 (July), 367-402.
A comprehensive article that surveys the philosophical bases of the movement and looks at the interrelationships of nongovernmental organizations, local level groups, and intergovernmental transnational organizations. Amnesty International, the Red Cross, and the International Commission of Jurists are described. The author looks toward the formation of networks as an effective way of developing this growing system of organizations.

Green, George. (1991). "The Felix Longoria Affair." *Journal of Ethnic Studies* 19, no. 3 (Fall), 23-49.
Using archival material, the author discusses how a 1949 incident in which an Anglo undertaker refused to allow funeral services for a Hispanic man galvanized a Hispanic civil rights movement in Texas and the Southwest. Documentation of the history of Hispanic civil rights issues and movements.

Kagarlitsky, Boris. (1992). "Russia on the Brink of New Battles." *New Left Review* 192 (March/April), 85-97.
A democratic socialist's view of the upheavals in Russia as the economy declines, nationalist currents grow, living standards fall, elites emerge and harden their control, and the institutionalization of democratic forms is embattled terrain. An interesting interim report.

Kelliher, Daniel. (1993). "Keeping Democracy Safe from the Masses: Intellectuals and Elitism in the Chinese Protest Movement." *Comparative Politics* 25, 379-396.
A critical perspective in which the author points to elitist themes in the movement. It was a movement of intellectuals that focused on issues such as freer circulation of ideas and information as well as students'

right to organize, with relatively little concern for the involvement of workers or the defense of their rights to form independent organizations.

Livezey, Lowell. (1989). "US Religious Organizations and the International Human Rights Movement." *Human Rights Quarterly* 11, no. 1 (February), 14-81.
The author describes the increasing role of U.S.-based Christian and Jewish organizations in the human rights movement and the activities of this growing constituency, as well as underlying philosophical and theological perspectives.

Lu Yuan. (1989). "Beijing Diary." *New Left Review* 177 (September/October), 3-26.
A moving and vivid account of a woman's visit to China at the time of the prodemocracy demonstration in Beijing, eventually crushed by the army. The daily entries reveal the ambivalent reactions of ordinary Chinese (including her family and friends) as well as the heroism and bitterness of the students.

McNitt, Andrew. (1986). "Measuring Human Rights: Problems and Possibilities." *Policy Studies Journal* 15, no. 1 (September), 71-83.
The author uses the descriptive portions of Amnesty International reports to create a data set that can be used to test comparative theories of human rights. Interesting methodological and theoretical discussion.

Smith, John. (1991). "Cultural Preservation of the Sea Island Gullah: A Black Social Movement in the Post-Civil Rights Era." *Rural Sociology* 56, no. 2 (Summer), 284-298.
Discussion of the organization and tactics of the Gullah movement to preserve their rural way of life, small property, and distinct culture in opposition to pressure from developers.

Thoolen, Hans. (1990). "Information and Training in an Expanding Human Rights Movement." *Development* 2, 86-90.
The article discusses the role of nongovernmental organizations in the expanding global human rights movement and draws attention to the need for transmitting public information and for communication among NGOs. The Human Rights Information and Documentation Systems, based in Norway, is described as a model of a center for networking, training, and communication.

Walicki, Andrzej (1991). "From Stalinism to Post-Communist Pluralism: The Case of Poland." *New Left Review* 185 (January/February), 92-121.

The author, who defines himself as a right-wing liberal democrat, argues that the end of Communism in Poland must be understood not as a sudden revolution against a totalitarian system but as the longterm outcome of a progressive loss of power, legitimacy, and ideological ground on the part of the Communist regime. The regime increasingly resorted to the depoliticization of the masses, virtually the opposite strategy from that of a truly totalitarian regime. He expresses hope for the formation of a moderate political direction, rather than a populistic and demagogic one. Interesting analysis of the entire historical sequence leading up to the collapse of Communism.

Wiseberg, Laurie. (1991). "Protecting Human Rights Activists and NGOs: What More Can Be Done?" *Human Rights Quarterly* 13, no. 4 (November), 524-544.

The author describes tactics used by governments to suppress human rights movement organizations as well as protection strategies such as urgent action networks, fact finding missions, and quiet diplomacy. She suggests establishing a legal defense fund.

Also of Interest

Ash, Timothy. (1989). *The Uses of Adversity: Essays on the Fate of Central Europe.* New York: Vintage Books.

Brysk, Alison. (1993). "From Above and Below: Social Movements, the International System, and Human Rights in Argentina." *Comparative Political Studies* 26 (October), 259-285.

Eagles, Charles W., ed. (1986). *The Civil Rights Movement in America.* Jackson: University of Mississippi Press.

Jelin, Elizabeth. (1994). "The Politics of Memory: The Human Rights Movement and the Construction of Democracy in Argentina." *Latin American Perspectives* 21 (Spring), 38-58.

Laski, Harold. (1936). *The Rise of European Liberalism.* London: Allen and Unwin.

Lin, Nan. (1992). *The Struggle for Tiananmen: Anatomy of the 1989 Mass Movement*. Westport, CT: Praeger.

Livingstone, Ken. (1992). "Can Democracy Survive in Russia?" *New Left Review* 192 (March/April), 98-104.

Lincoln, C. Eric, ed. (1984). *Martin Luther King: A Profile*. New York: Harper.

Lowi, Theodore. (1969). *The End of Liberalism*. New York: Norton.

McAdam, Doug. (1982). *Political Process and the Development of Black Insurgency*. Chicago: University of Chicago Press.

Morrison, Minion K. C. (1987). *Black Political Mobilization: Leadership, Power and Mass Behavior*. Albany: State University of New York Press.

Robinson, James, and Patricia Sullivan, eds. (1991). *New Directions in Civil Rights Studies*. Charlottesville: University of Virginia Press.

Chapter 6
THE LEFT

Socialism is an ideology characterized by the analysis that in class-stratified societies, the mode of production is an underlying sphere of inequality that constrains and limits human possibilities. Capitalism, the prevailing mode of production, contains a promise of human freedom and equality and represents a step forward from systems like feudalism. As long as the means of production are privately owned and the market is the regulating mechanism for the production and distribution of goods, however, this promise of freedom and equality cannot be fulfilled.

Socialists differ in their strategies for replacing capitalism by socialism. Revolutionary socialists, largely influenced by V. I. Lenin's thought, picture this transition as requiring the capture and reconstitution of the state. Many movements associated with revolutionary socialist ideology came to term themselves "Communist," and a number of these movements came to power as the ruling parties of twentieth century nation-states (most prominently in the Soviet Union and China). Social democrats, an important political force in Western Europe, picture a more gradual and peaceful transition that includes and extends the institutions of liberal democracy. Anarchists, the New Left, and many of the New Social Movements in Western Europe share the socialist critique of capitalism but eschew transformations that emphasize the state; their thought is more libertarian and antistatist.

Books and Book Chapters

Abendroth, Wolfgang. (1972). *A Short History of the European Working Class*. London: New Left Books.
A chronological summary of major working-class political movements in Europe from the nineteenth century to the 1970's. It focuses on the history of socialist movements and parties from an independent left-wing perspective.

Aronowitz, Stanley. (1973). *False Promises*. New York: McGraw-Hill.
See chapter 1 for an annotation.

Barkan, Joanne. (1984). *Visions of Emancipation: The Italian Workers' Movement Since 1945*. New York: Praeger.

The author provides a summary of the whole movement but focuses on the late 1960's and the 1970's, when younger workers in heavy industry brought a new vision to the labor struggle, a vision that emphasized democracy, autonomy, and building a society fundamentally different from capitalism. The most moving and remarkable part of the book is "Conversations in Turin," which contains interviews and life narratives of workers and others on the Left that give insight into the personal ideas, motivations, and experiences that fueled the new militancy. Important for a historical understanding of the European left and for tracing a major thread of left-wing ideology.

Bertsh, Gary, and Thomas Ganshow. (1976). *Comparative Communism.* San Francisco: Freeman.
    Although the cases are now mainly of historical interest, the analysis is clear and useful for obtaining a basic understanding of the major forms of single-party Communist systems in the post-World War II period, such as the Soviet and Chinese models and Yugoslav market socialism.

Blackburn, Robin. (1991). *After the Fall: The Failure of Communism and the Future of Socialism.* London: Verso.
    The author argues that although the single-party models of socialism no longer are relevant, the persistence of capitalism with all of its defects calls for the revitalization of socialism. Blackburn discusses the ways in which socialists must revise their tradition.

Blackmer, Donald, and Sidney Tarrow, eds. (1975). *Communism in Italy and France.* Princeton, NJ: Princeton University Press.
    A useful collection of essays on the development of Communist parties in two Western European countries after World War II. The analysis focuses on the processes that led both parties to accommodate themselves to the capitalist sphere of influence as well as on differences between the parties, such as the more open stance of the Italian Communist Party in contrast to the more rigid structure and outlook of the French Communist Party.

Boggs, Carl. (1986). *Social Movements and Political Power: Emerging Forms of Radicalism in the West.* Philadelphia, PA: Temple University Press.
    Written at the height of New Social Movement activism, with its wide range of peace, environmental, and urban mobilizations, the book argues for the vitality of a tradition of participation, democratic decentralization, and multifaceted mobilization. The author draws on the

experiences of left-wing populist electoral victories in Santa Monica that implemented reforms in urban development policies (for example, limits on condominium conversions and high-rises; innovative forms of rent control) but also notes the lack of a coherent agenda in some of these movements.

_____. (1995). *The Socialist Tradition: From Crisis to Decline.* New York: Routledge.
The author discusses the difficulties inherent in the project of bringing together socialism and democracy, from the beginnings of Marxist thought through the impact of Lenin, and finally to the post-World War II period. In this period, both the Euro-Communist and the Euro-Socialist projects of building democratic socialism and breaking with the vanguard model made some progress but ran into obstacles inherent in the new structures of European society. Democratic socialism may be revitalized in new forms within other movements, such as feminism or the environmental movement, but at present in a postmodernist period, the future for it is uncertain.

Boggs, James. (1963). *The American Revolution: Pages from a Negro Worker's Notebook.* New York: Monthly Review Press.
A remarkable essay on U.S. society and social structure, the interplay of class and race, and the experience of labor in heavy industry. Although the Fordist phase of capitalism appears to be in decline, with the reorganization of manufacturing and the stranding of African American communities in Rust Belt cities and neighborhoods, many of Boggs's insights remain powerful and worth a contemporary look. A must for anyone interested in developing a left-wing perspective that brings together labor and multicultural struggles.

Brecher, Jeremy. (1974). *Strike!* New York: Fawcett.
A spirited and easy to read account of labor struggles in the United States, with an emphasis on worker autonomy and spontaneity. There may be an underestimation of the role of organized labor, the Communist Party, or the federal government in some phases of the author's narrative. The book might be a good choice as one of several texts in an introductory labor history course.

Breines, Wini. (1982). The *Great Refusal: Community and Organization in the New Left: 1962-1968.* New York: Praeger.
The author explores the emancipatory elements of New Left theory and practice as it emerged in the mid-1960's, focusing on its rejection of hierarchy, centralized power, and inequality whether these appeared

in radical movements or in the dominant culture. Her sympathetic analysis is necessary reading for students of the New Left.

Brovkin, Vladimir. (1987). *The Mensheviks After October: Socialist Opposition and the Rise of the Bolshevik Dictatorship*. Ithaca, NY: Cornell University Press.

As the Bolsheviks consolidated their hold on state power and established a revolutionary regime, they limited the participation of other forms of movements of the Left—moderate socialists, anarchists, and, most important, the Mensheviks, with whom they had shared the major socialist movement organization in prerevolutionary Russia. In limiting and eventually repressing these forces on the Left, above all the Mensheviks, the Bolsheviks cut themselves off from the criticism they needed in order to examine and correct their own subsequent practice. Brovkin examines the process of limitation and repression and its consequences for creating a single-party state that allowed no public discussion—and, for that matter, very little intraparty debate—on key issues of the socialist transformation of society.

Carr, Barry, and Steve Ellner, eds. (1993). *The Latin American Left: From the Fall of Allende to Perestroika*. Boulder, CO: Westview Press.

The volume contains detailed and informative articles on the Left in Argentina, Venezuela, Brazil, Colombia, Peru, Mexico, Bolivia, and El Salvador, as well as several comparative articles on different types of movements (guerrilla insurgencies, the labor movement). The volume as a whole tries to address the issue of how the Left shifted from Marxist and often sectarian positions to collective activism that seems more pluralistic, diffuse, and located at the grassroots and among the marginalized—in short, a Latin American form of New Social Movements. Particularly interesting are discussions of the problems facing the trade union movement in the face of economic restructuring, the growing importance of the informal economy, and the challenge of the New Social Movements.

Carr, E. H. (1967). "Revolution from Above: Some Notes on the Decision to Collectivize Soviet Agriculture." In Kurt Wolff and Barrington Moore, Jr. (eds.), *The Critical Spirit*. Boston: Beacon Press.

The author summarizes and analyzes the decision made by the Communist Party under the leadership of Joseph Stalin to collectivize Soviet agriculture, transferring it from individual ownership by peasants of varying degrees to wealth to collective ownership with fixed purchases of farm output by the state. This move introduced a greater degree of predictability in the level of food production available to sustain massive industrial development, but at enormous human, social, and economic costs: the deportation and murder of the *kulaks* (the stratum of rich peasants that most resisted collectivization), the conflict and discontent built into the heart of the relationship between collective farms and the state, and the lack of incentives and mechanisms for modernizing agriculture and rural society. Important reading for understanding postrevolutionary transformations of society.

_____. (1972). *The Bolshevik Revolution 1917-1923*. London: Macmillan.
A modern classic about the Russian Revolution. It provides a detailed chronological account of the revolution, the civil war that followed, and the policies of the Bolsheviks during the period. Any student of Russian history or the history of revolutions would do well to look at this volume.

_____. (1982). *Twilight of the Comintern 1930-1935*. New York: Pantheon.
A major historian of the Soviet Union and the Communist Party looks at a decisive phase of the history of the Left, the period in which the party leadership finally chose to spearhead the formation of the popular front, a broad coalition of democratic forces, against the growing threat of fascist and Nazi movements. The centrist parties of the market democracies were included in this coalition, which eventually formed the basis of the Allied forces in World War II (although only after a provisional, tactical reversal in the Hitler-Stalin pact). The formation of the coalition also involved a reorganization of the relationship between the Communist Party of the Soviet Union and the Communist parties that were integrated into the Comintern under its hegemony. Carr traces the changes in the party's analysis and strategy that led up to this historic shift. Essential reading for understanding twentieth century history.

Castañeda, Jorge. (1993). *Utopia Unarmed: The Latin American Left After the Cold War*. New York: Knopf.
Castañeda provides an analytic history of the Latin American Left, including nationalist populist regimes, labor organizing and coalition politics of the Communist parties, insurgencies patterned after the Cuban revolution, organization of guerrilla forces with a base in poor rural populations, the role of liberation theology and the Catholic Left, and a variety of popular movements. The author maintains a consider-

able critical distance from most of these forces, especially from the various revolutionary insurgencies, which he believes were not only undemocratic but also out of touch with the realities of Latin America. He seeks to solve a puzzle: Why does South America, a continent with an enormous weight of poverty, exploitation, and transnational dependency, lack a hegemonic Left? Yankee intervention provides only a partial explanation. Castañeda points to what he considers errors of both analysis and strategy on the Left. He remains guardedly optimistic about the long-term prospects of the Left if it forms social democratic parties and popular movements that seek gradual reforms, work within the electoral process, and develop an understanding of national conditions rather than mechanically applying highly abstract models of revolutions. A richly detailed book that provides a wealth of information and insight, though not all readers will agree with all parts of the analysis.

Caute, David. (1988). *Year of the Barricades*. New York: Harper and Row.
A readable account of the wide range of movements and insurgencies that flared in 1968, including antiwar activism in the United States, the May events in Paris, and the Prague Spring.

Chaliand, Gerard. (1989). *Revolution in the Third World: Currents and Conflicts in Asia, Africa, and Latin America*. New York: Viking/Penguin.
An important analysis for assessing the record of Third World revolutionary socialist regimes. The author argues that many of these regimes were unable to accomplish the transformations of social structure that they promised; once in power, the revolutionary movements tended to create inflexible, bureaucratized structures of political rule that created new forms of social inequality and failed to alleviate the older forms. In the author's view, Vietnam is an exception to this general pattern and shows that even under the hardships of a prolonged war of liberation, a ruling party can move ahead with a genuinely revolutionary project.

Cohen, Stephen F. (1975). *Bukharin and the Bolshevik Revolution: A Political Biography, 1888-1938*. New York: Random House.
The life of Nikolai Bukharin, a Russian revolutionary, is traced by a leading scholar in Soviet studies in order to provide insights into the revolution and its outcome. Bukharin was considered to be on the "right" of the Bolsheviks and believed that it was essential for the Soviet Union to move toward socialism gradually, in a process that

would integrate peasant-owners into the economy rather than impose collectivization on them. He fell afoul of the Stalinist regime and was condemned to death and executed in the purge trials of the late 1930's. The author shows that far from being a traitor to the revolution, Bukharin had a cogent and pragmatic vision of socialist transformation. The book includes detailed historical narrative and carefully presented accounts of disagreements in the party. It is highly readable for anyone interested in twentieth century history.

Davis, Mike. (1986). *Prisoners of the American Dream*. London: Verso. See chapter 3 for an annotation.

Deutscher, Isaac. (1974). *Stalin: A Political Biography*. 2d ed. London: Oxford University Press.
A definitive political biography from an independent socialist perspective. Its value to theory lies in the analysis of the social conditions and forms of movement organization that made possible Stalin's rise to power within the structure of the Soviet Union and the organizational apparatus of the Bolshevik movement/Communist Party.

Dubovksy, Melvin. (1969). *We Shall Be All: A History of the Industrial Workers of the World*. Chicago: Quadrangle.
A definitive history of the anarcho-syndicalist IWW, which reached the peak of its influence in the early decades of the twentieth century in the United States. Its members held a vision of the collapse of capitalism through a series of general strikes and the subsequent establishment of a decentralized form of socialism. The organization directed its appeals to workers whom the mainstream craft unions had ignored, such as timber workers, miners, farm laborers, female factory workers, and minorities. Its principled opposition to World War I led to systematic repression and the effective end of its role in the U.S. Left. Although a relatively short chapter in labor history, the IWW and its antiauthoritarian views are a noteworthy legacy.

Dunn, John. (1972). *Modern Revolutions*. Cambridge, England: Cambridge University Press.
The author emphasizes the problems for a revolutionary movement in establishing legitimacy in the process of forming a new regime. He examines eight cases of twentieth century revolutions (Mexico, Russia, China, Algeria, Vietnam, Yugoslavia, Turkey, and Cuba). It is the old regime's loss of legitimacy that links the rationalist plans of the revolutionary leadership with the masses' unplanned responses to growing strain. This triad of forces generates collective action but

152 Social Movement Theory and Research

leaves unanswered the basis of the new revolutionary state's legitimacy. A critique of Marxist and structuralist analyses.

Eckstein, Susan, ed. (1989). *Power and Popular Protest: Latin American Social Movements*. Berkeley: University of California Press.
A collection of articles of scholarly analysis of grassroots and left-wing movements in Latin America.

Elliot, Gregory. (1993). *Labourism and the English Genius: The Strange Death of Labour England*. London: Verso.
The author explores the problems of the British Labour Party, its structural ties to the trade union movement, divisions within the party, and its difficulties in reaching a changing class base in the context of massive economic restructuring.

Esping-Andersen, Gosta. (1985). *Politics Against Markets: The Social Democratic Road to Power*. Princeton, NJ: Princeton University Press.
A scholarly analysis of social democratic strategies and outcomes, emphasizing the social democrats as a force within capitalist systems that stands for limitation of markets in favor of more public, planned, and egalitarian forms of distribution. Important for the understanding of social democracy as a historical phenomenon, especially in Sweden.

Farber, Samuel. (1990). *Before Stalinism: The Rise and Fall of Soviet Democracy*. London: Verso.
When did the "original sin" of the Soviet Union's slide into dictatorship and repression take place? Was it already inherent in the Leninist model of the vanguard party, did it emerge from the events of the civil war and the problems of regime formation in the 1920's, or was it entirely owing to Stalin? The author argues that the Bolsheviks neglected the role of civil society from an early point on, yet a more democratic movement might not have survived the civil war.

Flacks, Richard. (1971). *Youth and Social Change*. Chicago: Markham.
A sociological analysis of the role of youth in movements of the 1960's, connecting various forms of activism to generational experiences.

Fletcher, Roger, ed. (1987). *Bernstein to Brandt: A Short History of German Social Democracy*. London: Edward Arnold.
A collection of scholarly essays that analyzes major phases and strategies of one of the world's largest and most influential socialist movements, institutionalized as a mass party during much of its history.

Important material for understanding the history of socialism in Europe in the twentieth century.

Georgakas, Dan, and Marvin Surkin. (1975). *Detroit: I Do Mind Dying.* New York: St. Martin's Press.

A lively, scrapbooklike collection of essays, poems, and photographs recording a variety of leftist and labor mobilizations in Detroit in the 1960's and 1970's. These include labor organizing among black workers in the auto industry, a militant movement against companies as well as the relatively conservative leadership of the union. This movement promised a linkage of labor to otherwise fragmented rebellions against the status quo—the Black Power movement and the ideological organizations of the predominantly white and youthful New Left. In the long run, the movement could not deliver on these promises, as industry pulled out of the Detroit area (and similar zones of manufacturing) and the African American community lost much of its foothold in industrial production. The book is a good resource for students of the movements of the 1960's.

Gitlin, Todd. (1987). *The Sixties.* Toronto: Bantam.

The author, a noted sociologist of the media as well as a former activist, covers the movements of the period, interweaving a chronological account, personal memoir, and critical analysis. The story moves from the disintegration of the Old Left and the Beat cultural currents of the 1950's to the early period of the peace movement and the formation of Students for a Democratic Society (SDS) to civil rights and community organizing to the antiwar movement to the final fragmentation of SDS into increasingly sectarian groups of self-styled revolutionaries. A major theme of Gitlin's analysis is the failure of the progressive movement as a whole to question and reject models of revolution that were drawn from periods and places (such as China or Cuba) that were irrelevant to the situation in the United States. The reader should note that Gitlin's account of the 1960's is based on his own experience as well as his own theoretical perspective. In any case, the book is a must for any scholar examining the 1960's or the history of social movements in the United States and is also good reading for high school and college students.

Gitlin, Todd, and Nanci Hollander. (1970). *Uptown: Poor Whites in Chicago.* New York: Harper and Row.

A description of community organizing in the Uptown neighborhood of Chicago, which in the 1960's had become the home of poor whites,

many of them migrants from Appalachia. Gitlin and his fellow organizers focused on developing community centers, especially for young
people, and articulating demands for jobs or guaranteed minimum
incomes. The book provides insights into grassroots activities of the
New Left in the period.

Gruber, Helmut. (1974). *Soviet Russia Masters the Comintern.* New York:
Doubleday.
An account of the dominance of the Communist Party of the Soviet
Union (CPSU) over the international Communist movement in the
1920's and 1930's. The agenda and strategy of Communist parties in
various nations became subordinated to the priorities of the Soviet
Union as defined by Joseph Stalin and a small group of leaders of the
CPSU. Useful historical material.

Gurley, John. (1975). *Challengers to Capitalism: Marx, Lenin, Stalin and
Mao.* New York: Norton.
An excellent introductory discussion of the basic ideas and programs
of four socialist revolutionaries, with attention to the historical settings
in which they formulated and tried to implement their revolutionary
ideologies. This book is a good starting place for anyone who wants to
understand the role of socialism and communism in twentieth century
history. The author is sympathetic to the revolutionaries and, perhaps,
in the light of the collapse of Communism is not critical enough of the
revolutionary projects and their implementation through states. Useful
capsule biographies are included.

Halliday, Fred. (1989). *From Kabul to Managua.* New York: Pantheon.
A key analysis for understanding how the Cold War ended and what
became of Third World revolutionary socialist regimes. The author
links the arms race to the growing burden on the Soviet Union of
supporting impoverished and unstable revolutionary states. The Reagan Administration was able to "put the squeeze" on both fronts with
increases in defense spending to escalate the arms race, while at the
same time backing counterinsurgencies and protracted antirevolution-
ary wars in the Third World states. The Soviet Union lacked the
resources—and eventually the will—to deal with both pressures. It
increasingly disengaged from support for "states of a socialist orientation," many of which were very small, poor, and under siege from
counterrevolutionaries. The book gives enormous insight into the
geopolitical dynamics that led to the collapse of communism. Far from
being a chess game in which socialism marched across the board and

small states were promoted as part of this historical movement, geopolitics turned out to be a poker game won by a strategy of relentless pressure in both arms development and Third World counterinsurgency.

Hane, Mikiso. (1988). *Reflections on the Way to the Gallows: Rebel Women in Prewar Japan*. Berkeley: University of California Press.
A moving description of the activities and fate of a number of women in pre-World War II Japan who were socialist or labor organizers as well as challengers of the subordinate status of women. The author provides a wealth of information on the activists and on a period that is not well understood by Westerners, offering a powerful corrective to the notion that Japanese are traditionally docile and conservative on both gender and class issues.

Healey, Dorothy, and Maurice Isserman. (1990). *Dorothy Healey Remembers*. New York: Oxford University Press.
A personal memoir of life in the Communist Party in the United States. Healey provides richly detailed reflections on individual experiences as well as the issues the party confronted. Having eventually left the party, she has many critical insights into its organization and modus operandi, but she offers these without bitterness and with a lasting commitment to socialism. Her memoir offers insight into the struggles of the 1930's and 1940's, the repression of the post-World War II period, the structure of decision making within the party, and her role as a woman in the party. A valuable memoir for anyone interested in the history of the Left, U.S. political history, and issues of gender and movement participation.

Heclo, Hugh, and Henrik Madsen. (1987). *Policy and Politics in Sweden*. Philadelphia, PA: Temple University Press.
The authors provide a good analysis of Swedish politics up to the late 1980's and the role of the social democrats in establishing a comprehensive welfare state.

Hellman, Stephen. (1988). *Italian Communism in Transition: The Rise and Fall of the Historic Compromise in Turin 1975-1980*. New York: Oxford University Press.
Using detailed empirical data based on his study of the Communist Party (PCI) in Turin, the author analyzes changes in party strategy, party organization, and the views of grassroots participants as the party saw hopes fade for the "historic compromise," an institutional arrangement with the Christian Democrats that would have enabled the PCI

to participate in governing Italy. Although the data are derived from a particular city, the study has broad implications for understanding the problems of Italian Communism and of Euro-Communism as well during this crucial historical period.

Hobsbawm, Eric. (1973). *Revolutionaries*. New York: NAL.
Essays by a major historian of the Left, covering communism in several European countries, anarchism, Marxist theory, and various roles in revolutionary movements such as those of intellectuals, military officers, and guerrillas. Some of these essays are engaged in a dialogue with perspectives of the European New Left and other currents. Although some of the issues covered are no longer vital, much of the book remains thought provoking.

Howard, Dick, and Karl Klare, eds. (1972). *The Unknown Dimension: European Marxism Since Lenin*. New York: Basic Books.
Essays that review a wide range of developments in Marxist theory, most of them outside the orthodox current defined by Soviet ideologues. The volume is not directly about movements or movement ideologies, but it is valuable for understanding the social thought that provided an intellectual foundation for the New Left in Western Europe.

Isserman, Maurice. (1987). *If I Had a Hammer: The Death of the Old Left and the Birth of the New Left*. New York: Basic Books.
The author discusses the roots of the New Left in the Old Left, including the influence of specific groups and movements of the Old Left, such as Trotskyite splinter groups and radical pacifism. He argues that in the United States, in contrast to England, the New Left was connected only weakly to the Old Left because the latter had been so marginalized in the United States. Those parts of the Old Left with which the New Left was familiar often were strongly anti-Communist, and this deepened divisions in the New Left. Isolation from the historical mainstream of the Left made the New Left susceptible to crude versions of Marxist-Leninist sectarianism, often quite inappropriate to the U.S. context.

Jäggi, Max, Roger Müller, and Sil Schmid. (1977). *Red Bologna*. London: Writers and Readers Publishing Co-operative.
A lively and engaging account of "socialism in one city," the policies and programs instituted by the Italian Communist Party in its stronghold in the central region of Emilia-Romagna. Virtually uninterrupted local electoral victories since the end of World War II allowed the party

to develop major programs to provide social services and improve city quality of life, demonstrating its effectiveness and accountability. The description is extremely favorable.

Katsiaficas, George. (1987). *The Imagination of the New Left.* Boston: South End Press.
Covers the emancipatory ideas and visions of the New Left, with attention to its transnational character. The author draws his approach from Herbert Marcuse and G. Hegel, emphasizing moments of emancipatory eruptions that contribute to the historical development of a collective, democratic vision (in 1848, 1905, and 1917-1919, as well as 1968). These moments are characterized by an "eros effect," a heightened collective and politicized state. For the author, the social base of the latest of these moments is the student movement and the new working classes.

Kornai, Janos. (1989). *The Economics of Shortage.* New York: Elsevier-North Holland.
A leading Hungarian economist analyzes the socialist economies, with their persistent problems of shortfalls, most noticeably in the production of routine consumer goods. Good background for understanding the problems of Communist systems.

Kornbluh, Joyce. (1964). *Rebel Voices: An IWW Anthology.* Ann Arbor: University of Michigan Press.
A wonderful collection of pamphlets, posters, songs, and memoirs of the Industrial Workers of the World, an early twentieth century anarcho-syndicalist labor movement organization. Well-edited primary materials.

Laslett, John, and Seymour Martin Lipset. (1974). *Failure of a Dream? Essays in the History of American Socialism.* Garden City, NY: Anchor.
A stimulating set of essays by social scientists and socialists that offers a postmortem on socialism in the United States. Commentaries and replies are built into the volume to open debates. Both factors internal to the movement and external ones associated with the structure of American society are discussed.

Lenin, V. I. (1975). *The Lenin Anthology.* Edited by Robert Tucker. New York: Norton.
A collection of the writings of the leading figure of the Russian Revolution. These essays lay out the foundations of Leninist theories

of the state, capitalist development, and the organization of the revolutionary movement. Essential reading for understanding communism.

Lens, Sidney. (1969). *Radicalism in America*. New York: Thomas Y. Crowell.
A history of movements on the left in the United States from the beginnings of the republic to the movements of the 1960's. Written for the general reader; informative and with a broad sweep. It includes movements of radical democracy, populist movements, labor organizing, anarchism, and socialism. A good choice for high school or college students looking for an introduction to the topic.

Marcuse, Herbert. (1961). *Soviet Marxism: A Critical Analysis*. New York: Vintage/Random.
An unorthodox Marxist view of the Soviet system, especially its repressive political and intellectual characteristics.

Medvedev, Roy. (1977). *On Socialist Democracy*. New York: Norton.
A democratic socialist dissident offers a sweeping critique of virtually all institutions in Soviet society.

Miliband, Ralph. (1969). *The State in Capitalist Society*. London: Weidenfeld and Nicolson.
An analysis of the functions of the state in market societies: integrating the working class, managing and stabilizing the accumulation process, and expressing in universal form the interests of capital as a whole. The author addresses the problems that socialist parties encounter when they win public office. Forming a government within a capitalist economy and class structure is not an easy route to a transformation of the system, because the state is inherently organized to sustain capitalism. Still a valuable perspective.

Miller, James. (1987). *Democracy Is in the Streets: From Port Huron to the Siege of Chicago*. New York: Simon and Schuster.
The book covers the influence on the New Left of radical, non-Marxist U.S. academics such as C. Wright Mills who called for the restoration of democracy in a bureaucratized mass society. The author also notes the problems that emerged from consensus-based organizational procedures as well as New Left failures in reaching poor white constituencies in its Economic Research and Action Program.

Milner, Henry. (1989). *Sweden: Social Democracy in Practice*. New York: Oxford University Press.

A sound, scholarly study of social democratic political, social, and economic policies during the heyday of social democratic government.

Moore, Barrington. (1965). *Social Origins of Dictatorship and Democracy*. Boston: Beacon Press.
The author's analysis includes the cases of Russia and China, where capitalist development increased pressure on the peasantry, which was already subject to precapitalist exploitation by landowners. The peasantry remained a politically marginalized class. Preconditions thus existed for revolutions, spearheaded by socialist movements but with a mass base in the peasantry.

Petras, James, and Morris Morley. (1975). *The United States and Chile*. New York: Monthly Review Press.
A case study of intervention by the United States to block the development of socialist programs and policies by the Unidad Popular government of Salvador Allende. The government was formed after the united left won a relative majority in Chilean elections. As it attempted to carry out reforms of nationalizing large enterprises and redistributing income and services to workers and peasants, opposition emerged in several sectors of society, such as the military, large business owners, and some small property owners such as independent truckers. The United States supported these counterreform forces and also intervened to block credit for Chile in international agencies, tactics that exacerbated economic difficulties associated with socialist reforms and helped to set the stage for the Pinochet coup in 1973. A partisan but insightful discussion of the problems of elected socialist regimes.

Piven, Frances Fox, and Richard Cloward. (1977). *Poor People's Movements: Why They Succeed, How They Fail*. New York: Pantheon.
A classic sympathetic analysis of the spontaneous and uncontrollable character of poor people's movements. These movements typically are local, weakly institutionalized, led by grassroots activists, inclined to use direct action as a strategy, and not committed to a highly theoretical belief system. The authors explicitly and implicitly contrast these movements to other models of movements on the Left, especially the Leninist vanguard party, the mass electoral party, and the institutionalized labor union. These models do not meet the immediate survival needs of the poor and are subject to cooptation or repression. In the long run, however, poor people's spontaneous and casually organized movements may have difficulties in sustaining reform efforts and building coalitions.

Przeworski, Adam. (1987). *Capitalism and Social Democracy*. New York: Cambridge University Press.
In a sophisticated analysis, the author discusses the limits of social democracy as a socialist strategy. As social democratic governing parties succeed in introducing elements of socialism into a system, investors discover that profit margins shrink, taxes rise, and regulations become more stringent. These limits to capitalist accumulation in turn touch off tendencies toward reducing investment or shifting it abroad, in turn narrowing margins for the society as a whole. The author remains favorably inclined toward social democracy but is alert to its systemic limits.

Richmond, Al. (1972). *A Long View from the Left*. New York: Delta.
A personal memoir of life in the Communist Party, from early memories of the Soviet Union to a lifetime of activism to final disillusionment with the party, but not with socialism as a larger ideal. A satisfying life narrative.

Sader, Emir, and Ken Silverstein. (1991). *Without Fear of Being Happy: Lula, the Workers Party and Brazil*. London: Verso.
A discussion of the leading force on the left in Brazilian politics. The authors analyze the overall political situation in Brazil, the conditions of electoral politics, and the Workers' Party, with its strong base in urban areas and among industrial workers in Brazil's growing but extremely uneven economy.

Sale, Kirkpatrick. (1973). *SDS*. New York: Random House.
An interesting and fast-moving account of Students for a Democratic Society, the largest and most influential of the movement organizations of the New Left in the United States. Sale especially provides insights into the breakup of SDS, its fragmentation into warring factions of increasingly doctrinaire and unrealistic sects of self-styled revolutionaries.

Sassoon, Donald. (1981). *The Strategy of the Italian Communist Party: From the Resistance to the Historic Compromise*. New York: St. Martin's Press.
The author covers a segment of PCI history, from its triumphant role in World War II to its disappointing attempt to form a governing coalition with the Christian Democrats in the 1970's. An important slice of Euro-Communist history.

Sayres, Sohnya, ed. (1984). *The Sixties, Without Apology*. Minneapolis: University of Minnesota Press.

The collection brings together accounts by activists in the New Left, the antiwar movement, the women's movement, and the cultural currents of the period. The essays differ in style and point of view but share enthusiasm for the ferment and dissent of the period. A good selection for contemporary undergraduates exploring the period.

Smith, Martin J., and Joanna Spear. (1992). *The Changing Labour Party*. London: Routledge.

An analysis of how the British Labour Party has to change in conjunction with changes in its support base and environment. Historically, it was tied closely to the trade unions, which formed its major—in some ways its only—transmission belt to its supporters. Weakening union strength and the need to reach new constituencies pose problems for this organizational model. The analysis has broad implications for the future of any leftist party constituted as a labor party.

Stacey, Judith. (1983). *Patriarchy and Socialist Revolution in China*. Berkeley: University of California Press.

Excellent coverage of gender issues in modern China, beginning with an outstanding chapter on traditional structures of patriarchy and then moving to an analysis of the impact of modernization on the gender system in the first part of the twentieth century and the policies of the Communist regime. Realistic in the assessment of reforms under Communism and the limits of these reforms.

Thompson, E. P. (1963). *The Making of the English Working Class*. New York: Random House.

A classic historical study of class formation. For the author, a class is not a static category in a structure but a process of defining identities, building institutions, and engaging in politics. Examining primary sources, he creates a portrait of the working class in the crucial period at the end of the eighteenth century and beginning of the nineteenth century as it moved from artisan status, religious dissent, and democratic radicalism to industrial work and forms of political organization associated with the union movement and the beginning of socialism.

Tucker, Robert. (1973). *Stalin as Revolutionary*. New York: Norton.

_____. (1986). *Stalin in Power: The Revolution from Above*. New York: Norton.

The volumes cover Stalin's role in the Bolshevik Revolution, his position in what the author calls the "radical right" of the revolution, and his leadership of the state-building process in the Soviet Union. The author sees this process as a revolution from above, designed to modernize the nation in terms of urbanization, industrialization, and technical education, and—most important—to enable it to survive in a period of international hostility. He notes the Great Russian nationalism promoted by Stalin.

Wright, Erik Olin. (1994). *Interrogating Inequality: Essays on Class Analysis, Socialism and Marxism.* London: Verso.
The author makes a case for the continuing value of Marxist analysis as theory, although the concept of social class requires revision in the light of changes in class structure, especially the proliferation of contradictory class positions and the changing relationship of class and gender.

Periodical Articles

Anderson, Benedict. (1993). "Radicalism After Communism in Thailand and Indonesia." *New Left Review* 202 (November/December), 3-14.
The author discusses the prospects for the Left in Southeast Asia after the fall of the Soviet Union, focusing on two countries in which socialist movements have been relatively weak and (especially in the case of Indonesia in 1964) violently repressed. He highlights the work of writers and intellectuals engaged in redefining the left tradition to address current problems of dictatorship and exploitation in their countries.

Berman, Paul. (1993). "The Future of the American Left." *Dissent* 40 (Winter), 97-104.
In the past, the American Left committed itself to anti-imperialist activism, based on its understanding of V. I. Lenin's thought. This perspective led to an increasingly isolationist stance and growing irrelevance to more recent global issues. In the view of the author, what is needed is a revitalized Left with an international focus on democracy and human rights.

Ceresota, Shirley, and Howard Waitzkin. (1986). "Economic Development, Political-Economic System, and the Physical Quality of Life." *American Journal of Public Health* 76 (June), 661-666.

The authors provide data that support their contention that socialist nations tended to have better a better physical quality of life, measured by standard indicators, than capitalist nations at a comparable level of development. Fewer people living in absolute poverty at the bottom of the social structure and relatively extensive public health and education services in the socialist systems probably are major factors in the difference. This article is valuable in assessing the practical outcomes of socialist transformations of society.

Jenson, Jane, and Rianne Mahon. (1993). "Representing Solidarity: Class, Gender and the Crisis in Social Democratic Sweden." *New Left Review* 201 (September/October), 76-100.
An excellent discussion of the history of social democracy in Sweden in terms of its vision of and impact on social structure. Having accomplished the building of a welfare state and a substantial reduction of income inequalities, the party saw itself as having created the sense of "people's home," a system of security and belonging. Within a restructuring economy and limits on the welfare state, new cleavages have appeared, and gender inequality is becoming an issue.

Jenson, Jane, and George Ross. (1988). "The Tragedy of the French Left: 1945-1988." *New Left Review* 171 (September/October), 5-44.
An examination of the marginalization of the PCF (French Communist Party) from the 1960's to the 1980's. The authors identify failures of the PCF leadership to chart new theoretical directions as a major reason for its electoral decline and its weakness vis-à-vis the Socialists. The PCF's failures include the inability to change its thinking when confronted by economic restructuring, deindustrialization, and changes in French class structure. Insightful analysis.

Naison, Mark. (1981). "Communism and Harlem Intellectuals in the Popular Front: Anti-Fascism and the Politics of Black Culture." *Journal of Ethnic Studies* 9, no. 1 (Spring), 1-25.
The organizational involvement of the Communist Party in Harlem in the 1930's and the importance of black cultural issues to the Communist Party are documented and discussed.

Padgett, Stephen, and William Paterson. (1991). "The Rise and Fall of the West German Left." *New Left Review* 186 (March/April), 46-77.
The authors trace the history of the SPD (Socialist Party of Germany), the New Left, the greens, and other forces in the German Left, especially in relation to one another. They offer a diagnosis, if not a postmortem, of the fortunes of the SPD, especially its failure to capture

the new currents of the "postmaterial left" that had goals including a higher quality of life, personal freedom, a changed status for women, and self-expression. The SPD also had difficulties in coping with the effects of economic restructuring and the unification of Germany. The authors discuss problems inherent in the structure of the SPD and provide statistics on party support by region and class.

Wohlforth, Tim. (1989). "The Sixties in America." *New Left Review* 178 (November/December), 105-123.
An insightful review article covering a number of publications about the New Left and the Civil Rights movement. One of the author's conclusions is that the discontinuity between the New and the Old Left in the United States made the New Left theoretically unsophisticated and vulnerable to Marxist-Leninist sectarianism.

Also of Interest

Collier, Ruth Berins, and David Collier. (1991). *Shaping the Political Arena: Critical Junctures, the Labor Movement, and Regime Dynamics in Latin America*. Princeton, NJ: Princeton University Press.

Derber, Charles. (1995). *What's Left: Radical Politics in the Postcommunist Era*. Amherst: University of Massachusetts Press.

Gottlieb, Roger S. (1992). *Marxism 1844-1990: Origins, Betrayal, Rebirth*. New York: Routledge.

Hill, Christopher. (1971). *Lenin and the Russian Revolution*. Harmondsworth, England: Penguin.

Hooks, Bell, and Cornell West. (1991). *Breaking Bread: Insurgent Black Intellectual Life*. Boston: South End Press.

Jacobs, Harold. (1970). *Weatherman*. Berkeley, CA: Ramparts Press.

Klehr, Harvey, and John Earl Hynes. (1992). *The American Communist Movement: Storming Heaven Itself*. New York: Twayne.

Pontusson, J. (1987). "Radicalization and Retreat in Swedish Social Democracy." *New Left Review* 165, 5-33.

Ranis, Peter. (1992). *Argentine Workers: Peronism and Contemporary Class Consciousness*. Pittsburgh: University of Pittsburgh Press.

Robinson, Cedric. (1983). *Black Marxism: The Making of the Black Radical Tradition.* London: Zed.

Tilton, Tim. (1990). *The Political Theory of Swedish Social Democracy.* New York: Oxford University Press.

Vilas, Carlos. (1986). *The Sandinista Revolution.* New York: Monthly Review Press.

Chapter 7
POPULISM

Populism means a movement "of the people." This term is inherently ambiguous and all-encompassing. Populism is best conceptualized as a large spectrum of movements, mobilizations, ideologies, and collective action linked only by a shared discourse of opposition to elites. Some versions of populism genuinely seek to expand democratic representation, political power, and economic equality. Others can be interpreted as antielitist discourses and mobilizations that are manipulated by political leaders. In the latter case, populist ideology often includes ethnocentric appeals, anti-intellectual positions, or uncritical support for charismatic leaders. The antistatist and grassroots orientation of populism can have left-wing versions (converging with the ideology of socialism, the New Left, and the New Social Movements) and right-wing versions (as in antistatist and antielitist discourses of the New Right). In short, there are many complexities inherent in the concept of populism. Populism has many forms and is interpreted in many different ways by scholars.

Books and Book Chapters

Boyte, H. C., and F. Riessman, eds. (1986). *The New Populism*. Philadelphia, PA: Temple University Press.
    The authors wrote at a historical moment of neighborhood activism, in which grassroots movements rallied against redlining, urban renewal, and closed procedures of decision making by coalitions of politicians, real estate developers, and corporate elites. Interesting as a historical portrait, the book can now be criticized for missing the potential for a right spin to some of these mobilizations; in this respect, it is perhaps best read together with Rieder's (1985) book on the growing conservatism of populist mobilizations in New York City.

Clanton, Gene. (1990). *Populism: The Humane Preference in America 1880-1900*. New York: Twayne.
    The author focuses on the populist movement in Kansas and provides a fairly detailed narrative of its development in this period. He emphasizes its origins in a long-standing tradition of radicalism with roots in the Enlightenment and a history in the United States associated with Jefferson, Jackson, and Lincoln. He counters the negative image that postwar historians developed of the movement.

166

Hall, Melvin. (1995). *Poor People's Movement Organizations: The Goal Is to Win*. Westport, CT: Praeger.

The author reviews several theories of social movements: classical social strain theories, resource mobilization, political process, and new social movements. He examines poor people's movements in terms of organizational processes such as the structure of the internal polity, the definition of goals, organizational maintenance, and relationships to other organizations and institutions; at a more concrete level, he looks at variables such as size, funding, and the extent of internal democracy. The movements he considers are at the boundary line between movements and community-based organizations. They operate in a complex opportunity structure that includes local political actors, federal block grants, and other new institutions of policy implementation. One of the conclusions is that the more rank-and-file poor people exercise control within the organization, the more contentious and confrontational it becomes in its tactics. External funding is not necessarily deradicalizing in its effect on tactics. The book is an empirical contribution to an understanding of a type of movement that has come to have a significant role in the last couple of decades.

James, Daniel. (1988). *Resistance and Integration: Peronism and the Argentine Working Class, 1946-1976*. New York: Cambridge University Press.

A scholarly analysis of the relationship between the populist-nationalist regime of Juan Perón (some might prefer to characterize it as left-wing fascism) and its working-class base. The Peronistas provided many benefits to the working class, but at the price of integrating it firmly into the party through a corporatist structure of labor unions that preempted more independent socialist or communist organization.

Lasch, Christopher. (1991). *The True and Only Heaven: Progress and Its Critics*. New York: Norton.

A historian and social theorist who appears to have moved from left to right in his views, the author decries the elitist, liberal, and technocratic idea of progress and calls for more popularly rooted movements that support change without imposing it from above. He weaves together themes from Burkean conservatism (the notion that change must come about gradually, without imposition of radical blueprints or state initiatives, and with little disruption of institutions) with populist ideas. As in many populist discourses, it is difficult to tell whether this is an argument on the left or the right.

Lo, Clarence. (1990). *Small Property Versus Big Government: Social Origins of the Property Tax Revolt*. Berkeley: University of California Press.

The author offers a key empirical study of why popular discontent in the 1970's ended up being turned against the Democrats and the expansion of the welfare state. Through a detailed analysis based on demographic data, interviews, and observation of events and organizations in California, he shows how this discontent was framed in terms of the dissatisfaction of small property owners and taxpayers. This framing contributed to the integration of these strata with large business interests rather than into a bloc of working and poor people. The author traces the formation of organizations that assembled the conservative bloc and eventually succeeded in passing a property tax cap. This book is essential for understanding the way populist discontent contains potentials for both the Left and the Right and the way movements frame and mobilize such discontent in one direction or another.

Mollenkopf, John. (1983). *The Contested City*. Princeton, NJ: Princeton University Press.

An important overview of urban development policies in the United States and their consequences, including the emergence of grassroots movements of opposition. The policies of the New Deal, which were oriented primarily to improving housing for the poor, gave way to postwar policies of suburban and Sunbelt development and urban renewal. These projects met neighborhood resistance, leading to an increasing showdown in cities between progrowth coalitions and populist forces.

Perlman, Janice. (1979). *The Myth of Marginality: Urban Poverty and Politics in Rio de Janeiro*. Berkeley: University of California Press.

A classic empirical study of the political activism of poor people in Brazil. Far from being apathetic, isolated, or atomized, they are involved in political relationships and organizations, most of them of a populist and clientelistic character. In this case, populism is expressed as an exchange relationship between politicians, who gain power in return for offering attention, and the poor, who receive small tangible benefits from politicians.

Phillips, Kevin P. (1990). *The Politics of Rich and Poor: Wealth and the American Electorate in the Reagan Aftermath*. New York: Random House.

The author surveys the cleavages opened between elites and masses during the Reagan period. His assessment of the shrinkage of opportunities for the U.S. middle class is that it will produce populist voting and a rebellion—at least at the ballot box—against elites. Both the election of the President Clinton in 1992 and the 1994 Republican congressional victories may reflect these shifts. These events also show the volatility and instability of such populist preferences, the way they can be spun to both the left and the right, and the disaffection reflected in low voter turnouts. The issues covered in the book are important and thought provoking, even if Phillips failed to predict events with complete precision.

Squires, Gregory, Larry Bennett, Kathleen McCourt, and Philip Nyden. (1987). *Chicago: Race, Class, and the Response to Urban Decline.* Philadelphia, PA: Temple University Press.
The book contextualizes grassroots movements in the changing economic and political fortunes of one American city. The grassroots activism of the late 1970's and the 1980's can be understood as a response to several changes: deindustrialization, the subsequent devastation of African American communities, gentrification, and the revival of the downtown area, based on real estate development and financial institutions, that failed to include the neighborhoods.

Taylor, J. M. (1979). *Eva Perón: The Myths of a Woman.* Chicago: University of Chicago Press.
The author explores the meanings of Eva Perón for Argentine public opinion, relating her charisma to issues of gender, class, the left-fascist welfare state created by Juan Perón, and populist discourses.

Periodical Articles

Abrahamian, Ervand. (1991). "Khomeini: Fundamentalist or Populist?" *New Left Review* 186 (March/April), 102-119.
Focuses on the similarity between the Islamic Revolution in Iran and other Third World populist and populist-nationalist movements. Includes a general characterization of these movements. A very important contribution to the theoretical literature on both populism and religious movements.

Adelman, Jeremy. (1994). "Post Populist Argentina." *New Left Review* (January/February), 65-91.

The author defines Peronism as a form of populism that elided the class nature of the system by bringing labor into an alliance with some sectors of capital, especially those engaged in manufacturing for the domestic market. State subsidies helped these fractions of capital, and labor was incorporated into the structure through the Peronist unions. This populist alliance cannot be reconstituted because processes of deindustrialization, foreign indebtedness, export promotion, and restructuring have made it politically and economically impossible. Peronist politicians now are forging new class alliances tilted toward capitalist interests committed to privatization, liberalization, and globalization.

Also of Interest

Fisher, R. (1984). *Let the People Decide: Neighborhood Organizing in America*. Boston: Twayne.

Perlman, Janice. (1976). "Grassrooting the System." *Social Policy* 7, no. 2, 4-20.

Chapter 8
MOVEMENTS OF FAITH: RELIGIOUS
FOUNDATIONS OF SOCIOPOLITICAL ACTIVISM

This chapter covers ideologies and movements that grow out of traditional religious faiths. Some movements have adherents who define their position as one of rejecting the modern world and engage in collective action in order to reconstitute a revitalized form of a traditional society organized according to the precepts of a religion. These movements are often described as fundamentalist. The term is used to place together Islamic and Christian movements that share themes of traditional revitalization, rejection of the modern, and an integralist goal of folding the political system and civil society into a religiously based social order.

The Islamic Revolution in Iran (1979) has been of enormous interest to social movement theorists, and a number of outstanding works of scholarly analysis offer competing explanations of the rise of the movement, its successful regime formation, and its social outcomes. Other religious movements focus on connecting traditional religious institutions to the liberal democratic political system (especially Christian Democracy as a movement). Liberation theology brings together socialist analysis with Christian values and forms the ideological basis of movements for social justice and the "preferential option of the poor." In some regions, religiously based collective action may fuse with and reinforce communal and ethnonationalist conflict.

Books and Book Chapters

Ahmed, Leila. (1992). *Women and Gender in Islam.* New Haven, CT: Yale University Press.
  The author argues that much of the gender inequality that currently appears in Islamic political thought and the practice of Islamic states is based on later interpretations and restatements of the Qur'an. Many of these later ideas and practices date from the period of the Abbasid caliphate and do not accurately represent the more egalitarian view inherent in the Qur'an and the practice of Muhammad. Important "view from within" of Islamic thought on the issue of gender.

Arjomand, Said, ed. (1984). *From Nationalism to Revolutionary Islam: Essays on Social Movements in the Contemporary Near and Middle East.* Albany: State University of New York Press.

_____. (1988ba). *Authority and Political Culture in Shi'ism.* Albany: State University of New York Press.

_____. (1988b). *The Turban for the Crown.* New York: Oxford University Press.
The author (authors, in the case of the 1984 edited volume) considers the connections between ideology and the social class base of the Iranian revolution. Also covered is the role of Islam as a force of social integration. The anomie and uprootedness faced by migrants to the city is addressed by the network of Islamic voluntary associations that create a new social and moral order. Excellent scholarly analysis of the underlying social structure and political culture of the Iranian revolution.

Beyer, Peter. (1990). "Privatization and the Public Influence of Religion in Global Society." In Mike Featherstone (ed.), *Global Culture.* Newbury Park, CA: Sage.
Although there have been trends toward making religion a more private matter, in keeping with an individualist-pluralist model of society, there are also trends toward the opposite outcome, namely a public or politicized role for religion. These in turn include both liberal directions (the author's characterization of liberation theology) and conservative (that is, fundamentalist) directions. Abstract but interesting reflections.

Boff, Leonardo, and Clodovis Boff. (1987). *Introducing Liberation Theology.* Maryknoll, NY: Orbis.
An exposition of the ideas of liberation theology, that is, the "preferential option of the poor," the struggle for social justice, and the need to shift religious practice from its de facto but often unacknowledged support of the powerful to a more forthrightly politicized commitment to the poor and powerless.

Boyer, Paul. (1992). *When Time Shall Be No More.* Cambridge, MA: Harvard University Press.
The author analyzes the apocalyptic tradition in American fundamentalist Christian thought throughout the twentieth century. He summarizes and discusses a number of the "end of the world" beliefs and books in this eschatological tradition, writings that often made connec-

tions between the Book of Revelation and contemporary political issues, such as anticommunism and the Cold War. These discourses, which circulate widely in the American public, attempt to read current political events and social trends as steps leading toward Armageddon. The book is highly readable, attractively illustrated, and a fascinating volume for the general reader or scholar interested in apocalyptic thought, Christian fundamentalism, and the political views of the religious right.

Burke, Edmund, III, and Ira Lapidus, eds. (1988). *Islam, Politics, and Social Movements*. Berkeley: University of California Press.
The collection as a whole explores the history of Islamic movements in political systems from the nineteenth century to the present in North Africa, South Asia, West Asia, and, with special attention, Iran. Coverage includes a discussion of how the differences between the 1979 Iranian revolution and other revolutions of the period—specifically, its religious ideology, its peaceful entry into power, and its urban character—led to revisions in the theory of revolutions. Several authors also address the question of the conditions under which socioeconomic grievances are channeled into Islamic, nationalist, or communist movements, as alternative options for collective action.

Burnham, Walter Dean. (1981). "The 1980 Earthquake: Realignment, Reaction, or What?" In Thomas Ferguson and Joel Rogers (eds.), *The Hidden Election*. New York: Random House.
In the appendix to this chapter, the author emphasizes the importance of religion to the American electorate, a level of religiosity that is disproportionately high compared to that of other industrialized nations and falls more closely into the range of developing nations such as Pakistan. The author suggests that this high level of religious orientation creates more conservative voting patterns in the United States compared to Western Europe and Japan, effectively blocking out socialist and social democratic ideologies.

Capps, Walter. (1990). *The New Religious Right: Piety, Patriotism, and Politics*. Columbia: University of South Carolina Press.
The author explores the leaders and ideas of the new religious right in a series of vignettes that includes Jerry Falwell and the Moral Majority, Pat Robertson, Jim and Tammy Bakker and their Christian theme park, and Bob Jones University's implementation of racially restrictive admissions policies. The book is not highly theoretical but rather conveys the climate of these situations and organizations. Some use is

made of Anthony Wallace's concept of revitalization movement, and the values of the new religious right are discussed in terms of neonationalism and as alternatives to the civic religion identified by Robert Bellah. The author cautiously concludes that a movement that seeks to introduce a salvation-oriented religion into government and politics has a potential for being antidemocratic.

Carlson, Jeffrey, and Robert Ludwig, eds. (1993). *Jesus and Faith.* Maryknoll, NY: Orbis.

A series of essays, largely by progressive Catholic social critics and theologians, that emphasize the revolutionary qualities and message of Jesus. Several of the writers comment on and amplify the work of Dominic Crossan, a scholar who approached the life of Jesus as the story of a revolutionary peasant. They draw on Crossan's historical research to develop a contemporary practice of social justice. The collection gives insight into the ideas of the Catholic left and the implications of these ideas for organizing communities of the poor and marginalized.

Cohen, Norman J., ed. (1990). *The Fundamentalist Phenomenon: A View from Within, a Response from Without.* Grand Rapids, MI: William Eerdmans.

An important collection of essays on fundamentalism within several faiths, most notably Islam and Christianity. It contains both outsider analysis and insider perspectives, a combination that is particularly valuable for the reader who seeks to understand fundamentalism on its own terms rather than merely judge it from an external viewpoint. One of the essays that stands out is Riffat Hassan's "The Burgeoning of Islamic Fundamentalism: Toward the Understanding of the Phenomenon." Also noteworthy is James Davison Hunter's discussion of fundamentalism as a reaction against the modern world.

Cole, Juan, and Nikki Keddie. (1986). *Shi'ism and Social Protest.* New Haven, CT: Yale University Press.

Scholarly essays on Shi'a and its role in movements in Lebanon, Afghanistan, Iran, and other countries. The basic tenets of Shi'a are discussed, and attention is given to their role in the Iranian revolution.

Dekmejian, R. Hrair. (1985). *Islam in Revolution.* Syracuse, NY: Syracuse University Press.

A good discussion of the political role of Islam, especially in Western Asia. The sections dealing with the social basis of Islamic movements are especially useful and continue to be valid, even though the specifics of movement organizations and strategies have changed in the last decade.

Embree, Ainslie. (1990). *Utopias in Conflict: Religion and Nationalism in Modern India*. Berkeley: University of California Press.
The author offers a useful scholarly guide to the role of religion in communal tensions in India, conflicts that are associated with particularistic identities and weaken national cohesion.

Eve, Raymond, and Francis Harrold. (1990). *The Creationist Movement in Modern America*. Boston: Twayne.
The authors use the value-added framework of Neil Smelser's theory of collective behavior to discuss a movement that opposes the teaching of evolution as scientific truth and seeks to replace it with a system of ideas based on the Bible. They review the history, ideas, and organizations of the movement and are particularly informative in their coverage of strategies such as the call for "equal time," challenges to textbooks chosen at the state level, grassroots mobilizations, specific cases of contention, and links to New Right networks. Although not supporters of the movement, they question the "easy" dismissals of it inherent in some psychological and sociological theories. They define it as part of a larger struggle over the means of cultural reproduction.

Fichter, Joseph, ed. (1983). *Alternatives to American Mainline Churches*. Barrytown, NY: Unification Theological Seminary.
This collection charts a fairly early point in the growing difficulties of mainline churches in the United States, when it was less the New Religious Right and more a mixed bag of other movements (Hare Krishna, scientology, and cults) that challenged the established denominations. Also included is a discussion of the growth of the "electronic church" and traditionalist innovation in the Catholic church.

Fields, Karen. (1985). *Revival and Rebellion in Colonial Central Africa*. Princeton, NJ: Princeton University Press.
A study of millenarian movements in the first part of the century in British colonies (now Malawi and Zambia), in which political and cultural issues were fused, according to the author. The focus is on the Watchtower movement and the threat that colonial authorities perceived from it. The detailed study concludes by addressing the question of the meaning to participants and the historical significance of millenarian movements, which often appear irrational to the outside observer.

Freire, Paolo. (1970). *Pedagogy of the Oppressed*. New York: Seabury.
A statement defining a radical pedagogy in which the oppressed and marginalized become aware of their dignity and their possibilities for exercising power in their lives as they become literate. The author sees literacy not as a skill for the labor market but as a process of political liberation. These ideas have been influential in shaping the practices of liberation theology.

Geertz, Clifford. (1971). *Islam Observed: Religious Development in Morocco and Indonesia*. Chicago: University of Chicago Press.
A leading anthropologist looks for similarities and differences within the complicated texture of Islam, a faith that spans a multitude of cultures and nations. The pre-Islamic cultures of North Africa and Indonesia were vastly different, and these differences continue to be visible and to influence belief and practice within the modern Islamic culture. An excellent corrective to the Western tendency to see Islam as a rigid, monolithically orthodox faith closely tied to Arab culture and history.

Hill, Christopher. (1972). *The World Turned Upside Down: Radical Ideas During the English Revolution*. New York: Penguin.
The author describes the various movements and ideologies of social leveling and primitive Christian socialism that were popular during the seventeenth century, a period when English society and politics were in upheaval.

Jorstad, Erling. (1990). *Holding Fast/Pressing On: Religion in America in the 1980's*. New York: Greenwood.
In the author's words, this book offers a retrospective view of the shift from "mainline to frontline," after a Great Awakening in the period from 1960 to 1979 set the stage for major changes in U.S. religious life, including the decline of mainline leadership, conflict over social issues such as feminism and race, the role of the New Christian Right, the mass media as a new method of evangelization, the increasing numbers of evangelical Christians, and the impact of New Age spiritualism. In a paradoxical mix, religion became both more privatized and more politicized. An excellent overview of issues that are important for understanding the emergence of religiously based collective action.

Keddie, Nikki, and Eric Hooglund, eds. (1986). *The Iranian Revolution and the Islamic Republic*. Syracuse, NY: Syracuse University Press.

A collection of scholarly papers that addresses several topics, including the revolutionary clergy as a social group, postrevolutionary changes in a rural community, economic policies of the republic, ideological issues and disagreements, and the international relations of the republic. Included is an article on women that points to interesting differences among Islamic leaders in their views of women and the issue of equality in difference. These views are, in turn, different from the everyday gender practices of the masses.

Lancaster, Roger Nelson. (1988). *Thanks to God and the Revolution: Popular Religion and Class Consciousness in the New Nicaragua.* New York: Columbia University Press.
Although historically left radicalism and religion were at odds, Latin America in recent decades saw a convergence and even unity of left-wing and religious movements. In Nicaragua, the Sandinista leadership included clergy, and at a mass level as well religious and left-wing ideals supported revolutionary changes.

Lasch, Christopher. (1965). "Jane Addams: The College Woman and the Family Claim." In *The New Radicalism in America, 1889-1963.* New York: Knopf.
Explores the role of Protestant faith in the Progressive movement in the United States, especially in terms of its impact on the middle-class women who were among its leading activists.

Leonardi, Robert, and Douglas A. Wertman. (1989). *Italian Christian Democracy: The Politics of Dominance.* New York: St. Martin's Press.
The authors offer a definitive analysis of the Christian Democratic Party as the ruling institution of Italy since the late 1940's. The book is important for understanding how a movement becomes transformed into a ruling party, in this case, a highly institutionalized, pragmatic, and clientelistic one. Inevitably, the party developed multiple currents, committed to its tradition of Catholic political involvement in markedly different degrees, ranging from technocratic secularism to the integralism of the conservative Communion and Liberation movement.

Lernoux, Penny. (1982). *Cry of the People: The Struggle for Human Rights in Central America—The Catholic Church in Conflict with U.S. Policy.* New York: Viking Penguin.

_____. (1990). *People of God: The Struggle for World Catholicism.* New York: Viking Penguin.

The author sees a growing tension within Catholicism between conservative forces that turn away from the struggle for social justice and forces that are influenced by liberation theology. In her view, the poverty of the global South and the international balance of power that maintains this inequality are central issues in these disagreements.

Liebman, Robert C., and Robert Wuthnow, eds. (1983). *The New Christian Right: Mobilization and Legitimation*. New York: Aldine.
Relatively early studies of Christian mobilization on the right, largely among evangelical Protestants, and more specifically, fundamentalists. The Moral Majority is a focus of the discussion, and the "electronic church" is considered. Articles address the character of underlying strains and competing movements. Good background for understanding contemporary activism.

Martin, David. (1991). *Tongues of Fire: The Explosion of Protestantism in Latin America*. Oxford, U.K.: Blackwell.
The author emphasizes the movementlike character of the growth of Protestantism. He covers phenomena such as evangelical advances in Brazil, Central America, Mexico, and Ecuador and the growth of the Pentecostal movement in Chile. He offers comparisons with related developments in South Korea and South Africa. The re-formations (the author's term) involved in these changes include experiences of healing, speaking in tongues, conversions, and spiritual ecstasy. He devotes some attention to the political implications, because these movements combine apolitical stands with some populist impulses and, especially in the case of Pentecostals, a strong anti-Left position. The conclusions at this point can only be tentative. He also looks at the economic restructuring that contributes to the growth of Protestantism, especially in view of its strong support base among workers and micro-entrepreneurs in the informal sector. A stimulating contribution to the growing literature on postmodern and (in a very broad sense) fundamentalist religiously based collective change.

Marty, Martin. (1984). *Pilgrims in Their Own Land*. Boston: Little, Brown.
The author provides a social and historical analysis of the central role of religion in American society. He emphasizes the persistence and continued vitality of the utopian, visionary side of the Protestant tradition, with its tendency to reject compromise.

Marty, Martin, and R. Scott Appleby, eds. (1993). *Fundamentalisms and the State*. Chicago: University of Chicago Press.

This is the third volume of a massive project on the rise of fundamentalism and its impact in the contemporary world. This volume includes twenty-five contributions on state-movement relationships, the policies of fundamentalist movements in power, the influence of fundamentalisms on the state, strategies of fundamentalist movements to influence or reconstitute states, and the restructuring of economies by fundamentalist regimes. Islamic, Jewish, and Christian fundamentalisms are highlighted, and there is some attention to Buddhist fundamentalism and Hindu revivalism. The overall perspective defines fundamentalism as a response to modern dislocations and crises and as a collective effort to rebuild personal and collective identity by the formation of new codes of behavior. The boundaries of the public and private are dissolved, and the organic unity of people and faith is a central principle. Lines are drawn between believer and unbeliever. As several contributors note, once the movement is in power, legal and social codes are more easily created and implemented than economic reforms within this framework. This volume is an impressive project and essential reading for anyone interested in the role of religion in the contemporary world.

Mernissi, Fatima. (1991). *The Veil and the Male Elite: A Feminist Interpretation of Women's Rights in Islam.* New York: Addison-Wesley.
A Moroccan scholar strongly affirms a tradition of gender equality within Islam, covering a number of issues on which conservative male elites have been able to impose their own antiwomen interpretations on Islamic institutions.

Moaddel, Mansoor. (1993). *Class, Politics and Ideology in the Iranian Revolution.* New York: Columbia University Press.
The author offers a highly sophisticated Marxist interpretation of the Iranian revolution that emphasizes ideology and processes of discourse in the formation of classes and their entry into collective action, a framework based on E. P. Thompson's study of the English working class. He begins the book with an incisive critique of several other theories of revolution and collective action, some of which are (in his view) too subjectivist and individual-based, others of which use "class" in too mechanical a way. He then analyzes the role of Islamic ideology in class formation in Iran, with attention to workers, peasants, and the merchant class, as well as to capitalists. His discussion also includes postrevolutionary divergences within the revolutionary bloc, as reform began to tilt away from the expectations of workers and peasants.

Munson, Henry, Jr. (1988). *Islam and Revolution in the Middle East.* New Haven, CT: Yale University Press.
A useful overview of the ideas of Islamic movements.

Nielsen, Niels. (1993). *Fundamentalism, Mythos, and World Religions.* Albany: State University of New York Press.
The author finds tendencies toward a fundamentalist outlook within the world's major religious traditions. The book is more oriented toward the structure of belief systems than toward a sociological analysis of the sources of these beliefs in specific social support bases or specific characteristics of modern societies.

Pope, Liston. (1965). *Millhands and Preachers.* New Haven, CT: Yale University Press.
A study of a pre-World War II community in the South that highlights the way Protestant religious teachings weaken labor organization.

Riesebrodt, Martin. (1993). *Pious Passion: The Emergence of Modern Fundamentalism in the United States and Iran.* Berkeley: University of California Press.
In this important theoretical contribution to the understanding of fundamentalism, the author uses a Weberian approach of examining the meaning of a belief system to social actors. Fundamentalism cannot be seen as a mere discursive veil over a form of fascism or populism. He explores two versions of fundamentalism: Protestant fundamentalism in the United States in the early part of the century, when fundamentalist ideas were first formulated and politicized, and Islamic fundamentalism in Iran prior to the revolution of 1979. He argues that these two movements can be brought together under the concept of "fundamentalism." He surveys a number of theories of fundamentalism and definitions of the term. His own definition focuses on fundamentalism as a radicalized traditionalism. A major element is patriarchy and patriarchal moralism, in which female sexuality is defined as sinful. Ethical monism, interclass organicism, and messianic or millenarian themes also are present. The author suggests that in both cases, rural to urban migrants seeking new forms of normative integration formed an important part of the support base. Essential reading for the student of contemporary movements.

Smith, Christian. (1992). *The Emergence of Liberation Theology: Radical Religion and Social Movement Theory.* Chicago: University of Chicago Press.

The author provides a history of liberation theology, an explanation of its ideas, and a discussion of the institutional processes within the Roman Catholic church that contributed to the transformation of liberation theology into a movement that mobilized new constituencies. Applying the work of Charles Tilly and Doug McAdam, he analyzes the movement as a political process. He includes interesting reflections of the future of the movement in a period of economic restructuring, the collapse of Communism, and the decline of military regimes, as both socialism and dependency theory, key elements of liberation theology, are being questioned.

Stacey, Judith. (1991). *Brave New Families.* New York: Basic Books.
See chapter 4 for an annotation.

Stoll, David. (1990). *Is Latin America Turning Protestant? The Politics of Evangelical Growth.* Berkeley: University of California Press.
The author considers the causes and consequences of the movementlike sweep of Protestant conversion in many regions of Latin America (for example, Guatemala). Adherence to evangelical and Pentecostal churches often is associated with an apolitical stance, rejection of labor unions and the Left, and individualistic views of self and society. Although apparently apolitical and salvation-oriented at the level of individual worldviews, evangelical growth has political consequences at the collective level in a devaluation of public, collective action. In some cases, conservative and military regimes have encouraged evangelical growth for precisely these reasons.

Weber, Max. (1963). *Sociology of Religion.* Boston: Beacon Press.
A classic in sociological theory, in which the author discusses world religions and their historical development from the perspective of sociology, with attention to the social origins of their ideas and the effects of the belief systems on economies, stratification systems, and forms of action in societies.

Wilcox, Clyde. (1992). *God's Warriors: The Christian Right in the Twentieth Century.* Baltimore: Johns Hopkins University Press.
An empirical study of participants and support bases of right-wing fundamentalism, especially the Christian Anti-Communist Crusade, the Moral Majority, and Pat Robertson's Pentecostal/Charismatic right. Wilcox provides a short history of the Christian right in twentieth century America and identifies some important distinctions between evangelical Christians, fundamentalists, and right-wing fundamentalists. The potential support bases are not all mobilized by the Christian

right. Participants in the Christian right, such as the Moral Majority, are not markedly different from other Americans—especially white, small-town, moderate-income Americans—either demographically or in their psychological profiles.

Wills, Garry. (1990). *Under God: Religion and American Politics.* New York: Simon and Schuster.
Essays on the topic by an author who is sympathetic to religion as a force in human society but unsympathetic to the role that Protestant fundamentalists have in U.S. political and cultural life. He argues that religion is a foundation for American political behavior. He profiles a variety of religious/political activists and gives insight into the specific beliefs of fundamentalists that propel them into political action. Very readable.

Wuthnow, Robert. (1988). *The Restructuring of American Religion: Society and Faith Since World War II.* Princeton, NJ: Princeton University Press.
Excellent background for understanding the emergence of the New Christian Right as well as less politicized movements within Christianity in the United States. The author considers various disagreements within religious institutions, especially the fundamentalist/modernist split, the impact of social issues such as feminism and abortion on these continuing cleavages, and the emergence of the New Right. His discussion of the decline of denominationalism is interesting and suggests certain parallels to the decline of political party organization.

Periodical Articles

Abrahamian, Ervand. (1991). "Khomeini: Fundamentalist or Populist?" *New Left Review* 186 (March/April), 102-119.
Focuses on the similarity between the Islamic Revolution in Iran and other Third World populist and populist-nationalist movements. The article includes a general characterization of these movements and is an example of an analysis of the Iranian revolution that assimilates it to other forms of social movements (populism, fascism, and so on) while downplaying its distinctively Islamic ideology.

Ammerman, Nancy. (1991). "Southern Baptists and the New Christian Right." *Review of Religious Research* 32 (March) 213-236.

A 1985 survey study of twelve hundred pastors and eighteen hundred other leaders in the church suggests that opposition to modern values is related to support for both denominational and secular conservative agendas.

Bruce, Steve, and Wesley Miller. (1987). "Status and Cultural Defense: The Case of the New Christian Right." *Sociological Focus* 20, no. 3 (August), 242-246.
In an article and response, the two authors debate status politics versus resource mobilization models for explaining the rise of the New Christian Right, based in part on content analysis of conservative Protestant publications.

Dekmejian, R. Hrair. (1985). "Fundamentalist Islam: Theories, Typologies, Trends." *Middle East Review* 17, no. 4 (Summer), 28-33.
A broad discussion of Islamic resurgence that criticizes theories that explain the phenomenon largely in terms of economic stress rather than cultural factors. Considers international security implications.

Hatem, Mervat. (1985). "Conservative Patriarchal Modernization in the Arabian Gulf." *Contemporary Marxism* 11 (Fall), 96-109.
The author analyzes social change in the states of the Arabian peninsula. As petroleum wealth and changes in social structure threatened traditional patriarchal control, the state stepped in to transform a private system of patriarchy into a publicly monitored and enforced structure of gender segregation and male dominance. Middle-class women, many of them well educated, have been particularly affected by this public perpetuation of traditional private control and dominance. Also affected are expatriate female workers in the region. The author underlines how economic development and modernization do not automatically produce Western forms of gender stratification, in the cases in which deliberate action is taken by means of the state to prevent this outcome.

Howe, John. (1992). "The Crisis of Algerian Nationalism and the Rise of Islamic Integralism." *New Left Review* 196 (November/December), 85-100.
The nationalist movement that came to power after Algeria's war of independence from France has failed to meet the expectations of the mass of Algerians, especially the growing numbers of young people who remain under- and unemployed. Wealth from energy resources has not been distributed fairly or used effectively to develop the economy. The government is seen as bureaucratic and often repressive. These

objective conditions create a climate in which Islamic integralism has grown, because it addresses issues of equity, social justice, and autonomy from Western economic and cultural dominance. Although opposed to the ascendance of the religious movement, the author explains its strength by offering a scathing critique of the postcolonial regime.

Jelen, Ted. (1992). "Political Christianity: A Contextual Analysis." *American Journal of Political Science* 36 (August) 692-714.
Using data from fourteen rural midwestern Christian churches, the author explores the interaction of individual-level variables and characteristics of congregations in explaining support for the Republican Party and New Christian Right leadership.

Kabbani, Rana. (1992-1993). "Gender Jihad." *Spare Rib* 239 (December, 1992/January, 1993), 35-41.
In an article addressed to a Western feminist readership, the author argues that Islam is not as uniformly patriarchal and oppressive to women as many Westerners believe. Some of these negative tenets are later additions to Islam, not part of its original foundation in the Qur'an and the life of Muhammad. It is possible, says the author, to be both a feminist and a Muslim, and Western feminists would do well to make their critique of Islamic gender practice more nuanced and informed.

Kellstedt, Lyman, John Green, James Guth, and Corwin Smidt. (1994). "Religious Voting Blocs in the 1992 Election: The Year of the Evangelical?" *Sociology of Religion* 55, no. 3 (Fall), 307-326.
Data from the 1960, 1988, and 1992 elections suggest that the Republican Party gained votes of evangelical Protestants, while the Democrats absorbed votes of "seculars" and some mainline Protestants. This trend is linked to the responses of the parties to cultural conflicts.

Lechner, Frank. (1989). "Fundamentalism Revisited." *Society* 26, no. 2, (January/February), 51-59.
A broad theoretical and historical discussion of fundamentalism as a modern movement dedicated to the overturn of "the modern."

Mathisen, Gerald, and James Mathisen. (1988). "The New Fundamentalism: A Sociorhetorical Approach to Understanding Theological Change." *Review of Religious Research* 30, no. 1 (September), 18-32.
Examines the discourse of fundamentalism by a content analysis of one hundred articles in the *Fundamentalist Journal*; explores the renegotiation of the symbolic boundaries between secular and religious culture.

Midgley, James. (1990). "Religion, Politics, and Social Policy: The Case of the New Christian Right." *Journal of Social Policy* 19, no. 3 (July), 397-403.

An important review article in which the author discusses several books written about the Christian right in the late 1980's that shed light on its ideology, its effect on social policies, its countermovement activism, and its role in international politics.

Perry, James. (1994). "The Christian Coalition Crusades to Broaden Its Rightist Political Base." *Wall Street Journal*, July 19, p. A1.

A good journalistic article on the expansion of a conservative Christian movement. Attention is given to the social bases of the movement and various strategies for mobilizing at the grassroots.

Reese, William. (1985). "Soldiers for Christ in the Army of God: The Christian School Movement in America." *Educational Theory* 35, no. 2 (Spring), 175-194.

The author examines the curriculum, training, and methods of the staff as well as the daily life of students in a study of Christian schools, primarily run by evangelical Protestants. There were about five thousand to six thousand such schools, with approximately 1 million pupils, at the time of the study. Their curriculum is organized by religious values and beliefs.

Vanaik, Achin. (1992). "Reflections on Communalism and Nationalism in India." *New Left Review* 196 (November/December), 43-63.

The author examines the intertwining of religious communal identity and ethnonationalism in India, examining a number of cases of conflict. He argues that as Islam and Christianity influence Hindus and other South Asian communities, the practices of these communities have become more politicized, integralist, and exclusive, contributing to communal conflict.

Also of Interest

Esposito, J., ed. (1983). *Voices of Resurgent Islam.* New York: Oxford University Press.

Fern, D. W., ed. (1987). *Third World Liberation Theologies.* Maryknoll, NY: Orbis.

Fleet, Michael. (1985). *The Rise and Fall of Chilean Christian Democracy*. Princeton, NJ: Princeton University Press.

Galanter, Marc. (1989). *Cults, Faith, Healing and Coercion*. New York: Oxford University Press.

Gutierrez, Gustavo. (1988). *A Theology of Liberation*. Maryknoll, NY: Orbis.

Hill, Samuel, and Dennis Owen. (1982). *The New Political Right in America*. Nashville, TN: Parthenon Press.

Hiro, Dilip. (1989). *Holy Wars*. New York: Routledge.

Jelen, Ted. (1993). "The Political Consequences of Religious Group Attitudes." *The Journal of Politics* 55 (February), 178-190.

Jelen, Ted, and Clyde Wilcox. (1992). "The Effects of Religious Self-Identification on Support for the New Christian Right: An Analysis of Political Activists." *The Social Science Journal* 29, no. 2, 199-210.

Levine, Daniel. (1992). *Popular Voices in Latin American Catholicism*. Princeton, NJ: Princeton University Press.

Mortimer, Edward. (1982). *Faith and Power: The Politics of Islam*. New York: Random House.

Poloma, Margeret. (1982). *The Charismatic Movement: Is There a New Pentecost?* New York: Twayne.

Watt, William. (1988). *Islamic Fundamentalism and Modernity*. London: Routledge.

Weber, Max. (1958). *The Protestant Ethic and the Spirit of Capitalism*. New York: Scribner.

Chapter 9

NATIONALISM

This chapter covers movements and ideologies that claim there should be correspondence between a nation or people with a shared history, on one hand, and a territory, on the other. They seek to establish a nation-state, a centralized political entity that expresses the political unity of the nation within the territory. By extension, cultural nationalist movements confirm the historical integrity and unity of a people but in situations in which its territorial claims may be difficult to establish.

Books and Book Chapters

Anderson, Benedict. (1991). *Imagined Communities: Reflections on the Origin and Spread of Nationalism.* London: Verso.
One of the most important contemporary treatments of nationalism. The author views nationalism as a socially constructed community. Nationalist sentiments emerged with print and the sense of community shared by readers of a vernacular language. Movements of national independence appeared first in the Americas as creoles (American-born persons of European origin) felt excluded from political control by the European imperial governments, primarily Spain and Great Britain. Similar processes took place in other colonial empires, most recently in decolonization movements in the twentieth century, which the author illustrates primarily with Southeast Asian examples. The academic subjects of history and geography were used by nationalist intellectuals to construct a sense of nationhood.

Birch, Anthony. (1989). *Nationalism and National Integration.* London: Unwin Hyman.
The author reviews some ideologies of nationalism (which he labels theories, in a somewhat nonstandard usage) and then proceeds to discuss three cases of national integration in successor states of the British empire—the United Kingdom, Canada, and Australia. For each, linguistic and cultural diversity, immigration-related issues, and the rights of indigenous peoples (Scots and Welsh, as well as Native Canadians and Australians) are covered, and the prospects of secessionist movements are addressed.

Camilleri, Joseph, and Jim Falk. (1992). *The End of Sovereignty?: The Politics of a Shrinking and Fragmenting World*. Brookfield, VT: Edward Elgar.
A thought-provoking analysis that suggests that the nation-state is declining in importance as the basic unit of the global political system. Transnational markets and movements, as well as entities like the European Union, are creating new bases of identity and political action, both supernational and subnational.

Davidson, Basil. (1992). *The Black Man's Burden: Africa and the Curse of the Nation State*. New York: Random House.
The author argues that the colonial imposition of the nation-state as the basic political form is a major cause of the political and social problems that now beset many African states. These units did not match the distribution of ethnic groups, nor did they fit into African political culture.

Denitch, Bogdan. (1994). *Ethnic Nationalism: The Tragic Death of Yugoslavia*. Minneapolis: University of Minnesota Press.
An excellent discussion of the background of ethnic warfare in the former Yugoslavia. The author focuses less on traditional animosities (which he believes could have been overcome) and more on the recent process of breakdown associated with the precipitous transition out of socialism and intervention by foreign powers and exile communities. Important for understanding how ethnic difference can deteriorate into ethnonationalism and ethnic violence.

Fanon, Frantz. (1967). *The Wretched of the Earth*. Harmondsworth, England: Penguin.
A reflection on the decolonization movements of the postwar period. The author sees nationalism as a necessary, though hardly sufficient, ingredient of the formation of revolutionary socialist states. Based on his French-Caribbean background, his profession as a psychiatrist, and his experience in the Algerian war of independence, Fanon focuses on the formation of autonomous identities in the struggle for national liberation. This book—more a prose poem about identity and struggle than an empirical study—was considered a key text for understanding anticolonial movements.

Febvre, Lucien, and Henri-Jean Martin. (1976). *The Coming of the Book: The Impact of Printing, 1450-1800*. London: New Left Editions.
An analysis of the role of print in cultural and political change during the early modern period in Europe, with emphasis on its association

with the formation of national political systems and national markets. The community of readers of a vernacular language (that is, not Latin) began to define the basis of political identity.

Gellner, Ernest. (1983). *Nations and Nationalism.* Ithaca, NY: Cornell University Press.
A key contemporary text in the theoretical analysis of nationalism. The author associates nationalism with language communities and explores the processes that have led to the formation of political units (nation-states) that claim to correspond to language communities. At the core of this transformation is the shift from agrarian empires with traditional ruling classes to capitalist economies with new types of relationships between dominant classes and subordinate strata. These new class structures are associated with modern educational systems (hence the decline of the traditional, universalistic, and religious elite language) and new forms of social integration between classes (based on nationalist ideology). The author offers a highly abstract characterization of this historical transition, and readers will find the argument theoretically complex.

Gottlieb, Gidon. (1993). *Nation Against State.* New York: Council on Foreign Relations Press.
An analysis of those forms of nationalist conflict in which groups that share a sense of nationhood make claims against existing states that are defined as mismatching the geographical distribution of the ethnic group. A dispassionate overview, illustrated with contemporary cases.

Greenfeld, Liah. (1992). *Nationalism: Five Roads to Modernity.* Cambridge, MA: Harvard University Press.
The author offers a complex analysis of the intertwining of nationalism with modernity, arguing that nationalism forms modern societies and not—as is commonly stated by theorists—that nationalism is a product of modernity. She analyzes five cases of nationalism: England, the United States, France, Russia, and Germany. In all five cases, structural changes (which were not purely economic, though classes may have been one of the groups affected by such changes) precipitated a crisis of traditional identity, experienced as anomie. The social groups implicated in this crisis searched for new identities, generating nationalist ideology in the process of creating meaning out of their situation. In part, this process was international, and elements of nationalist ideology were imported in the formation of new identities. Each national case had its own characteristics, however, and especially in the cases

of Germany and Russia, the formation of national identity was organized around ethnicity and powered with a strong charge of *ressentiment*. In England and the United States, the new identities were more individualistic and civic in character, leading to a more inclusive and less ethnicized form of nationalism. France is intermediate in this regard. The analysis is strongly informed by Weberian theory; in other words, human beings are seen as social actors, engaged in the creation of symbolic reality, rather than as the vehicles for structurally determined outcomes. The theoretical grounding leads the author to a method similar to Weber's, that is, the detailed reading and interpretation of texts produced by literate strata as the key to understanding the production of meaning and identity. An important theoretical contribution for the serious student of the subject.

Gurr, Ted Robert. (1993). *Minorities at Risk*. Washington, DC: United States Institute of Peace Press.

A review of contemporary cases in which minority ethnic groups within nation-states are targeted in a variety of ways, ranging from restriction of civil rights to informal social and economic discrimination to expulsion and violent attacks.

Hobsbawm, Eric. (1992). *Nations and Nationalism Since 1780*. New York: Cambridge University Press.

An important overview of the phenomenon by a leading Marxist historian. Hobsbawm confronts what to Marxists is an exasperating puzzle—the persistence of nationalist identity as an alternative to class consciousness. He traces processes of nationalism "from above" (the formation of national states and institutions by modernizing elites and ruling classes) as well as nationalist movements and mass sentiments of nationalism. Far from a vulgar dismissal of nationalism as a mere "false consciousness," this analysis shows how nationalism and the nation were integral structural elements of the development of modern capitalism.

Hobsbawm, Eric, and Terence Ranger, eds. (1992). *The Invention of Tradition*. New York: Cambridge University Press.

Major essays in the social construction of nationalism. The authors focus primarily on Great Britain and the British empire and show how "age-old traditions" actually were recent inventions designed to create precisely this sense of reverence, custom, and venerability. In some cases, such as the outfits of regiments from colonies and the Celtic regions of Britain, the invented traditions also had the function of representing integration into a multiethnic empire. The "archaic and organic" trappings of nationhood, so beloved by conservatives, often are deliberately designed mechanisms with ideological purposes. The book is witty, and many readers will be quite surprised how recent and synthetic these beloved traditions really are.

Hockenos, Paul. (1994). *Free to Hate: The Rise of the Right in Postcommunist Eastern Europe.* New York: Routledge.

The author covers a number of movements, most of them with an ethnonationalist ideology, that are developing in the postcommunist states. These movements are responses to economic tensions associated with the transition to market economies. In some cases, the new governments have tacitly or explicitly supported these movements and ideological currents. A good current overview.

Horowitz, Donald. (1992). *Immigration and Group Relations in France and America.* New York: New York University Press.

The author compares two multiethnic societies in terms of their policies of immigration and assimilation. Historically, French policy has been oriented more strongly toward assimilation of immigrants to French culture. These assimilative processes, in the United States, have been left to market and social pressures, but in France they have been more carefully included in government policies. Useful as background for understanding the framework and history within which ethnic movements, anti-immigration movements, and immigrant rights movements are forming in the two societies.

Kolko, Gabriel. (1988). *Confronting the Third World.* New York: Pantheon.

The author reviews a large number of instances in which the United States became involved, overtly or covertly, in the developing nations after World War II. Anti-Communism became a blanket excuse for these interventions, but many of them were targeted at decolonization and nationalist movements as well as socialist revolutions. A partisan book that questions U.S. interventions and argues that they distorted political and economic development in the Third World.

Leonardi, Robert, and R. Nanetti. (1994). *Tuscany in Europe.* London: Pinter.

The authors look at regional development in the European Community, using Tuscany as their key case study. The example suggests that sub- and supernational units ("Tuscany"/"Europe" in contrast to "Italy") are becoming increasingly important as economic entities. Although not directly related to social movements, the book will stimulate reflection on the decreasing role of the nation as the dominant economic unit, with possible consequences for nationalism.

Levin, Michael, ed. (1993). *Ethnicity and Aboriginality: Case Studies in Ethnonationalism.* Toronto: University of Toronto Press.
Scholarly essays on the development of ethnonationalist movements in multiethnic states. Examples include First People and francophones in Canada, aborigines in Australia, and several ethnic groups in Nigeria. The authors examine the conditions for the emergence of such movements and the types of government policy that develop to accommodate their demands.

Lijphart, A. (1977). *Democracy in Plural Societies: A Comparative Exploration.* New Haven, CT: Yale University Press.
The author looks at arrangements in multiethnic societies that sustain civil rights, equity, and participation; in many cases, "one person, one vote" rules have to be adjusted through other, politically negotiated, mechanisms to protect the rights of minorities. A baseline analysis that continues to shape scholarly discussions of these types of polities.

McGarry, John, and Brendan O'Leary, eds. (1993). *The Politics of Ethnic Conflict Regulation: Case Studies of Protracted Ethnic Conflicts.* London: Routledge.
An outstanding collection of articles on conflict and accommodation in multiethnic states. The case studies include Burundi, India, Fiji, Malaysia, Yugoslavia, Spain, South Africa, Northern Ireland, and the former Soviet Union. The introduction develops a useful typology of ethnic conflict regulation. The level of analysis in the case studies is uniformly high, and the treatment generally is evenhanded. The case studies underline the fragility of ethnic conflict regulation and the complex processes by which accommodation breaks down. The volume would be an excellent choice for an upper-level undergraduate or graduate course.

Magas, Branka. (1993). *The Destruction of Yugoslavia.* London: Verso.
Traces the distribution of groups in the territory of the former Yugoslavia and discusses the political processes that produced and sustain the current conflicts. The author believes that the death of Yugoslavia was not a natural one and could have been prevented. The author is especially critical of the ideology and territorial ambitions of the Greater Serbia movement and its supporters in Belgrade.

Nairn, Tom. (1988). *The Enchanted Glass: Britain and Its Monarchy.* London: Radius.

The analysis focuses on the conservative ideological and integrative functions of the monarchy, especially the connection between the monarchy and the archaic character of British political culture.

O'Donnell, Guillermo. (1979). *Modernization and Bureaucratic Authoritarianism.* Berkeley: University of California Press.

An influential study at the time of its publication, but some political scientists have turned away from its key concept, bureaucratic authoritarianism, as the best conceptualization of modernizing regimes, perhaps because statist interventions in guiding economic development have themselves lost ground recently.

Smith, Anthony. (1986). *The Ethnic Origins of Nations.* Oxford, England: Basil Blackwell.

Taking an approach that is different from the one that identifies nationalism as a modern form of identity construction, the author argues that in some cases, ethnic identity has a long-standing history. Ethnically defined nations often produce the exclusion of minorities.

Thompson, Mark. (1992). *A Paper House: The End of Yugoslavia.* New York: Vintage.

The discussion places weight on expansionist sentiments among Serbs, beginning during the Communist period, as a major source of the conflict in the former Yugoslavia.

Tibi, Bassam. (1990). *Arab Nationalism: A Critical Inquiry.* New York: St. Martin's Press.

An essay on the historical development of Arab nationalism, with contrasts to European nationalist texts. Attention is given to Frantz Fanon and the influence of socialism and opposition to colonialism on nationalist thought.

Yergin, Daniel, and Thane Gustafson. (1993). *Russia 2010.* New York: Random House.

The authors let their imaginations run loose and produce a series of scenarios to stimulate thought on what the future may hold in store for Russia. Many of these scenarios revolve around different forms of nationalism, both Russian nationalism and opposed movements of ethnic separatism. A provocative and highly readable book.

Periodical Articles

Malek, Mohammed. (1989). "Kurdistan in the Middle East Conflict." *New Left Review* 175 (May/June), 79-94.

A good interim report on the conflicts concerning Kurdistan. It includes brief histories of the territorial issues and the various factions and currents of the Kurd nationalist movement. The Kurds are an ethnic group currently located primarily in Iran, Turkey, Iraq, and Azerbaijan; their claims to a nation-state implicate the entire region and have called forth repressive measures, especially in Iraq and Turkey.

Spektorowski, Alberto. (1994). "The Ideological Origins of Right and Left Nationalism in Argentina, 1930-43." *Journal of Contemporary History* 29, no. 1 (January), 155-184.

Discussion of how and why nationalist ideology in Argentina developed in a right-wing direction. The author notes the influence of right-wing European ideologies as well as indigenous forces.

Žižek, Slavoy. (1990). "Eastern Europe's Republic of Gilead." *New Left Review* 183 (September/October), 50-62.

The importance of this article lies in its challenge to the conventional wisdom that ethnonationalism exploded in the postcommunist regions because Communist regimes were no longer keeping a tight lid on "age-old" ethnic hatreds and rivalries; from the conventional, naturalistic view of ethnic relations, "naturally" these long-standing conflicts burst forth once Communist parties were ousted. On the contrary, the author argues, the Communist regimes themselves were expressions of ethnic dominance and acted in such a way as to construct the politics of ethnic rivalry and competition for hegemony.

Also of Interest

Balibar, Etienne, and Immanuel Wallerstein. (1991). *Race, Nation, Class: Ambiguous Identities*. London: Routledge.

Coakley, John, ed. (1992). *The Social Origins of Nationalist Movements*. London: Sage.

Harris, Nigel. (1990). *National Liberation*. New York: St. Martin's Press.

Rock, David. (1993). *Authoritarian Argentina: The Nationalist Movement, Its History, and Its Impact.* Berkeley: University of California Press.

Townson, Michael. (1992). *Mother-Tongue and Fatherland: Language and Politics in German.* Manchester, England: Manchester University Press.

Chapter 10
THE FAR RIGHT: FASCISM, NAZISM, AND ETHNORACISM

The following entries cover movements of the Right that converge in their rejection of all liberal and liberal democratic forms of political institutions, a characteristic that distinguishes them from conservatives and the New Right. Historically, these movements are characterized by ideologies of nature as a system of domination. Closely associated with this central concept is the idea of superior and inferior races and the notion of absolute obedience to a leader who expresses the will of the people without any need for institutions of democratic representation. Italian Fascism (which was relatively nonracist) and German Nazism (with an elaborated racist ideology) are the two major historical examples. Contemporary forms include "skinhead" movements, neo-Nazis, and right-wing militias and survivalists, as well as ultranationalist and anti-immigrant movements. These movements generally express racist ideologies and emphasize domination and violence in their actions.

Books and Book Chapters

Abraham, David. (1986). *The Collapse of the Weimar Republic*. New York: Holmes and Meier.

The author uses the concept of hegemony to analyze the inability of the Weimar Republic to withstand the growing power of the Nazis. The absence of unity within the capitalist class and its weak ideological cohesion combined with the persistence of an agrarian elite (the Junkers, or Prussian estate owners) with antidemocratic orientations produced a political system that could not sustain liberal democracy in the face of a growing right that operated both within and outside the parliamentary process. The book links processes within conservative right-wing elites to the formation of extreme right-wing movements with a mass base.

Arendt, Hannah. (1973). *The Origins of Totalitarianism*. New York: Harvest.

A political philosopher reflects on the structure and social bases of totalizing political systems characterized by single-party rule, repressive social control, ideological closure, and the absence of civil society.

196

In this regard, she groups together under the concept of "totalitarianism" the Soviet Union under Stalin (and other Communist states) and Nazi Germany. Still of interest.

_____. (1977). *Eichmann in Jerusalem*. New York: Viking/ Penguin.

The author, a leading political philosopher, argues that Adolf Eichmann was only one element in the Nazi bureaucracy designed to implement the genocide of European Jews. She describes the many levels of complicity in the "final solution," detailing the bureaucracy's complicated functions of gaining access to records of Jewish communities, arranging the compliance of local authorities, organizing deportations, and running death camps and gas chambers. Denmark and Bulgaria (and at a more individualistic level, Italy) are notable exceptions in a dismal record of collaboration with the Nazis, and it was only in these countries that a substantial proportion of Jews survived. The book remains informative and powerful.

Bettelheim, Bruno, and Morris Janowitz. (1964). *Social Change and Prejudice*. New York: Free Press.

A psychoanalyst and a sociologist teamed up in an empirical study of ethnocentrism and anti-Semitism in veterans in the United States after World War II, looking for sources of these attitudes in personal experiences such as downward mobility. Some of the conclusions are largely of historical interest, but part of the analysis can be transferred to contemporary patterns of attraction to racism and ethnic intolerance.

Cardoza, Anthony L. (1982). *Agrarian Elites and Italian Fascism: The Province of Bologna 1901-1926*. Princeton, NJ: Princeton University Press.

A historian's detailed analysis of participation in the growing Fascist movement in a central Italian province from the beginning of the century to the consolidation of Fascist rule. The author finds a strong connection between the rise of the Fascist movement and agrarian elites' efforts to control left-wing organizing of peasants and rural laborers. Although Fascism gained adherents across the class spectrum, it was disproportionately concentrated among small property owners and other middle strata and functioned on behalf of larger agrarian interests. An important scholarly study for understanding the social support base of Italian Fascism in historical perspective.

Carsten, F. L. (1967). *The Rise of Fascism*. Berkeley: University of California Press.

A readable historical account of fascism, Nazism, and related movements of the extreme right in Europe between World War I and World War II. The author emphasizes the ubiquity of these movements, though they did not attain a large size or come to power in most of the countries. During the Nazi occupation, fascist movements often formed Axis-aligned puppet regimes. Most of the movements were characterized by virulent anti-Semitism, support bases of dislocated students and military officers, a violent action orientation, and ambiguous rhetoric addressed to the discontents of middle strata who pictured themselves as trapped between finance capital and Communism. The chapters are organized by country and are highly informative.

Cheles, Luciano, Ronnie Ferguson, and Michalina Vaughan. (1995). *The Far Right in Western and Eastern Europe*. London: Longman.
A useful collection of articles about different forms of the far right in Europe, including neo-Nazis and other violent groups, anti-immigration movements, and ultranationalists.

Childers, Thomas. (1983). *The Nazi Voter: The Social Foundations of Fascism in Germany 1919-1933*. Chapel Hill: University of North Carolina Press.
An empirical study of the social support base of Nazism. The author puts less credence in the notion that the working class was greatly underrepresented in the Nazi support base than did some earlier analyses.

Coates, James. (1987). *Armed and Dangerous: The Rise of the Survivalist Right*. New York: Hill and Wang.
The author examines the formation in the United States of extreme right-wing groups with an antigovernment ideology and a penchant for stockpiling arms in anticipation of some type of final, cataclysmic conflict. Racist themes also are often present. In many ways, these movements are forerunners and related phenomena to the militias that formed the nurturing environment for the Oklahoma City bomber.

Corcoran, James. (1990). *Bitter Harvest: Gordon Kahl and the Posse Comitatus: Murder in the Heartland*. New York: Viking/Penguin.
An account of violence associated with a midwestern paramilitary movement on the far right, the Posse Comitatus, that tried to organize farmers who felt alienated by the wave of bankruptcies, farm foreclosures, and farm failures in recent decades.

Erikson, Erik. (1964). *Childhood and Society*. New York: Norton.

A psychoanalytically oriented scholar discusses cultural variation in socialization and the formation of adult personality types. The relevant chapter is an analysis of Adolf Hitler as he portrayed his own childhood, highlighting themes of repression, conventionality, the weight of the authoritarian family, and a sense of dismemberment associated with German identity.

Fischer, Conan. (1982). *Stormtroopers*. London: Allen and Unwin.
Analysis of the organization and social support base of the SA, the Stormtroopers, a paramilitary formation of Nazism. The author documents its crucial function in the Nazi rise to power. In 1932, it had about 450,000 members. The author discusses the problems of control and structural integration that it created for the party (stormtroopers were not, strictly speaking, members of the party organization), leading to its eventual violent suppression in the Night of the Long Knives, when the SS decimated the leadership.

_____. (1995). *The Rise of the Nazis*. Manchester, England: Manchester University Press.
An excellent concise summary of the latest research and analysis of the Nazi movement. The book covers the ideological basis (centered on ethnic populism, as the author translates *völkisch*), movement organization, policies and propaganda, and class constituencies. In keeping with recent research, he points to its substantial working-class base, constituting perhaps as much as 40 percent of its membership and voting strength. These workers were, however, disproportionately concentrated in crafts, agriculture, and small firms. Also valuable is the discussion of intramovement rivalries and tensions in the organizational structure. The volume includes annotated documents and bibliographical notes.

Flynn, Kevin, and Gary Gerhardt. (1989). *The Silent Brotherhood: Inside America's Racist Underground*. New York: Free Press.
A fascinating journalistic account of the small movement of Aryan Nations activists and Christian survivalists that culminated in the murder of Alan Berg in 1984. The book includes many details of the everyday lives and background of the adherents (for example, leader Robert Jay Mathews' early involvement with the John Birch Society), providing a valuable sense of how this extremist movement was grounded in a larger milieu of the radical right, survivalism, and anti-Semitism.

Gregor, A. James. (1974). *Interpretations of Fascism*. Morristown, NJ: General Learning Press.

The author concentrates on Italian Fascism and reviews a number of types of theories, including psychological, mass society, and Marxist-influenced, that point to class structure and/or economic determinations, as well as theories of totalitarianism. He presents strengths and flaws in all these approaches.

Guerin, Daniel. (1973). *Fascism and Big Business*. Garden City, NY: Anchor Books.

A Marxist analysis that links the rise of fascism to large capitalist interests that sponsored the movements, supported their entry into government, and benefited from their development policies, suppression of labor and the Left, and military buildup.

Hamm, Mark. (1993). *American Skinheads: The Criminology and Control of Hate Crime*. Westport, CT: Praeger.

A discussion of the social and psychological origins of what the author (a criminologist) terms a terrorist youth subculture. Topics include facets of this subculture such as antifeminism, "beer and bonding," racism, rebellion, and the social context in which hate crimes are committed. An excellent analysis that will engage students as well as scholarly and general readers.

Hitler, Adolf. (1962). *Mein Kampf*. Boston: Houghton Mifflin.

The English edition of the reflections of the Führer. Although the contemporary reader is likely to find much of it to be tedious ramblings about Aryan virtues, Jewish viciousness, and the sad state of the German people, there are occasional flashes of insight into what makes a right-wing mass movement successful, especially when Hitler discusses flags, insignias, and the ways in which a speaker can exert power over an audience.

Hockenos, Paul. (1994). *Free to Hate*. New York: Routledge.

See chapter 9 for an annotation.

Kershaw, Ian. (1987). *The "Hitler Myth" : Image and Reality in the Third Reich*. Oxford, England: Oxford University Press.

The author explores the limits of Hitler's charismatic authority and the disruptive consequences of charismatic authority for orderly decision making.

_____, ed. (1990). *Weimar: Why Did German Democracy Fail?* London: Weidenfeld and Nicolson.
A collection of essays that analyze Hitler's rise to power. The focus is on party structure and the role of incumbent conservative elites as well as voting data that show the increasing constriction of options across the political spectrum as the Nazis consolidated their hegemony over the Right.

_____. (1993). *The Nazi Dictatorship: Problems and Perspectives of Interpretation.* New York: Routledge.
A leading contemporary analyst of the Nazi phenomenon focuses on the structure of power in the Nazi state, with its anomalous mix of bureaucratic and charismatic authority, its hyperdevelopment of coercive apparatuses, and its often chaotic policy outcomes. Excellent theoretical analysis.

Laqueur, Walter. (1993). *Black Hundred: The Rise of the Extreme Right in Russia.* New York: HarperCollins.
The author examines the emergence of a nationalist, anti-Semitic, antidemocratic, and ethnonationalist right in Russia after the collapse of Communism, showing the origins of these movements in longstanding belief systems.

Mayer, Arno. (1971). *Dynamics of Counterrevolution in Europe, 1870-1956.* New York: Harper and Row.
The author places fascism into a broader perspective of counterrevolution and opposition to socialism. Fascism is a form of opposition to radical democracy and socialism that came into power where weak conservative elites felt under pressure to secure their rule by support from a mass right-wing movement. An important theoretical analysis of the entire spectrum of the Right by a leading modern European historian.

Moore, Barrington. (1965). *Social Origins of Dictatorship and Democracy.* Boston, MA: Beacon Press.
Moore's work provides a perspective on the types of social structure and political modernization that resulted in fascist political systems, namely those in which landed elites and a modernizing bourgeoisie joined forces in preempting and suppressing democratic mass movements.

Neumann, Franz. (1972). *Behemoth.* New York: Octagon Books. (Originally published in 1942)

A Marxist-influenced analysis of the Nazi state and its relationship to large capital.

Nolte, Ernst. (1966). *Three Faces of Fascism*. New York: Holt, Rinehart and Winston.

An analysis of fascist ideology in twentieth century Europe, in Italy, Germany, and France. The author leans toward the perspective of "totalitarian" as a concept that bridges repressive state/party structures on the Left and the Right.

Poulantzas, Nicos. (1974). *Fascism and Dictatorship*. London: Verso.

A Marxist analysis of the class base of fascism and the role of the movement in capitalist societies. The author discusses the relationship between the petite bourgeois mass support base of the movement and the way it functioned to cope with problems of the capitalist system in the interwar period. Complicated exposition.

Ridgeway, James. (1990). *Blood in the Face: The Ku Klux Klan, Aryan Nations, Nazi Skinheads, and the Rise of a New White Culture*. New York: Thunder's Mouth Press.

The author documents with photographs, poster reproductions, interview material, and quotations from books and pamphlets the ideology, projects, and actions of the racist extreme right in the United States. Very vivid and likely to be interesting to students.

Schoenbaum, David. (1966). *Hitler's Social Revolution*. Garden City, NY: Anchor/Doubleday.

A historian analyzes Nazism in terms of its social structural outcomes, examining programs and policies in a number of areas. He concludes that despite its radical rhetoric and repressive violence, it accomplished relatively little fundamental social change in German society.

Speer, Albert. (1970). *Inside the Third Reich*. New York: Macmillan.

Hitler's favorite architect presents his own version of life at the top in Nazi Germany. Apart from the fact that Speer is eager to establish his own innocence and rarely is a reliable witness on matters in which he was directly involved, there is a wealth of telling little details of everyday life with the Führer. From a theoretical perspective, the most important feature of the book is the confirmation that the structure of decision making was highly personalistic, inconsistent, and disorganized.

Sternhell, Zeev, with Mario Sznajder and Maia Asheri. (1994). *The Birth of Fascist Ideology: From Cultural Rebellion to Political Revolution.* Princeton, NJ: Princeton University Press.

The authors trace the origins of fascism in a cultural movement that questioned and reformulated many features of modernism at the turn of the century. They suggest that it began by confronting issues in modernity that socialism and nationalism also addressed, but that it offered a more heroic and elitist set of answers. The analysis offers new theoretical approaches to fascism and is in keeping with trends in the study of collective behavior that place increasing emphasis on cultural processes rather than social structural strains and political opportunities. Some readers may find the argument too long and repetitious.

Trotsky, Leon. (1944). *Fascism: What It Is and How to Fight It.* New York: Pathfinder Press.

Emphasizing the relationship between fascism (including the Nazi state) and large capital, a Marxist (and exiled Russian revolutionary) discusses the threat of fascism.

Tucker, Henry Ashby. (1985). *German Big Business and the Rise of Hitler.* New York: Oxford University Press.

The author provides detailed descriptions of the actions of big business leaders in relation to the Nazi Party in and out of power. Contrary to Marxist theorists, he concludes that big business was not a leading factor in Hitler's rise to power and that business leaders went along with the Nazis rather than actively promoting them. Marxists are likely to disagree with the entire framework of analysis, arguing that it leaves out structural outcomes and ideological vision, while focusing too much on day to day behavioral details.

University of Colorado, Department of Philosophy. (1952). *Readings on Fascism and National Socialism.* Chicago: Swallow Press.

A short but well-selected collection of fascist and Nazi documents that illustrates major ideological themes such as the notion of the people or *volk* as a natural group, the glorification of the leader, and the substitution of leadership and unreasoning obedience for the rule of law.

Periodical Articles

Clark, Cynthia. (1992). "Deviant Adolescent Subcultures: Assessment Strategies and Clinical Interventions." *Adolescence* 27, no. 106 (Summer), 283-293.

The author discusses clinical practice to assist clinicians working with neo-Nazi skinheads, as well as teen Satanists and violent street gang members. The concept of alienation forms part of this psychological perspective on destructive youth cultures.

Dobratz, Betty, and Stephanie Shanks-Meile. (1988). "The Contemporary Ku Klux Klan and the American Nazi Party: A Comparison to American Populism at the Turn of the Century." *Humanity and Society* 12, no. 1 (February), 20-50.

The authors suggest that evidence from the movements under consideration supports the view that these movements have a mixed class base and serve finance capital's interests rather than being exclusively movements of the petite bourgeoisie against both large capital and the proletariat. The authors point to similarities among the movements' ideologies, such as a rhetoric of hostility to big business, racial intolerance, and an emphasis on community, tradition, and morality.

Fields, Barbara. (1990). "Slavery, Race, and Ideology in the United States of America." *New Left Review* 181 (May/June), 95-118.

A good article for understanding the formation of racist ideologies. The author argues that slavery as a class structure preceded the formation of racist ideologies, not the other way around. Racist ideology was diffused throughout the practices of everyday life, as well as explicitly articulated.

Freedman, Carl. (1992). "Louisiana 'Duce': Notes Toward a Systematic Analysis of Postmodern Fascism in America." *Rethinking Marxism* 5, no. 1 (Spring), 19-31.

The author discusses David Duke's appeal (he polled close to 44 percent of the vote in the 1990 U.S. Senate race), including his ability to define himself as an outsider, his manipulation of discourse, and his success at disassociating himself from his past. The depressed local economy is also a factor. The article is interesting as an effort to identify "postmodern fascism."

Gerth, Hans. (1940). "The Nazi Party: Its Leadership and Composition." *American Journal of Sociology* 45 (January), 517-541.

A classic in the analysis of the social origins of a party/movement. The author looks at the social strata to which leadership cadres and members belonged; his conclusion remains largely undisputed—that they were disproportionately located in middle strata such as self-employed artisans, white-collar workers, and small proprietors, although recent studies have indicated a somewhat larger support base in the working class than previously noted.

Grass, Gunter, and Krishna Winston. (1993). "On Loss: The Condition of Germany." *Dissent* 40, no. 2 (Spring), 178-188.
The authors discuss the role of right-of-center political leaders in creating an atmosphere of opinion and discourse in which radical right-wing violence has emerged.

Moore, David. (1990). "Drinking, the Construction of Ethnic Identity, and Social Process in a Western Australian Youth Subculture." *British Journal of Addiction* 85, no. 10 (October), 1265-1278.
Skinhead behavior is observed, in particular the interplay of drinking with the expression of English ethnic identity. Insights at a micro level into the formation of ethnic identity and skinhead youth culture.

Oestreicher, Emil. (1974). "Fascism and the Intellectuals: The Case of Italian Futurism." *Social Research* 41, no. 3 (Autumn), 515-533.
A case study in the attraction of artists and writers to fascism, elitism, and terrorism. Italian intellectuals, in response to the slow and uneven modernization of Italy, turned to the fascist movement with its emphasis on nationalism, technology, and violence as a solution to these problems of development.

Rogowski, Ronald. (1977). "The Gauleiter and the Social Origins of Fascism." *Comparative Studies in Society and History* 19, no. 4 (October), 399-430.
Using empirical data based on the sixty-three pre-1933 Gauleiter, the author concludes that these were not men drawn from the socially and economically threatened or downwardly mobile petite bourgeoisie; rather, they were generally upwardly mobile, although blocked mobility may have been one element in their recruitment to the NSDAP.

Stollmann, Rainer, and Ronald Smith. (1978). "Fascist Politics as a Total Work of Art: Tendencies of the Aesthetization of Political Life in National Socialism." *New German Critique* 14 (Spring), 41-60.
Theoretical discussion utilizing the concept of the "beautiful illusion" and examining the role of aestheticized politics in the Third Reich.

Suall, Irwin, and David Lowe. (1988). "Shaved for Battle: Skinheads Target America's Youth." *Political Communication and Persuasion* 5, no. 2, 139-144.
A description of violent antiblack, anti-Semitic youth gangs. The authors include a discussion of "white power" music and a comparison with Great Britain.

Vajda, Mihaly. (1971). "On Fascism." *Telos* 8 (Summer), 43-63.
The author identifies fascism as a mass movement with a base in the middle strata and key characteristics such as an ideology of "natural" groups, veneration of authoritarian figures, intense hostility to out-groups, and paramilitary organizations as dominant forces within the party. It attempts to smash working-class organizations and ends up implementing the policies of large capital because its petty bourgeois support base is not capable of formulating independent solutions to capitalist crises. The article is an important theoretical statement that helps to define fascism and provide a sophisticated Marxist-influenced perspective.

_____. (1972). "Crisis and the Way Out: The Rise of Fascism in Italy and Germany." *Telos* 12 (Summer), 3-26.
The author argues against mechanical economic explanations of the rise of the historical instances of fascism and favors an approach that emphasizes agency on the part of the bourgeoisie in both countries. Germany and Italy differed, however, in the functions that the fascist movement was expected to serve. Good theoretical analysis.

Also of Interest

Gillingham, John. (1985). *Industry and Politics in the Third Reich: Ruhr Coal, Hitler, and Europe*. London: Methuen.

Müller, Klaus-Jürgen. (1987). *The Army, Politics, and Society in Germany, 1933-45*. New York: St. Martin's Press.

Noakes, Jeremy, and Geoffrey Pridham, eds. (1990). *Nazism 1919-1945: A History in Documents and Eyewitness Accounts*. New York: Schocken.

Singer, Daniel. (1991). "The Resistible Rise of Jean-Marie Le Pen." *Ethnic and Racial Studies* (special issue on migration and migrants in France) 14 (July), 368-381.

Sohn-Rethel, Alfred. (1987). *The Economy and Class Structure of German Fascism.* London: Free Associates.

Southern Poverty Law Center. (1989). *Hate, Violence and White Supremacy: A Decade Review.* Montgomery, AL: Author.

"Symposium on the Extreme Right." (1992). *Parliamentary Affairs* 45 (July).

Togliatti, Palmiro. (1976). *Lectures on Fascism.* New York: International Publishers.

Zellner, William W. (1995). *Counter Cultures: Skinhead, Satanism, the Unification Church, KKK, the Church of Scientology, Survivalists.* New York: St. Martin's Press.

Chapter 11
GENDER AND SEXUAL ORIENTATION AS FOCAL POINTS OF MOVEMENTS

This chapter covers social and political movements and movement organizations. It is not a bibliography of feminist theory or gender studies, nor does it cover research into the conditions of the lives of women and persons with a homosexual sexual orientation. The movements under consideration include three distinct types. One is feminism, which can be defined as a movement that addresses the entire issue of gender inequality. There are several different forms of feminist ideology, explored in the listed works. Second, women's movements are forms of collective action that seek to alter or redress specific problems faced by women, but often without feminism's discourse about gender inequality. Third, movements focused on inequalities between people of different sexual orientations are included in this section. These movements include a variety of perspectives, ranging from civil rights mobilizations to end discrimination against homosexuals to more radical movements that call into question institutions of compulsory heterosexuality.

Books and Book Chapters

Adam, Barry. (1987). *The Rise of a Gay and Lesbian Movement*. Boston Twayne.
Good introductory coverage of the emergence of movements for civil rights and liberties of persons with a same-sex sexual orientation.

Afshar, Haleh, ed. (1993). *Women in the EastMiddle East: Perceptions, Realities and Struggles for Liberation*. New York: St. Martin's Press.
Excellent articles about both the conditions of women's lives in a range of Middle Eastern nations and various movements concerning women. The articles offer a nuanced analysis of the situations, dispelling Western stereotypes without losing a critical edge toward the status quo.

Andreas, Carol. (1986). *When Women Rebel: The Rise of Popular Feminism in Peru*. Westport, CT: L. Hill Brooks.
The author gives an overview of feminism among poor and working people in Peru, women for whom gender issues are necessarily intertwined with class issues.

Backhouse, Constance, and David Flaherty, eds. (1992). *Challenging Times: The Women's Movement in Canada and the United States.* Montreal: McGill-Queen's University Press.
Scholarly articles about the emergence and forms of mobilization of the women's movement. The attention to Canada and the comparative analysis offer a corrective to the typical focus on the United States.

Balser, Diane. (1987). *Sisterhood and Solidarity: Feminism and Labor in Modern Times.* Boston: South End Press.
United by experiences of subordination and political marginalization, but often divided by social class and economic interests, women and the labor movement have not consistently merged or even coordinated their struggles. The author traces these divergences and convergences from a position of critical support for both types of movements.

Bawer, Bruce. (1993). *A Place at the Table.* New York: Simon & Schuster.
The author makes a case for liberal and inclusionary goals for the gay and lesbian movement. In his view, the movement should focus on civil rights and civil liberties for all people, regardless of their sexual orientation, which in any case is and should be largely a private concern, not a public issue of cultural diversity. He takes a critical view of ideologies that focus on accentuating and celebrating cultural differences between "gays" and "straights." A readable book for the general public.

Beauvoir, Simone de. (1974). *The Second Sex.* New York: Random House.
A modern classic about women and gender inequality. First published after World War II, it is dated and European-oriented in some respects, but many of its claims and insights will still engage the contemporary North American reader. The author, an existentialist philosopher, debunks naturalistic explanations of women's marginalized condition, dissects the image of women in Western thought and literature, traces the social construction of "secondariness" throughout a woman's life course, and reflects on the problems of organizing women across class and ethnic divisions.

Berger, Iris. (1992). *Threads of Solidarity: Women in South African Industry, 1900-1980.* Bloomington: Indiana University Press.
In a scholarly study, the author traces the complex interrelationships of labor, gender, and ethnic/racial issues in South Africa.

Black, Naomi. (1989). *Social Feminism.* Ithaca, NY: Cornell University Press.

The author discusses the ideas of social feminism, an ideology that calls for the valorization of the sphere of social reproduction—child rearing, care of the sick and elderly, and homemaking. Arguing that women's entry into the paid labor force cannot be on equal terms with men as long as there is no collective, societal responsibility for women's traditional caretaking functions, the movement calls for public attention to these areas of life. There are fascist, conservative, liberal, and socialist variants of these ideas, and the author discusses some specific movements and government policies, especially in Europe.

Bouvard, Marguerite Guzman. (1994). *Revolutionizing Motherhood: The Mothers of the Plaza de Mayo*. Wilmington, DE: Scholarly Resources. The author features the women who called the world's attention to the "disappearance" of their children at the hands of the Argentine military regime from 1976 to the early 1980's. The regime kidnapped, tortured, and murdered community activists, labor union members, and intellectuals with the excuse that a "dirty war" was necessary to suppress left-wing guerrillas. The author brings a spirit of admiration and warmth to her essays about the despair and courage of the women who stood in front of the presidential palace to demand the return of their children, or at least knowledge of their fate. The book gives insight into their experiences and feelings, and it stresses the left-wing anarchism of the movement.

Bridenthal, Renate, Claudia Koonz, and Susan Stuard, eds. (1987). *Becoming Visible: Women in European History*. Boston: Houghton Mifflin. An excellent collection of scholarly articles by historians, covering women in Europe from classical antiquity to the twentieth century. Careful, detailed analysis dispels myths and misconceptions, showing the complex, contradictory situations of women in society and their contested images in religion, art, and ideology. A number of articles cover women's involvement in change, both in premodern forms and in modern social movements including feminism, labor organization, and socialism.

Bunch, Charlotte. (1987). *Passionate Politics: Feminist Theory in Action*. New York: St. Martin's Press. A lively series of essays that offers a feminist perspective on politics and global issues. Feminism is presented as a positive and coherent vision of a future in which dominance, violence, and hierarchy are replaced by egalitarian relations, to the benefit of men as well as women.

Chafetz, Janet Saltzman, and Gary Dworkin. (1986). *Female Revolt: Women's Movements in World and Historical Perspective*. Totowa, NJ: Rowman and Allanheld.
A major theoretical study that attempts to answer the question, When do women form women's movements and feminist movements? The answer is an empirically grounded structural one, based not on an analysis of women's attitudes but on the characteristics of the occupational structure of the societies in which such movements emerge. Women's movements are associated with increasing female participation in the paid labor force, and feminist movements with increasing entry into previously male occupations. Essential reading for social movement theory and for an understanding of feminism that goes beyond subjective concerns.

Cochran, Jo Whitehorse, Donna Langston, and Carolyn Woodward, eds. (1991). *Changing Our Power*. Dubuque, IA: Kendall/Hunt.
A lively series of essays, memoirs, and poems celebrating women and diversity among women along lines of ethnicity and sexual orientation.

Collison, Helen. (1990). *Women and Revolution in Nicaragua*. London: Zed.
A sympathetic but not uncritical look at the role of women in the Sandinista revolution, Sandinista gender policy, and women's organizations during the Sandinista period.

Davis, Flora. (1991). *Moving the Mountain: The Women's Movement in America Since 1960*. New York: Simon & Schuster.
A detailed narrative history of second wave feminism. The author provides detailed information about movements, movement organizations, public policy issues, and leadership. The book is particularly strong in coverage of what some might call "liberal feminism," focused on equal rights, individual rights, political participation, and economic equality. There is relatively less about ethnic and class diversity within the movement and about currents of radical, cultural, and lesbian feminism.

D'Emilio, John. (1992). *Making Trouble*. New York: Routledge.
Perceptive personal and theoretical essays on gay identity and the gay movement, by a sociologist and gay activist. The most interesting pieces for the social movement scholar are those in which the author

traces the formation of a gay movement in capitalist societies. Only within the economic and social structure of capitalist societies was it possible to move historically from homosexual acts (condemned or tolerated, as varied from culture to culture) to distinct homosexual communities and ultimately to a movement making claims to both civil rights and cultural diversity. Important theoretical analysis.

Echols, Alice. (1989). *Daring to Be Bad: Radical Feminism in America, 1967-1975*. Minneapolis: University of Minnesota Press.
The author provides lively insights into radical feminism, a short-lived current that had an influence on later developments in cultural feminism. Radical feminism itself grew out of a reaction to the New Left's sexism in discourse and practice. It preserved the left-wing and anarchist elements of New Left ideology but added to them a far-reaching critique of gender inequality in contemporary society.

Faludi, Susan. (1991). *Backlash: The Undeclared War Against American Women*. New York: Crown.
An angry, detailed, and wide-ranging look at countermovements against feminism as well as government policies and media messages that sought to undo reforms accomplished by the women's movement in the United States. It has reached a large readership.

Fernandez-Kelly, Maria P. (1984). *For We Are Sold: I and My People: Women and Industry in Mexico's Frontier*. Albany: State University of New York Press.
A pioneering study of women in factory work in low-wage economies, a situation likely to expand with free trade zones and the globalization of production. The analysis raises the question of what types of movements and movement organizations might be able to mobilize workers in these conditions.

Fisher, Jo. (1993). *Out of the Shadows: Women, Resistance and Politics in South America*. New York: Monthly Review Press.
The author highlights grassroots struggles of women that are distinct from middle-class feminist movements in terms of organization and issues. Case studies include organizers of communal kitchens in Chile, union activists in Uruguay, and mothers of the disappeared in Argentina. Many of these movements developed in response to the destruction of the traditional male-oriented Left by military regimes. The grassroots movements challenge both the middle-class feminists and the male-oriented Left and have changed gender consciousness in the region.

Fox-Genovese, Elizabeth. (1991). *Feminism Without Illusions: A Critique of Individualism.* Chapel Hill: University of North Carolina Press.
Essays on the subject of what types of feminist ideologies and mobilizations are of value in the conditions of the contemporary United States. The author argues that individualistic feminism contributes to the attenuation of social bonds, especially those of families and communities; what is needed is a feminism that enhances the rights of women in a framework of collective commitment.

Freeman, Jo. (1975). *The Politics of Women's Liberation.* New York: McKay.
A key early study of second wave feminism that uses concepts from resource mobilization theory to analyze the preexisting networks and organizations that contributed to the rise of the feminist movements in the United States.

Friedan, Betty. (1984). *The Feminine Mystique.* New York: Dell.
A later edition of the 1963 book that sparked public discussion of the discontent that educated women felt in the homemaker roles they entered after World War II.

Funk, Nanette, and Magda Mueller, eds. (1993). *Gender Politics and Post-Communism.* New York: Routledge.
A collection of articles that provide valuable insights into gender politics in the post-Communist states, where increased opportunities for autonomous feminist organizing go hand in hand with increasing public expression of misogyny, shrinking employment opportunities, and constricted social services.

Herdt, Gilbert, ed. (1991). *Gay Culture in America.* Boston: Beacon Press.
Theoretical and empirical studies on a variety of facets of contemporary gay culture and distinct subcultures within the larger gay community. Most of the authors are sociologists or anthropologists and bring rigorous qualitative methods, such as participant observation and collection of life narratives, to bear on the topic. The groups and communities studied by the researchers include several that function as movements.

Hewlett, Sylvia. (1986). *A Lesser Life.* New York: Warner.
An angry but thought-provoking critique of liberal, equal rights feminism from a social feminist viewpoint. The author argues that the women's movement in the United States has not supported the interests of women who have child-care responsibilities. She contrasts the more

214 Social Movement Theory and Research

supportive social welfare policies and union-based initiatives of Western European countries.

Katzenstein, Mary Fainsod, and Carol McClurg Mueller. (1987). *The Women's Movements of the United States and Western Europe*. Philadelphia: Temple University Press.
Good sociological analysis of the rise of second wave feminism in the developed Western political economies, movement goals and ideologies, organization and strategies, and policy accomplishments.

Liebman, Marvin. (1992). *Coming Out Conservative: A Founder of the Modern Conservative Movement Speaks Out on Personal Freedom, Homophobia, and Hate Politics*. San Francisco: Chronicle.
The author argues that a genuine conservatism that cherishes liberty has no room for the homophobia found in some currents of cultural conservatism.

Luker, Kristin. (1984). *Abortion and the Politics of Motherhood*. Berkeley: University of California Press.
An important empirical study in which the author presents data that contextualizes activism on both sides of the abortion issue within a larger set of values, experiences, and concerns. Women in the two opposing movements had distinct educational and occupational experiences and markedly different views of the meaning of womanhood, pregnancy, and maternity.

Mansbridge, Jane. (1986). *Why We Lost the ERA*. Chicago: University of Chicago Press.
The author is both an advocate and an empirical researcher, and the study offers an in-depth discussion that will be of interest to both scholars and activists for women's rights. She presents data and analysis supporting the view that a combination of factors led to the eventual defeat of the ERA by negative votes in a small number of key state legislatures, despite considerable public opinion in favor of it. One of the most important reasons was that anti-ERA forces on the cultural right were able to reach legislators in these states, while convincing sizable numbers of women that the legislation would have far-reaching negative consequences for their status and security.

Marcus, Eric. (1992). *Making History: An Oral History of the Struggle for Gay and Lesbian Civil Rights 1945-1990*. New York: HarperCollins.

The author provides the recollections of activists, some of them high-profile leaders, others "ordinary people." The material is organized into pre-1960's, 1961-1968, 1968-1973, 1973-1981, and 1981-1990, helping the reader see the struggles in their historical context. Not heavily theoretical, but engaging.

Matteo, Shirley, ed. (1993). *American Women in the Nineties: Today's Critical Issues*. Boston: Northeastern University Press.
A collection of articles on various topics including AIDS, abortion, equality in education, the feminization of poverty, and women and pornography. Most are written from a moderate, liberal perspective. Although most are not directly about movements, the material has implications for activism and the formation of social policy.

Melzer, Sara, and Leslie Rabine, eds. (1992). *Rebel Daughters: Women and the French Revolution*. New York: Oxford University Press.
The revolution that opened the door to the formation of modern political systems involved women as revolutionaries, redefined the gender system, and in many ways narrowed the privileges of women at the top of the social structure. These complex and inconsistent forces are explored in studies by social historians.

Mernissi, Fatima. (1991). *The Veil and the Male Elite: A Feminist Interpretation of Women's Rights in Islam*. New York: Addison-Wesley.
See chapter 8 for an annotation.

Miller, Francesca. (1991). *Latin American Women and the Search for Social Justice*. Hanover, NH: University Press of New England.
A careful overview of a variety of movements in Latin America, including feminist movements and organizations as well as those that link women's issues with a more generalized challenge to social inequality. The author believes that there is a valid role for several types of movements.

Molyneux, Maxine. (1986). "Mobilization Without Emancipation: Women's Interests, State, and Revolution." In Richard Fagen, Carmen Deere, and J. L. Coraggio (eds.), *Transition and Development*. New York: Monthly Review Press.
The author examines in comparative perspective the outcomes of Third World revolutions for women. She argues that women often were included in revolutionary fronts and in regime-sponsored organizations and that some gains in their situation resulted from these transitions, but that in many cases women's issues ultimately were

subordinated to priorities of economic development and political consolidation.

Momsen, Janet Henshall, and Janet G. Townsend, eds. (1987). *Geography of Gender in the Third World.* Victoria, Australia: Hutchinson and State University of New York Press.
A collection of scholarly articles about the conditions under which women live in developing nations, especially in South Asia. Many articles focus on problems including gender-related malnutrition and neglect, and some on movements for change, especially local and small-scale initiatives to improve women's access to economic resources.

Moraga, Cherrie, and Gloria Anzaldua, eds. (1983). *This Bridge Called My Back: Writings by Radical Women of Color.* New York: Kitchen Table Press.
Essays by women in situations of multiple jeopardy—color, class, gender, and/or sexual orientation.

Morgan, Robin, ed. (1984). *Sisterhood Is Global: The International Women's Movement Anthology.* New York: Anchor/Doubleday.
Essays by feminists reporting from a large range of countries that address issues (for example, economic opportunities, violence, sexual and reproductive rights) and the progress made by women's movements. Some of these reports are no longer up to date, but the volume provides a sense of the beginnings of a transnational women's movement.

_____. (1992). *The Word of a Woman: Feminist Dispatches, 1968-1992.* New York: Norton.
The author represents a relatively radical position in the spectrum of feminism. The essays document her involvement in the movement and express her ongoing concerns.

Peters, J. S., and Andrea Wolper, eds. (1995). *Women's Rights, Human Rights.* New York: Routledge.
In recent years, the women's movement on a transnational scale increasingly has turned to a human rights discourse to frame the discussion of problems such as juridical inequality, the denial of property rights to women, formally and informally condoned domestic violence, genital mutilation, restrictions on travel and movement in public spaces, and various forms of sexual coercion. This framing shifts "women's issues" into a more inclusive legitimizing framework.

The volume makes a major contribution to this new framing, which is likely to expand and gain support, as became evident at the September, 1995, U.N. conference in Beijing. The book covers a wide range of issues in many countries.

Radcliffe, Sarah, and Sallie Westwood. (1993). *VIVA: Women and Popular Protest in Latin America.* New York: Routledge.
Women historically have been marginalized in Latin American politics, but in recent years a wide spectrum of women's movements has emerged that bring women into formal and informal political processes and challenge the genderized nature of the states in the region.

Rowbotham, Sheila. (1974). *Women, Resistance, and Revolution.* New York: Vintage.
At the height of decolonization movements and Third World socialist revolutions, the author looked at the involvement of women in these movements and the outcomes for women. Women made some concrete gains and participated in political change, but many problems remained. Women were unable to sustain their political roles, and autonomous organizations committed to women's rights were eliminated or marginalized.

_____. (1992). *Women in Movement.* New York: Routledge.
An overview of women's movements on a global scale, from a Marxist-feminist perspective.

Rupp, Leila, and Verta Taylor. (1987). *Survival in the Doldrums: The American Women's Rights Movement, 1945 to the 1960's.* New York: Oxford University Press.
A work of theoretical importance that provides insights into how a movement survives a period of becalmment. The authors analyze the organizations and individuals who gave continuity to the women's movement in a period when it was marginalized.

Sawicki, Jana. (1991). *Disciplining Foucault: Feminism, Power, and the Body.* New York: Routledge.
The author transposes Michel Foucault's theoretical work to feminist issues, focusing on how power is exercised and resistance asserted in an ongoing process of struggle in discourse and interaction. Foucault's perspective is particularly cogent for feminism, insofar as women generally do not live in separate communities of interest that can easily form movement organizations and articulate distinct ideologies. The

book is valuable as a synthesis and explanation of Foucault's work as well as an application of it to feminism.

Shilts, Randy. (1982). *The Mayor of Castro Street: The Life and Times of Harvey Milk.* New York: St. Martin's Press.
A biography of Milk, one of the first openly gay elected public officials, and a description of the social context of his activism.

Smith, Barbara, ed. (1983). *Home Girls: A Black Feminist Anthology.* New York: Kitchen Table Press.
A collection of essays, poems, short memoirs, and other pieces by black feminists. Includes attention to issues of sexual orientation as well as class, race, and gender.

Smith-Ayala, Emilie. (1991). *The Granddaughters of Ixmucané.* Toronto: Women's Press.
The author edited and compiled short reflections and life narratives of women in the popular movement in Guatemala, who risk their lives in a struggle against the military regimes (and their civilian fronts) in power since the coup of 1954. The women include peasant organizers, union officials, religious activists, and indigenous leaders. The accounts are moving. An excellent selection for students at the secondary and college level.

Walker, Alice. (1984). *In Search of Our Mothers' Gardens: Womanist Prose.* New York: Harcourt Brace.
Essays and reflections on defining a feminism of African American women. A contribution to the growing recognition of diversity in the women's movement.

Willis, Ellen. (1993a). *Beginning to See the Light: Sex, Hope, and Rock and Roll.* Middletown, CT: Wesleyan University Press.
In a lively memoir, the author describes her participation in the New Left and analyzes the radical sources of the women's movement.

_____. (1993b). *No More Nice Girls: Countercultural Essays.* Hanover, NH: University Press of New England.
The author reflects on the origins and continuing contributions of radical feminist movements and ideology.

Wollstonecraft, Mary. (1975). *A Vindication of the Rights of Women.* New York: Norton.

The French revolutionary "Rights of Man" declaration was appropriated as well as challenged by the author, whose work was published in 1792 as a call for equal rights for women. It marks the beginning of modern feminist movements and ideologies.

Yee, Shirley. (1992). *Black Women Abolitionists: A Study in Activism 1828-1860*. Knoxville: University of Tennessee Press.
Although overshadowed in mainstream history books by abolitionists who were male and/or white, black women had a vital role in the movement as organizers, spokespeople, and guides for slaves escaping north. A good overview of their part in the abolitionist movement.

Periodical Articles

Andersen, Margaret. (1991). "Feminism and the American Family Ideal." *Journal of Comparative Family Studies* 22, no. 2 (Summer), 235-246.
The author argues that the feminist movement has affected as well as reflected family life across racial and class groups, but that the ideology of the ideal U.S. family persists and hinders development of effective social policies to solve family problems.

Andreas, Carol. (1989). "People's Kitchens and Radical Organizing in Lima, Peru." *Monthly Review* 41, no. 6 (November), 12-21.
The author looks at the role of women in movements and community organizations of poor people in marginal areas of Lima, giving attention to people's kitchens, where food is prepared and distributed on a communal basis. A good example of the intertwining of class struggles with women's movements.

Bawer, Bruce. (1994). "Notes on Stonewall." *The New Republic* 210 (June 13), 24-27.
The author uses the Stonewall riot of 1969 as a benchmark for measuring what has happened in the United States to the rights, activism, and identities of people with a same-sex sexual orientation. He finds some progress in inclusion in the rights and liberties of civil society (his own goals for the movement) and expresses his doubts about tendencies in the movement to publicize and accentuate cultural differences between gays and straights.

Beccalli, Bianca. (1994). "The Modern Women's Movement in Italy." *New Left Review* 204 (March/April), 86-112.

An important article surveying the history of the women's movement in post-World War II Italy, with a focus on the last few decades. The author gives special attention to the complex relationship between the women's movement and the forces of the Left, such as organized labor and the Communist Party. She takes a critical view of how the women's movement became part of the New Social Movements, left-libertarian movements with decentralized structures. This New Social Movement involvement, along with the extremely high level of introspective theorizing, are tendencies that have reduced the movement's ability to organize a mass support base to pursue concrete goals. Essential reading for understanding women's movements in comparative perspective.

Berger, Ronald, Patricia Searles, and Charles Cottle. (1990). "Ideological Contours of the Contemporary Pornography Debate: Divisions and Alliances." *Frontiers* 11, no. 2-3, 30-38.
Discussion of the debate between antipornography and anticensorship feminists, including the topic of the unexpected alliance between the former and religious conservatives.

Bishop, Brenda. (1990). "From Women's Rights to Feminist Politics: The Developing Struggle for Women's Liberation in Poland." *Monthly Review* 42, no. 6 (November), 15-34.
A good interim report on the women's movement in Poland during the transition from Communism to capitalism. Although women now have the right to form autonomous organizations, their actual economic and social position has deteriorated because of both a difficult economic situation and the role of conservative forces such as the Catholic church.

Bobroff, Anne. (1976). "The Bolsheviks and Working Women, 1905-1929." *Radical America* 10, no. 3 (May/June), 51-73.
Charts changes in party policy toward the issue of whether women's situation requires special attention. The author suggests that more attention to women's issues was the result of pressure and competition from the "bourgeois feminist movement," despite Bolsheviks' tendency officially to deny an advanced or independent level of consciousness among women workers.

Boles, Janet K. (1991). "Form Follows Function: The Evolution of Feminist Strategies." *Annals of the American Academy of Political and Social Science* 515 (May), 38-49.

The author suggests that both radical women's groups and the liberal feminist movement have adapted their strategies to fit into the U.S. federal structure in terms of influencing legislative policy, developing policy networks, and pursuing local and issue-specific advocacy work. The article exemplifies theories of political opportunity structure.

Brenner, Johanna. (1993). "The Best of Times, the Worst of Times: U.S. Feminism Today." *New Left Review* 200 (July/August), 101-159.
A key article featuring a leftist perspective on women's movements in the United States. The author summarizes and analyzes a wide spectrum of movements and ideological currents within feminism, looks at the complex intertwining of class and ethnic/racial issues with gender issues, assesses the force of conservative countermovements, and critically examines the prospects for a larger progressive movement that would include women as a leading force.

Brown, Ruth Murray. (1984). "In Defense of Traditional Values: The Anti-Feminist Movement." *Marriage and Family Review* 7, no. 3-4 (Fall/Winter), 19-35.
An Oklahoma-based sample of pro- and anti-ERA persons provided questionnaire and interview data that showed that the antis are predominantly fundamentalists and Mormons and that 96% of them stated that religion is very important in their lives, as compared to 53% of the pros. The author concludes that the anti-ERA orientation is part of a traditional culture that interprets the Bible literally, objects to sexual permissiveness and the use of alcohol and tobacco, and has conservative views on family authority and women's labor force participation. Antis believe that traditional gender roles reflect inborn differences between men and women. The study offers interesting insights into the conservative countermovement to feminism and the ways in which positions on a specific issue are part of a larger cultural framework.

Chinchilla, Norma Stoltz. (1991). "Marxism, Feminism, and the Struggle for Democracy in Latin America." *Gender and Society* 5, no. 3 (September), 291-310.
The author believes that new understandings of the situation in the region now create openings for the convergence of movements and struggles. The concept of a plurality of social subjects, recognition of the autonomy of popular movements from political parties and the state, and more focus on the concerns of everyday life in the struggle for socialism contribute to the possibility of a more productive relationship between feminism and Marxist movements.

Cockburn, Cynthia. (1991). "Democracy Without Women Is No Democracy: Soviet Women Hold Their First Autonomous National Conference." *Feminist Review* 39 (Winter), 141-148.
A report on the beginnings of a feminist movement in Russia, a movement that has to contend with a difficult situation left by the unfulfilled promises of Communism as well as current misogynist efforts to reverse the economic and social gains that had been accomplished.

Cowan, Gloria, Monja Mestlin, and Julie Masek. (1992). "Predictors of Feminist Self-Labeling." *Sex Roles* 27, no. 7-8 (October), 321-330.
The authors used questionnaire data to explore attitudinal correlates of self-labeling as a feminist. Some of the results seem unsurprising or even tautological, but the study contributes to an understanding of attitudes in movement support bases.

Creevey, Lucy. (1991). "The Impact of Islam on Women in Senegal." *Journal of Developing Areas* 25, no. 3 (April), 347-368.
Describes the historical and current socioeconomic and educational status of women in Senegal. Though not an Islamic republic, Senegal's population is 85-90 percent Muslim. The author concludes that as Senegalese women enter educational institutions and employment, a feminist movement is developing. The general outlook for women is positive.

Ferree, Myra Marx. (1991). "Political Strategies and Feminist Concerns in the United States and Federal Republic of Germany: Class, Race, and Gender." *Research in Social Movements, Conflicts, and Change* 13, 221-240.
An important theoretical contribution to the analysis of transnational movements that operate in different national political cultures. In Germany, gender issues are seen in the light of the history of class politics; in the United States, it is race that structures the framework. The author looks at how issues of employment policy, reproductive rights, and women in the military are construed differently in the two countries because of these differences in national political culture.

_____. (1993). "The Rise and Fall of 'Mommy Politics': Feminism and Unification in (East) Germany." *Feminist Studies* 19, no. 1 (Spring), 89-115.
After 1972, a phase of gender policy focused on women's labor force participation came to an end, and the GDR pursued policies of accommodating women's special needs as mothers. These policies created

contradictions experienced by women in their everyday lives and thus contributed to the rise of a feminist movement. The movement now has to contend with the post-Communist situation and with the rejected legacy of "mommy politics"; consequently, it has yet to find a popular discourse for addressing the condition of women. The case study points to the long-term political implications of gender policies based on discourses of difference and special needs.

Gardezi, Fauzia. (1990). "Islam, Feminism, and the Women's Movement in Pakistan." *South Asia Bulletin* 10, no. 2, 18-24.
The author discusses improvements that resulted from both grassroots groups and a more development-oriented institutionalized movement. She also identifies issues that continue to divide and weaken the movement, including the disputed relationship to Islam, bureaucratic structures in the movement, and a lack of attention to the material problems of everyday life.

Hutchins, Vicky. (1992). "The Woman Question." *New Statesman and Society* 5, no. 232 (December), 16-17.
An overview of fragmentation in the feminist movement that surfaced at an international conference at the University of Sussex, England, celebrating two hundred years of feminism. These divisions include those between intellectuals and movement professionals, on one hand, and the mass support base, on the other, because of a focus on different issues and different types of discourse.

Jancar, Barbara. (1988). "Neofeminism in Yugoslavia: A Closer Look." *Women and Politics* 8, no. 1, 1-30.
As the country entered a period of protracted economic and social crisis in the mid-1970's, a modern feminist movement emerged and became increasingly militant in its challenge to the notion that socialism solved "the woman question." Although this article is out of date as reportage, it is still of historical interest in providing an example of the emergence of feminism within the Communist societies.

Kabeer, Naila. (1988). "Subordination and Struggle: Women in Bangladesh." *New Left Review* 168 (March/April), 95-121.
An excellent overview of the condition of women in a South Asian, predominantly Islamic country, as well as an assessment of the women's movement there. Given the poverty of the country, informal traditions of subordination, and the tendencies toward fundamentalist interpretations of Islam, women's organizations have to work within narrow margins. Reducing violence against women and improving

access to economic resources are priorities. Both autonomous feminist organizations and left-wing movements are engaged in these struggles.

Kesselman, Amy. (1991). "The 'Freedom Suit': Feminism and Dress Reform in the United States, 1848-1875." *Gender and Society* 5, no. 4 (December), 495-510.
The case of dress reform has theoretical implications for understanding tension between the politics of personal transformation and movements for political change. Dress reformers used an "exemplary action model" that called for courageous individuals to promote social change by undertaking personal changes in behavior.

Kimmel, Michael S. (1993). "Sexual Balkanization: Gender and Sexuality as the New Ethnicities." *Social Research* 60 (Fall), 571-587.
The author criticizes what he perceives to be a form of essentialism that is emerging in gay (and some feminist) discourse. These quasi-biological discourses lead into political strategies that fragment progressive movements. Essentialist discourses are incompatible with political efforts to develop a radical critique of gender inequality and heterosexism. Institutional change requires an underlying model of the social construction of institutions, not biological determination of individual behavior. Thought provoking.

McClain, Edwin. (1978). "Feminists and Nonfeminists: Contrasting Profiles in Independence and Affiliation." *Psychological Reports* 43, no. 2 (October), 435-441.
An effort to understand psychological correlates of feminist and nonfeminist attitudes of seventy-eight women, based on responses to a questionnaire and personality inventories.

Mackie, Vera. (1988). "Feminist Politics in Japan." *New Left Review* 167 (January/February), 53-76.
A good overview of feminism and women's movements in Japan, with attention to women's challenges to barriers in education and labor markets as well as historical continuity in debates about prostitution, an issue that now has transnational dimensions. Women also are a major force in peace and environmental movements.

Massell, Gregory. (1968). "Law as an Instrument of Revolutionary Change in a Traditional Milieu: The Case of Soviet Central Asia." *Law and Society Review* 2, 179-228.
An article with important theoretical conclusions concerning cultural and political barriers to implementing juridical changes at the grass-

roots level. The case study focuses specifically on laws that were designed to bring about gender equality in accordance with socialist ideology, in traditional, largely Islamic societies in the Soviet Central Asian republics. These laws often were ignored, circumvented, or politically negotiated into ineffectiveness. The article continues to be of interest in the contemporary climate of defining women's rights as human rights and seeking juridical change as a foundation of change in social relations.

Matsui, Machiko. (1990). "Evolution of the Feminist Movement in Japan." *NSWA Journal* 2, no. 3 (Summer), 435-449.
An overview of the history of the movement since the 1960's. The movement has moved from small decentralized grassroots groups to national and regional organizations. Concerns have expanded to include the condition of women in other Asian countries and the development of more sophisticated theoretical formulations.

Molyneux, Maxine. (1990). "The 'Woman Question' in the Age of Perestroika." *New Left Review* 183 (September/October), 23-49.
An excellent overview of the achievements and failures of the Communist systems (including China as well as the former Soviet Union and Eastern Europe) with regard to the emancipation of women. In the author's view, the record is mixed: Many traditional limitations in culture, the economy, and sexual rights were not forcefully addressed and ended. The transition to capitalism opens possibilities for autonomous feminist organizing but also undoes some of the economic and cultural advances achieved under socialism.

_____. (1991). "Interview with Anastasia Posadskaya." *Feminist Review* 39 (Winter), 133-140.
An interview that provides insight into the beginnings of an autonomous feminist movement in Russia, a movement that faces powerful odds in a climate of traditional misogyny, outdated ideas of femininity, and a weak economy.

Morgen, Sandra. (1990). "Contradictions in Feminist Practice: Individualism and Collectivism in a Feminist Health Center." *Comparative Social Research*, Suppl. 1, 9-59.
A case study of conflicting ideologies and bases of action, focused on the firing of a staff member defined as unable to function according to collective norms. In spite of the explicit emphasis on collectivism, the center functioned tacitly according to individualistic norms. The case

study gives insight into the role of ideology and patterns of conflict at the micro level of movements.

Oakley, Ann. (1987). "The Woman's Place." *New Society* 79, no. 1262 (March 6), 14-16.
A brief analysis of the effects of the feminist movement on British society. The author concludes that although many changes have taken place in marriage, the family, and women's labor force participation, ideology has not changed accordingly and remains highly traditional. State intervention in family life has reinforced patriarchal institutions. The feminist movement points out that society uses the ideology of the family to divide the sexes and perpetuate inequality.

Poole, Keith, and L. Harmon Ziegler. (1981). "The Diffusion of Feminist Ideology." *Political Behavior* 3, no. 3, 229-256.
Using 1972-1976 panel data from the National Election Studies, the authors conclude that three items regarding women's social and political equality gained awareness and support, including support from less advantaged social classes (vertical diffusion). As this expansion of attitudinal awareness and support increased, there also was increasing constraint between the items—that is, the items increasingly were seen as a connected package. This article is an empirical exploration of an important theoretical issue, the patterns of diffusion of ideology in mass publics.

Posadskaya, Anastasia. (1992). "Self-Portrait of a Russian Feminist." *New Left Review* 195 (September/October), 3-19.
The author discusses experiences that led her to feminism and prospects for a feminist movement in contemporary Russia.

Reeves, Joy. (1990). "A Structural Explanation of Why a Feminist Movement Has Not Developed in Indonesia." *Free Inquiry in Creative Sociology* 18, no. 2 (November), 181-189.
Janet Chafetz and Gary Dworkin's structural theoretical work is used together with an analysis of political institutions and ideologies in order to explain the virtual absence of a feminist movement. Interesting application of theory in a national case study.

Renzetti, Claire. (1987). "New Wave or Second Stage: Attitudes of College Women Toward Feminists." *Sex Roles* 16, no. 5-6 (March), 265-277.
The author administered an attitudinal inventory to 398 women at a small U.S. university. She found that although women support feminist

ideas and the notion of gender role equality and had positive attitudes toward the women's movements (and that all these attitudes are positively correlated with length of time in college), they do not call themselves feminists and believe women no longer need collective action to improve their position in society. This article supports informal and anecdotal evidence that the support base of feminism is not being mobilized effectively into movement participation.

Riger, Stephanie. (1983). "Vehicles for Empowerment: The Case of Feminist Movement Organizations." *Prevention in Human Services* 3, no. 2-3 (Winter/Spring), 99-117.
A good historical study of social service movement organizations associated with feminism. The author examines the short-lived nature of many of these organizations and specifies conditions that are conducive to greater organizational longevity.

Robinson, Jean C. (1985). "Of Women and Washing Machines: Employment, Housework, and the Reproduction of Motherhood in Socialist China." *China Quarterly* 101 (March), 32-57.
Although major strides in women's rights and opportunities were made following the Communist revolution, the regime tended to subordinate women's issues to development priorities, at some points bringing women into the labor force to increase production and at other times emphasizing their role in social reproduction. Increasing economic well-being and access to consumer goods have benefited women. The overall picture remains one of considerable social progress for women, but without any autonomous political power.

Rosenberg, Dorothy. (1991). "Shock Therapy: GDR Women in Transition from a Socialist Welfare State." *Signs* 17, no. 1 (Autumn), 129-151.
A review article that provides a feminist critique of gender policies in the GDR and analyzes problems that the feminist movement is having after unification in preserving positive features of the socialist system, such as legal and economic rights.

Sanger, Susan, and Henry Alker. (1972). "Dimensions of Internal-External Locus of Control and the Women's Liberation Movement." *Journal of Social Issues* 28, no. 4, 115-129.
On the basis of a factor analysis of responses from a sample of one hundred women, the authors conclude that the situation with respect to an internal or external sense of control is quite complex, with feminists both feeling that the condition of women needs to be transformed from its present state (demonstrating externality) and that it is

possible for their own efforts as activists to contribute to these changes (demonstrating internality). An empirical, psychologically oriented contribution to the agency and structure debate.

Sarti, Cynthia. (1989). "The Panorama of Brazilian Feminism." *New Left Review* 173 (January/February), 75-90.
An overview of women's movements in Brazil, their relationship to government and to the Left, and the cultural setting within which feminism develops.

Segura, Denise, and Beatriz Pesquera. (1989-1990). "Beyond Indifference and Apathy: The Chicana Movement and Chicana Feminist Discourse." *Aztlan* 19, no. 2 (Fall), 69-92.
The authors discuss a typology of Chicana feminist discourses (liberal, insurgent, and cultural nationalist). Drawing on a mail questionnaire from 101 Chicanas in higher education, they conclude that there are differences with respect to views of Chicano culture, gender oppression, and forms of political struggle among women who identify themselves as Chicana feminists. The recent history of relations between U.S. feminism and Chicano cultural nationalism is discussed.

Skjeie, Hege. (1991). "The Uneven Advance of Norwegian Women." *New Left Review* 187 (May/June), 79-102.
The author evaluates the situation of women in Norway, finding advances in the public sector (associated with left-of-center parties and policies) but relatively weak integration into corporations and the private sector in general. Shrinkage of welfare state functions could affect women negatively.

Snider, Laureen. (1990). "The Potential of the Criminal Justice System to Promote Feminist Concerns." *Studies in Law, Politics, and Society* 10, 143-172.
An examination of nineteenth and twentieth century reforms in criminal law (in areas such as prostitution, sexual violence, and delinquency) suggests that the aims of feminism have not been well promoted because such changes are oriented to the individual level, often strengthen state control and bureaucratic power, and target working- and lower-class women. A thought-provoking examination of the limits of reform.

Snitow, Ann. (1989). "Pages from a Gender Diary." *Dissent* (Spring), 205-224.

Included in a variety of personal observations on gender issues are some interesting remarks about women's movements of survival in Latin America.

Sorrentino, Constance. (1990). "The Changing Family in International Perspective." *Monthly Labor Review* 113, no. 3 (March), 41-58.
A short article that covers some of the institutionalized arrangements promoting gender equality that were implemented in the context of social democratic governments in the Nordic countries. Useful comparison with the more backward conditions in the United States.

Stamiris, Eleni. (1986). "The Women's Movement in Greece." *New Left Review* 158 (July/August), 98-112.
A report on the growth of feminism and women's movements in Greece, a European country with traditionally patriarchal institutions and a relatively low rate of female labor force participation. Although no longer up to date, it provides a useful interim account.

Stein, Arlene. (1992). "Sisters and Queers: The Decentering of Lesbian Feminism." *Socialist Review* 22, no. 1 (January-March), 33-55.
The author offers a critical history of lesbian feminism and suggests that the current greater interest in global issues and lesser focus on lesbian identity issues are positive developments in the lesbian feminist movement.

Sternbach, Nancy Saporta, Marysa Navarro Aranguren, Patricia Chuchryk, and Sonia Alvarez. (1992). "Feminisms in Latin America: From Bogota to San Bernardo." *Signs* 17, no. 2 (Winter), 393-434.
The authors discern a broad-based, heterogeneous, and active movement. They trace its history from the 1970's and discuss the Encuentros—biannual forums for activists—as a framework for providing an overview of the movement.

Stevens, Beth. (1988). "Women in Nicaragua." *Monthly Review* 40, no. 4 (September), 1-18.
An account of the situation of women in Nicaragua shortly before the defeat of the Sandinista government. Covers gains made during the Sandinista period as well as limitations.

Taylor, Verta, and Leila Rupp. (1993). "Women's Culture and Lesbian Feminist Activism: A Reconsideration of Cultural Feminism." *Signs* 19, no. 1 (Autumn), 32-61.
Although some feminists have conflated lesbian feminism and cultural feminism, accusing both of essentialism and separatism, a more nu-

anced analysis is necessary. Lesbian feminism is not necessarily essentialist. It often includes separatism as a strategy, but in a carefully limited way. The primacy of relationships between women can have both a political and an erotic meaning. Lesbian feminism offers feminist rituals associated with women's culture and celebrations. The authors use the lesbian feminist community in Columbus, Ohio, as an example of these characteristics and document some changes taking place, such as more playful, diversified, and pro-sex values and the formation of an ideology of Third Wave feminism. They emphasize that lesbian feminism offers a permanent community that sustains the values and goals of the larger women's movement during periods of abeyance; it has important political functions as a reservoir of feminist values. Good overview and analysis.

Tronto, Jean. (1991). "Changing Goals and Changing Strategies: Varieties of Women's Political Activism." *Feminist Studies* 17, no. 1 (Spring), 85-104.
A review article of books on women's political activism. Gains have been made, but what is still lacking is an overall political strategy that brings women together with other forces that challenge social inequalities and individualistic ideologies.

Vargas, Virginia. (1992). "The Feminist Movement in Latin America: Between Hope and Disenchantment." *Development and Change* 23, no. 3 (July), 195-214.
The author examines the proceedings of five post-1981 feminist conferences, in Peru, Colombia, Mexico, Brazil, and Argentina. She concludes that feminists are moving toward recognition and integration of diversity into the movement but that more needs to be done in this regard.

Watson, Peggy. (1993). "The Rise of Masculinism in Eastern Europe." *New Left Review* 198 (March/April), 71-82.
The author discusses the rise of masculinism as a counterideology to feminism in the former Communist states. This misogynistic ideology attacks those gains in women's rights and progress toward gender equality that were made during the Communist period and seeks to undo these reforms. Useful for understanding the dynamics of a countermovement.

West, Lois. (1992). "Feminist Nationalist Social Movements: Beyond Universalism and Towards a Gendered Cultural Relativism." *Women's*

Studies International Forum 15, no. 5-6 (September-December), 563-579.

Using the feminist-nationalist movement in the Philippines as an example, the author argues that feminism can be reconciled with nationalism and cultural particularism, especially in identity rights movements and struggles against colonialism and neocolonialism.

White, Kendall. (1985). "A Feminist Challenge: 'Mormons for ERA' as an Internal Movement." *Journal of Ethnic Studies* 13, no. 1 (Spring), 29-50.

Using a resource mobilization model, the author looks at the relationship between MERA and other institutions within the Mormon community as well as MERA's relationship to the feminist movement.

Women's Studies International Quarterly. (1981). Volume 4, no. 4.

Articles on women's movements in France, The Netherlands, and Germany, tracing their emergence and their role as elements of the New Social Movements. Useful historical baseline material.

Also of Interest

Bonepath, Ellen, ed. (1982). *Women, Power and Policy.* New York: Pergamon.

Bouchier, David. (1984). *The Feminist Challenge.* New York: Schocken.

Bystydzienski, Jill. (1992). *Women Transforming Politics.* Bloomington: Indiana University Press.

Cruikshank, Margaret. (1992). *The Gay and Lesbian Liberation Movement.* New York: Routledge.

Duberman, Martin. (1994). *Stonewall.* New York: Plume.

Ferree, Myra Marx, and Beth B. Hess. (1985). *Controversy and Coalition: The New Feminist Movement.* Boston: Twayne.

Gelb, Joyce. (1989). *Feminism and Politics: A Comparative Perspective.* Berkeley: University of California Press.

Kuppers, Gaby. (1994). *Compañeras: Voices from the Latin American Women's Movement.* New York: Monthly Review Press.

Chapter 12
ENVIRONMENTAL MOVEMENTS

This chapter covers movements that are concerned with the relationships between human activity and other processes on the planet. They focus on issues such as pollution, waste disposal, topsoil and water depletion, declining biodiversity, population growth and its impact on the environment, animal rights, nuclear power development, global warming, and ozone layer depletion. They approach these issues from a number of different perspectives. Some ideologies are markedly more anthropocentric than are others, in that they are concerned primarily with the future of humanity; other ideologies reject this view and claim to represent Earth or the biosphere as a whole. There also are divisions between various combined movements, such as ecofeminism, eco-anarchism, ecosocialism, and so on. NIMBYs ("not in my backyard") defend local interests. Some movements work primarily within existing political and economic institutions, whereas others are more committed to direct action or to developing alternative sustainable economies. Powerful countermovements, representing industries and property owners, have formed.

Books and Book Chapters

Abbey, Edward. (1975). *The Monkeywrench Gang*. New York: Avon.
  In a work of the imagination, the author calls for direct action—some might say sabotage—in defense of the environment. A classic work of the radical side of the movement.

Adams, Carol, ed. (1993). *Ecofeminism and the Sacred*. New York: Continuum.
  Articulation of an ideology that develops the convergence of feminist opposition to dominance and hierarchy, goals of respecting the environment, and spiritual values.

Biehl, Janet. (1991). *Rethinking Ecofeminist Politics*. Boston: South End Press.
  The author discusses the ideas of ecofeminism from a critical point of view. The following elements of ecofeminism are identified as problematic: antimale bias and an essentialist notion of "women's values"; moralistic obscurantism; New Age mysticism and a celebration of the irrational; a "neolithic mystique"; and neovitalism, which has been

used historically to defend inequality. Her own environmentalist position is one of gender equality, participatory democracy, criticism of capitalism, and an emphasis on citizenship in the *polis*. Her view of humanity is more dialectical, evolutionary, and historical than are the positions she finds in ecofeminism. A thought-provoking discussion of environmental ideologies.

Bookchin, Murray. (1990). *Remaking Society: Pathways to a Green Future*. Boston: South End Press.
An important statement by an eco-anarchist who calls for an environmental movement that breaks with the logic of capitalist and state socialist exploitation of nature, but without a rejection of secular, rational, and humanistic values.

Bullard, Robert. (1990). *Dumping in Dixie: Race, Class, and Environmental Quality*. Boulder, CO: Westview Press.
A major study of the uneven impact of environmental pollution in the U.S. South. As "environmental racism" became more evident—the locating of waste sites and polluting industrial processes near communities of people of color as well as working-class people of all ethnic backgrounds—the environmental movement expanded its support base from a largely white, educated, middle-class base to new, more immediately threatened constituencies.

Campbell, John. (1988). *Collapse of an Industry*. Ithaca, NY: Cornell University Press.
Documents the decline of the nuclear industry in the United States, in part as the result of the action of environmentalists and their role in making the public aware of the costs of nuclear power development.

Carson, Rachel. (1962). *Silent Spring*. Boston: Houghton-Mifflin.
One of the first books directed to a mass readership that drew attention to the effects of pesticides on the environment. It helped spark a new wave of environmental action, restarting a movement that had been dormant since the conservation movement of the turn of the century.

Commoner, Barry. (1990). *Making Peace with the Planet*. New York: Pantheon.
A statement of concern about the environment and discussion of needed programs and policies, by a leading activist.

Davis, John, and David Foreman. (1991). *The Earth First Reader: Ten Years of Radical Environmentalism.* Salt Lake City, UT: Peregrine Smith.

Essays that reflect radical environmental positions and concerns.

Devall, Bill, and George Sessions. (1985). *Deep Ecology.* Salt Lake City, UT: Peregrine Smith.

A statement of a radical environmental position that questions the anthropocentric view of more mainstream environmentalists and considers direct action in defense of the environment.

Diamond, Irene, and Gloria Orenstein, eds. (1990). *Reweaving the World: The Emergence of Eco-Feminism.* San Francisco: Sierra Club Books.

Statements from a perspective that associates feminism's opposition to dominance, hierarchy, and violence with environmental themes.

Ehrenfeld, David. (1978). *The Arrogance of Humanism.* New York: Oxford University Press.

A relatively early statement that criticizes anthropocentric views of nature and humanity. Anthropocentrism evaluates actions (such as the eradication of the smallpox virus) in terms of outcomes for human beings, not in terms of a biocentric or Earth-centered frame of reference in which humans do not have claims to survival that are more legitimate than those of other species.

Faber, Daniel. (1993). *Environment Under Fire: Imperialism and the Ecological Crisis in Central America.* New York: Monthly Review Press.

Military regimes, the forms of economic development they promote, and the general pattern of dependent regional specialization in agro-export commodities are causing a growing environmental crisis in Central America, with destruction of forests.

Flavin, Christopher. (1987). *Reassessing Nuclear Power: The Fallout from Chernobyl.* Washington, DC: World Watch Institute.

Covers some of the scientific issues associated with the disaster at Chernobyl (former Soviet Union, now Ukraine) and briefly documents the growing opposition to nuclear power in Western Europe.

Foreman, Dave. (1991). *Confessions of an Eco-Warrior.* New York: New Harmony.

Personal memoirs of a radical environmental activist.

Foreman, David, and Bill Haywood, eds. (1987). *Ecodefense: A Field Guide to Monkeywrenching*. Tucson, AZ: Ned Ludd Books.
Some tips for radical environmentalists who might be interested in getting involved in direct action against environmental abuse.

Gorz, Andre. (1985). *Paths to Paradise*. Boston: South End Press.
This engaging little quasi-utopian book depicts a possible future of sustainable development, a healthy environment, and liberation from work.

Hecht, Susanna, and Alexander Cockburn. (1989). *The Fate of the Forest: Developers, Destroyers and Defenders of the Amazon*. London: Verso-Routledge.
The authors describe the destruction of the Amazon forest by developers, ranchers, miners, timber companies, and so on, as well as the growth of local environmental activism, often at great risk of violence to those who undertake the defense of the forest.

Hulsberg, Werner. (1988). *The German Greens: A Social and Political Profile*. New York: Verso.
Analyzes the growth and strategies of the German environmental movement/party, one of the largest in Europe.

Jasper, James, and Dorothy Nelkin. (1993). *The Animal Rights Crusade*. New York: Free Press.
The authors cover the growth of the animal rights movement, its key issues—such as lab testing, animal fur as clothing, and the destruction of dolphins—and the major animal rights organizations (most notably, People for the Ethical Treatment of Animals). They discuss the elements that contributed to the movement ideology, including New Age ideas, civil rights discourses, and a distrust of instrumentalism. In moving from a position of "compassion" and "animal protection" to one of "animal rights," the movement has become more fundamentalist (the authors' term) and crusadelike; it uses dramatic discursive framing and demonization of opponents.

Lovelock, James. (1988). *The Ages of Gaia: A Biography of Our Living Earth*. New York: Norton.
Introduces the concept of Gaia, the totality of Earth's biological and physical processes viewed as a system. The concept is favored by some environmental activists.

Merchant, Carol. (1992). *Radical Ecology: The Search for a Livable World*. New York: Routledge.
An excellent overview of a wide range of radical ecological/environmental ideologies, including ecofeminism, deep ecology, and ecosocialism.

Nelkin, Dorothy. (1971). *Nuclear Power and Its Critics: The Cayuga Lake Controversy*. Ithaca, NY: Cornell University Press.
A case study of activism against nuclear power.

Paehlke, Robert C. (1989). *Environmentalism and the Future of Progressive Politics*. New Haven, CT: Yale University Press.
The author provides a discussion of the ideas of environmentalism and explores where it lies on the political spectrum. He decides that it is closest to a moderate-progressive position but is not incompatible with a certain type of conservative thought that emphasizes limits, self-restraint, and the good of the whole. Includes Canadian as well as U.S. examples.

Papadikis, Elim. (1984). *The Green Movement in West Germany*. London: Croom Helm.
Good theoretical analysis of the origins and early phases of contemporary environmentalism in Germany, as the Greens formed a party and entered electoral politics.

Parkin, Francis. (1968). *Middle Class Radicalism: The Social Bases of the British Campaign for Nuclear Disarmament*. Manchester, England: University of Manchester Press.
The author studied the CND, a movement that in many ways was a prototype of both the New Left and later New Social Movement activism, and found that supporters were both middle class and left of center. This study is an early documentation of the postwar shift of left radicalism from a working-class mass base to a support base in the middle strata.

Peterson, D. J. (1993). *Troubled Lands: The Legacy of Soviet Environmental Destruction*. Boulder, CO: Rand.
Documentation of extensive pollution and environmental disasters in the former Soviet Union, many of them associated with weapons testing and poorly planned industrial and agricultural development.

Price, Jerome. (1990). *The Antinuclear Movement*. Boston: Twayne/G. K. Hall.

An excellent, readable, and comprehensive overview of the movement, including summaries of sociological research, identification of major themes and issues, and a review of work on pronuclear countermovements.

Sale, Kirkpatrick. (1993). *The Green Revolution: The Environmental Movement Since 1962*. New York: Hill and Wang.

An excellent, readable overview of the movement, from a perspective that is sympathetic but not uncritical. The author begins with a time line of events and organizations. The analysis covers the origins of the movement, the 1960's, the "doomsday" discourses of the 1970's, the Reagan reaction, and the emergence of radical ecological ideologies. The author offers an incisive analysis of problems of the movement, including structural and institutional limitations. At the level of ideology, he sees a need to connect the NIMBYs to mainstream activism and piecemeal reform to larger systemic issues. The movement also has to deal with a tendency to define it as a "special interest," participating mostly in lobbying and electoral politics. The shortest, but the most analytic and critical, of the overviews of U.S. environmentalism.

Scheffer, Victor. (1991). *The Shaping of Environmentalism in America*. Seattle: University of Washington Press.

After reviewing a number of environmental problems, the author discusses the history of the movement—especially in the 1970's—its growth, and its relationship to other movements. The focus is on citizens' groups and mobilizations.

Shabecoff, Philip. (1993). *A Fierce Green Fire: The American Environmental Movement*. New York: Hill and Wang.

A readable, nontechnical account of the rise and growth of the movement. Coverage includes the period of the Reagan counterrevolution and the expansion and diversification of the movement into new communities by the late 1980's. The author describes some of this expansion and reformulation as a "third wave" of environmentalism that is exploring a wide spectrum of new approaches such as market solutions, more radical action, and links to social equity movements. Social bases and organizational forms also are becoming more diversified.

Periodical Articles

Baugh, Joyce. (1991). "African Americans and the Environment: A Review Essay." *Policy Studies Journal* 19, no. 2 (Spring), 181-191.
A review essay on evidence that African American communities (as well as the poor and working class of all ethnic backgrounds) have borne a disproportionate share of environmental damage. The essay also covers their growing involvement in the movement. Organizational structure and strategies are discussed. The work of Robert Bullard on environmental racism is highlighted.

Benton, Ted. (1992). "Ecology, Socialism and the Mastery of Nature." *New Left Review* 194 (July/August), 55-74.
The author argues that even though Communist states caused environmental damage, ultimately socialism is more congruent with ecological values and goals than is capitalism.

Cockburn, Alexander. (1989). "Trees, Cows and Cocaine: An Interview with Susanna Hecht." *New Left Review* 173 (January/February), 34-45.
The interview covers the destruction of the Amazon rain forest, the economic dislocations in Latin America that have led to the extension of coca farming, and movements in the region to protect the environment.

_____. (1993). "'Win-Win' with Bruce Babbit: The Clinton Administration Meets the Environment." *New Left Review* 201 (September/October), 46-59.
The author presents a sarcastic picture of compromises that the Clinton Administration made with anti-environmental forces, especially in the timber and ranching industries. The article also contains interesting reflections on the way major industries "think ahead" of the movement and manage to move their operations into areas where opposition is weak.

Connell, Robert. (1990). "A Whole New World: Remaking Masculinity in the Context of the Environmental Movement." *Gender and Society* 4, no. 4 (December), 452-478.
The author interviewed six men involved in the Australian environmental movement. The interviews reveal a process of disengagement from hegemonic masculinity and the attempt to undo oedipal masculinization while moving toward collective politics. The discussion gives insight into the interconnection between environmental activism and new forms of gender practice.

Davis, Mike. (1993). "The Dead West: Ecocide in Marlboro Country." *New Left Review* 200 (July/August), 49-73.
The author describes environmental problems in the U.S. West, especially those associated with nuclear and chemical weapons testing. He also touches on growing environmental activism in local communities, including Mormons and Native Americans.

Devall, Bill. (1991). "Deep Ecology and Radical Environmentalism." *Society and Natural Resources* 4, no. 3 (July-September), 247-258.
The author gives an overview of a number of major environmental groups, including Earth First!, Greenpeace, the Sea Shepherd Society, and the Rainforest Action Network, outlining organization, strategies, and tactics. The countermovement to the environmental movement is considered, and the prospects for the radical environmental movement as a whole are discussed.

Dunlap, Riley, and Angela Mertig. (1991). "The Evolution of the U.S. Environmental Movement from 1970 to 1990: An Overview." *Society and Natural Resources* 4, no. 3 (July-September), 209-218.
The article provides an overview of the contents of the special issue on the environmental movement marking the twentieth anniversary of the first Earth Day. The authors emphasize the growing diversity of the movement.

Foster, John. (1993). "The Limits of Environmentalism Without Class: Lessons from the Ancient Forest Struggle of the Pacific Northwest." *Capitalism, Nature, Socialism* 4, no. 1 (March), 11-41.
The author argues that ecological destruction is inherent in capitalist accumulation. Using the example of the timber industry and the environmental movement in the Pacific Northwest, he argues that the movement must give attention to the social class context of environmental issues and consider strategies for ecological conversion that are rooted in an awareness of local and global social inequality.

Freudenberg, Nicolas, and Carol Steinsapir. (1991). "Not in Our Backyards: The Grassroots Environmental Movement." *Society and Natural Resources* 4, no. 3 (July-September), 235-245.
The authors discuss the expansion of the environmental movement, which increasingly encompassed local activism, a broader cross section of ethnic and class support bases, and women as leaders. Grassroots groups are likely to see their efforts as protection of public health. They express some distrust of experts in government and scientific institutions. Their accomplishments are notable (cleanup of contami-

nated sites, blocking of polluting projects, and a preventive approach to environmental problems). The authors defend the role of local groups and criticize the negative view that some observers express about the "not in my backyard" perspective.

Galtung, Johan. (1986). "The Green Movement: A Socio-historical Exploration." *International Sociology* 1, no. 1 (March), 75-90.
The green movement is analyzed in a broad historical perspective, in terms of its recruitment profiles, its ability to serve as an umbrella for a variety of new partial movements and currents (peace, ecology, and women's movements), and its role as the fourth phase in a series of major political transformations of Western societies (church-state separation, bourgeois hegemony, and working-class inclusion being the preceding ones). A valuable and theoretically provocative macro level overview.

Hay, P. R., and M. Haward. (1988). "Comparative Green Politics: Beyond the European Context?" *Political Studies* 36, no. 3 (September), 433-448.
Contrasts European green politics to its counterparts in North America and Australia/New Zealand, arguing that differences in political culture and opportunity structure have created differences in the movements.

Hecht, Susanna. (1989). "Chico Mendes: Chronicle of a Death Foretold." *New Left Review* 173 (January/February), 47-55.
The author reviews the work of Chico Mendes, a rubber tapper in Acre, Brazil, who sought to secure the integrity of the forest as a source of life for forest workers and indigenous people. Murdered by ranchers, he has become a symbol of the expansion of environmental activism to larger, more economically marginal support bases.

Hutton, Drew. (1992). "From the Moral High Ground to Political Power: Environmental Ethics and Green Politics." *Social Alternatives* 11, no. 3 (October), 13-15.
The author discusses the shift in Australian environmentalism from an outsider activism to increasingly institutionalized forms focused on public policy and coalition building.

Kitschelt, Herbert. (1986). "Political Opportunity Structures and Political Protest: Anti-Nuclear Movements in Four Democracies." *British Journal of Political Science* 16, 57-85.

An important theoretical article that looks at the structure of environmental movements in terms of the political systems in which they operate. The movements in the relatively open systems of Sweden and the United States accommodated themselves more to working within these systems, whereas in the more closed political structures of Germany and France, they were more confrontational.

Lange, Jonathan. (1990). "The Refusal to Compromise: The Case of Earth First!" *Western Journal of Speech Communication* 54, no. 4 (Fall), 473-494.

An interesting puzzle for social movements has been whether bizarre, destructive, offensive, and uncompromising behavior and rhetoric are always detrimental to a movement or whether such discourses and practices can be used to draw public attention to the irrationalities of the status quo. The author explores this issue in a case study of a radical environmental group, with emphasis on its rhetoric, its culture, and its self-representation in its main communication link, a newsletter/journal.

Lincoln, David. (1991). "Despatches from a Natural Site of Struggle: Environmentalism in a 'New' South Africa." *South African Sociological Review* 4, no. 1 (October), 2-12.

The author describes the emergence of the environmental movement in South Africa and discusses structural constraints and economic and political processes that might limit further growth of the movement.

McCloskey, Michael. (1991). "Twenty Years of Change in the Environmental Movement: An Insider's View." *Society and Natural Resources* 4, no. 3 (July-September), 273-284.

The author reviews the literature on the movement and draws the conclusion that it has now divided into three currents—radical, mainstream, and accommodationist—distinguished by their attitudes toward government and industry, by their goals, and by their strategies and tactics. He suggests a need for improved communication among these three currents and emphasizes the importance of green consumerism as a way of directly influencing corporate behavior, rather than consistently relying on governmental regulation as the main strategy of protecting the environment. An interesting analytical overview.

Matthiessen, Peter. (1991). "The Blue Pearl of Siberia." *The New York Review of Books* 38 (February 14), 37-47.

Describes the growing environmental movement in Russia, its focus on Lake Baikal as an endangered zone, and its reactionary and obscurantist as well as progressive ideological themes.

Mitchell, R. C. (1981). "From Elite Quarrel to Mass Movement." *Society* 18, no. 5, 76-84.
Analyzes the growth of the movement against nuclear power from its origin as a dispute among scientists to a movement with a mass base.

O'Connor, James, and T. Barry. (1992). "Red Green Politics." *Capitalism, Nature, Socialism* 3, no. 4 (December), 1-17.
Prospects for an alliance between socialists and environmentalists are discussed, at a global level (O'Connor) and in Ireland (Barry).

Pettit, Dean, and Jerry Paul Sheppard. (1992). "It's Not Easy Being Green: The Limits of Green Consumerism in Light of the Logic of Collective Action." *Queen's Quarterly* 99, no. 2 (Summer), 328-350.
Using Mancur Olson's theoretical work, the authors discuss green consumerism as a movement strategy and note reasons for engagement and apathy.

Research in Social Movements, Conflicts, and Change: Supplement 2. (1992).
This issue contains articles that describe environmental activism in a number of countries and regions (Brazil, Japan, Asia, the United States, the USSR, and Eastern Europe) and analyze it in global perspective, especially in terms of differences between its form in the North and South, the formation of nongovernmental organizations, and new types of coalitions.

Rootes, Chris. (1992). "The New Politics and the New Social Movements: Accounting for British Exceptionalism." *European Journal of Political Research* 22, no. 2 (August), 171-191.
The political opportunity structure of Great Britain has constrained the formation of the environmental movement. The movement is both less radical and less effectively organized as a party than are the movements in continental Western Europe. The Labour Party became the vehicle for environmental activism. The article provides a good example of the use of political opportunity structure theory to account for national differences in the form of a transnational movement.

Sarkar, Saral. (1986). "The Green Movement in West Germany." *Alternatives* 11, no. 2 (April), 219-254.

The author traces the history of the movement over a fifteen-year period, from its origins to a shift in the mid-1970's, when the ideology became increasingly critical of "the system," and later to a phase of electoral involvement. The author predicts (accurately, it turns out) that the movement may have a difficult future because of changing attitudes in its middle-class voting base.

Schmid, Carol. (1987). "The Green Movement in West Germany: Resource Mobilization and Institutionalization." *Journal of Political and Military Sociology* 15, no. 1 (Spring), 33-46.
The author analyzes resources and constraints associated with the German political structure to explain the form of the environmental movement and its electoral victories in the 1980's.

Sherkat, Darren, and Jean Blocker. (1993). "Environmental Activism in the Protest Generation: Differentiating 1960's Activists." *Youth and Society* 25, no. 1 (September), 140-161.
A discussion of differences and similarities in social background and socialization patterns of two categories of 1960's activists: community environmentalists and others (civil rights, antiwar, and student protesters). The data are based on more than fifteen hundred high school students and their parents and provide insights into individual and family-level processes.

Taylor, Dorcetta. (1993). "Minority Environmental Activism in Britain: From Brixton to the Lake District." *Qualitative Sociology* 16, no. 3 (Fall), 263-295.
Minority participation in the British environmental movement is growing slowly. Up until now, ethnic minorities have not been included in white environmental organizations and have not benefited directly from public funds for countryside and wildlife preservation. Issues of environmental racism and city development projects are beginning to involve people of color in various aspects of the larger movement.

Useem, Bert, and Mayer Zald. (1982). "From Pressure Group to Social Movement: Organizational Dilemmas of the Effort to Promote Nuclear Power." *Social Problems* 30, no. 2, 144-156.
An important theoretical article on the formation of a countermovement to the antinuclear movement. The analysis focuses on efforts to establish the legitimacy of the pronuclear movement as a social movement using strategies such as recruiting women and African Americans as symbols of grassroots involvement and appealing to the value of American independence from foreign energy sources.

Van der Heijden, Hein Anton, Ruud Koopmans, and Marco Giugni. (1992). "The West European Environmental Movement." *Research in Social Movements, Conflicts, and Change* Suppl. 2, 1-40.

The authors make a strong case for the role of political opportunity structures in shaping the forms, discourses, and outcomes of movements. Using newspaper reports on environmental actions in four countries (France, Germany, The Netherlands, and Switzerland), the authors test the hypothesis that changes in country-specific political preconditions are a major factor in movement activism, which mediates and modifies other factors such as ecological and cultural conditions. The authors found that national branches of major transnational associations such as Greenpeace, Friends of the Earth, and the World Wildlife Fund are among the most important actors in the West European environmental movement.

Walsh, Edward. (1988). "New Dimensions of Social Movements: The High-Level Waste-Siting Controversy." *Sociological Forum* 3, 586-605.

Western European New Social Movement theory defines the novelty of contemporary collective action in terms of changes in the nature of the capitalist state and in value systems of citizens. Here the authors suggest that the most important new feature of environmental movements and, more broadly, "technology movements" is the type of problems that they address—the long-term and irreversible catastrophic potential of certain technological changes such as creation of nuclear waste sites.

Walsh, Edward, Rex Warland, and Clayton Smith. (1993). "Backyards, NIMBYs, and Incinerator Sitings: Implications for Social Movement Theory." *Social Problems* 40 (February), 25-38.

The authors conducted a survey study of residents at two locations to understand why activists defeated the building of an incinerator at one site but not at the other. The data are used to develop the concept of "technology movements" with characteristics that are distinct from those of equity movements of minority populations.

Yanitsky, Oleg. (1991). "Environmental Movements: Some Conceptual Issues in East-West Comparisons." *International Journal of Urban and Regional Research* 15, no. 4 (December), 524-541.

The author discusses differences in the forms of the two movements that developed in the two opposing blocs. In the East, movements saw the "administrative-command system" as the main opponent and had to operate in a political system that did not accord civil rights to citizens. Now that Russia is moving toward a market economy, environmental movements may actually experience a period of decline as they readjust their strategies and goals to new problems and opportunities.

Yearly, Steven. (1992). "Green Ambivalence About Science: Legal-Rational Authority and the Scientific Legitimation of a Movement." *British Journal of Sociology* 43, no. 4 (December), 511-532.
Using case study data, the author explores the paradox that environmental movements rely on scientific data but are distrustful of scientific authority, expertise, and technology.

Also of Interest

Adato, Michael, and the Union of Concerned Scientists. (1987). *Safety Second: The NRC and America's Power Plants*. Bloomington: Indiana University Press.

Brown, Michael, and John May. (1991). *The Greenpeace Story*. New York: Dorling Kindirsly.

Druce, Nell. (1990). *Green Globalism: Perspectives on Environment and Development*. Oxford, England: Third World First.

Fradkin, Philip. (1989). *Fallout: An American Nuclear Tragedy*. Tucson: University of Arizona Press.

Freudenberg, N. (1984). *"Not in Our Backyards!" Community Action for Health and the Environment*. New York: Monthly Review Press.

Fuller, John. (1984). *The Day We Bombed Utah: America's Most Lethal Secret*. New York: NAL.

Gallagher, Carole. (1993). *American Ground Zero: The Secret Nuclear War*. Boston: MIT Press.

Gorz, Andre. (1993). "Political Ecology: Expertocracy Versus Self Limitation." *New Left Review* 202 (November/December), 55-67.

McDermott, Jeanne. (1987). *The Killing Winds: The Menace of Biological Warfare*. New York: Morrow.

Medvedev, Zhores. (1979). *Nuclear Disaster in the Urals*. New York: Norton.

_____. (1990. *The Legacy of Chernobyl*. New York: Norton.

_____. (1990). *The Legacy of Chernobyl*. New York: Norton.

Parsons, Howard. (1977). *Marx and Engels on Ecology*. Westport, CT: Greenwood.

Rensenbrink, John. (1992). *The Greens and the Politics of Transformation*. San Pedro, CA: R. and E. Miles.

Touraine, Alain, Zsuzska Hegedus, Francois Dubet, and Michael Weviorka. (1982). *Anti-Nuclear Protest: The Opposition to Nuclear Energy in France*. Cambridge, England: Cambridge University Press.

Wallace, Aubrey. (1993). *Eco-Heroes*. San Francisco: Mercury House.

PART III

SOCIAL MOVEMENTS IN FILMS AND NOVELS

Chapter 13
SOCIAL MOVEMENTS IN FEATURE FILMS, DOCUMENTARIES, AND NOVELS

Social Movements in the Lens of the Camera

Documentaries and feature films reflect the social movements and ideologies of their times, as well as the movements they explicitly portray. Film representations are always "through a glass, darkly" because the movement is transformed by the director's imagination, the actors' choices, the pressures of the box office and the market, and the demands of producers who are in turn responding to their own notions about the market (or perhaps to government censors). The climate of the times inevitably shapes the style and content of a film; thus, films cannot be taken as "reality" but only as images of it, images that tell as much or more about the conditions of creative production as they do about actual historical times and movements portrayed.

Classic works of cinema dating from before World War II take sharply opposed views of fascism and communism. *Potemkin* (1925), based on a rebellion by sailors of the Black Sea fleet early in the century, and *Ten Days That Shook the World* (1928, also known as *October*), based on John Reed's sympathetic account of the Bolshevik Revolution, are Soviet director Sergei Eisenstein's tributes to revolutionary forces in Russia. *Kühle Wampe* (1932), available only in an incomplete print, is a salute by playwright Bertold Brecht (and others) to the German Communist Party on the eve of the Nazi takeover. Leni Riefenstahl celebrates Hitler and the Nazis in *Triumph of the Will* (1935), a tediously fascinating film of a party rally. Among classics of the cinema that deal with social movements, it is probably also necessary to mention, if not recommend, the thoroughly reprehensible work of D. W. Griffith, *Birth of a Nation* (1915), which depicts the formation of the Ku Klux Klan in favorable terms.

During and after World War II, filmmakers continued to give attention to ideological conflicts. One of the first World War II-era films with this type of subject matter was *For Whom the Bell Tolls* (1943), based on Ernest Hemingway's novel and its sympathetic treatment of the Spanish Republic's fight for survival against the invasion of General Francisco Franco. *Salt of the Earth* (1953) describes the struggle of Mexican American miners for better living conditions. *Paisà* (1946; also released as *Paisan*) and *Roma, Città Aperta* (1945; also released as *Rome, Open City*) provide a near-documentary form for the story of the partisans in the Italian resistance to fascist rule and German occupation. *All the King's Men* (1949) offers a fictionalized and rather critical portrait of the populist currents that swept Huey Long into the governorship of Louisiana.

The onset of the Cold War led to the casting of conflicts largely in terms of Communism versus anti-Communism. Films such as *My Son John* (1952) and *The Manchurian Candidate* (1962) use the theme of a threat posed by Communist movements and regimes to the United States. Emile d'Antonio's *Point of Order*, a documentary made after the peak of the Cold War, includes footage of the Army-McCarthy hearings and the final discomfiture of Senator Joseph McCarthy. A distant reflection of the American Communist movement appears in *The Way We Were* (1973), a romance about the lifelong entanglement of a left-wing Jewish activist and her bourgeois, WASP lover.

The "second cold war," as some termed a period of increased friction between the United States and the Soviet Union in the 1980's, was marked by an escalation of the arms race and a round of U.S.-backed counterinsurgencies. It became the impetus for films such as Sylvester Stallone's Rambo series, celebrating counterinsurgencies, and the political fantasy *Red Dawn* (1984), in which young Americans rebel against a Soviet occupation of the country. Less action packed but more thought-provoking criticisms of "real socialism" were made by directors within Communist countries, as were Andrzej Wajda's *Man of Iron* (1980) and *Man of Marble* (1977), or were based on works of dissidents and exiles, such as *The Unbearable Lightness of Being* (1988), a film version of the novel by Czech émigré Milan Kundera. In the 1990's, Gianni Amelio's *Lamerica* (1995) offered heartrending images of Albania as the final nightmare ending of the Communist dream.

As movements of the New Left came to prominence in both Western Europe and the United States, films appeared that depicted student movements and the growing restiveness of young workers. *La Chinoise* (1967, Jean-Luc Godard) and *La Cina é vicina* (1967, Marco Bellocchio; also released as *China Is Near*) explore the wanna-be Maoism of European youth in a somewhat tongue-in-cheek manner. Equally satiric is *The Working Class Goes to Heaven* (1971), which presents the tribulations of an Italian automobile worker as the visionary hopes and emancipatory dreams of the late 1960's faded away.

Third World revolutions, national liberation movements, Latin American guerrilla insurgencies, and counterinsurgencies were the topics of several films. One of the most notable of these is *Battle of Algiers* (1965, G. Pontecorvo), a fictional re-creation of urban terrorism and counterterrorism in Algeria that has the look of documentary footage in its portrayal of bombings by the nationalist insurgency and torture carried out by the French armed forces. Constantin Costa-Gavras' *State of Siege* (1973), based on the left-wing guerrilla insurgency in Uruguay, presents a more ambiguous picture of self-defined revolutionaries. His earlier *Z* (1969) is a gripping, lightly fictionalized reference to Greece under the regime of the right-wing colonels. *Memories of Underdevelopment* (1968) deals with a middle-class Cuban intellectual's reluctance to come to terms with the revolution; while reflecting the Cuban government's criticism of such a position, the film also develops a degree of sympathy with the hero. More directly propagandistic but visually stunning is *I Am Cuba* (1964), a Soviet-Cuban coproduction that traces the lives and deaths of revolutionaries against the Batista regime.

As the guerrilla insurgencies and revolutionary regimes of the 1970's increasingly gave way to counterinsurgencies, these too were captured in more or less fictionalized form. *Missing* (1982) tells the story of the 1973 Pinochet coup in Chile; it focuses on the fate of a U.S. citizen and the family members who search desperately for him. *The Official Story* (1985) is based on the "dirty war" in Argentina, with its disappearances and kidnappings carried out by the military against activists, intellectuals, and union members. Told in the format of a "woman's movie," it allows the political analysis to unfold through a middle-aged, middle-class woman's tale of personal discovery, family conflict, and impending heartbreak. Also based on the Argentinean dirty war (though cinematically transposed to Brazil) is *Kiss of the Spider Woman* (1985), in which two imprisoned men, one of them gay and one of them leftist, come to share their dreams of liberation.

The experiences of fascism, Nazism, the Resistance, and World War II continued to grip filmmakers, who returned to these experiences in many forms. In this context, particularly noteworthy are Bernardo Bertolucci's 1971 *The Conformist* (the psychosexual foundations of fascist obedience) and 1976 *1900* (a sweeping Italian *Gone with the Wind* that covers forty-five years of Italian history and the decline and fall of the class of large landowners after their involvement with fascism); Louis Malle's *Lacombe, Lucien* (1974), a miniature about French collaboration with the Nazis; and *Army of Shadows* (1969) and Francois Truffaut's *The Last Metro* (1980), both about the Resistance. Ettore Scola's *C'eravamo tanto amati* (1975; released as *We All Loved Each Other So Much*, 1977) offers a story about the postwar breakup of the Resistance coalition of Communists, the non-Communist left, and centrist forces, each represented by one of the three male leads whose comradeship and friendship gradually fade away as each responds to the demands of his own social position.

Resistance to the Japanese occupation, the role of this resistance in the Chinese Communist revolution, and the engagement of women in the resistance are the subjects of a more recent, very powerful Chinese movie, *Red Sorghum* (1987). *Night and Fog* (1956), *The Sorrow and the Pity* (1970), and *Shoah* (1985) use documentary techniques to confront Nazi genocide and the record of European collaboration with the Nazis. Quite different in tone is A. Holland's *Europa, Europa* (1991), a postmodern Holocaust comedy about the misadventures and secret identity of a Jewish boy. In typically postmodern fashion, it deconstructs and satirizes the Nazi project of racial identity. *To Die in Madrid* (1965, documentary) and Alain Resnais' *La Guerre est Finie* (1966) returned to the story of the Spanish Civil War, now seeing it from a position of historical distance. A similar elegiac tone was set in *The Good Fight* (1983), a U.S. documentary on North Americans who had fought on the side of the Republic.

The Civil Rights movement and subsequent movements of African Americans received attention in films, although until recently Hollywood was reluctant to feature anyone other than a white man as the hero of the narrative. For example, *Mississippi Burning* (1988) featured white FBI agents investigating the murder of civil rights workers. *The Long Walk Home* (1990) diverged from this formula by focusing on two women caught up in the Montgomery bus boycott in the mid-1950's, a wealthy white woman and her black maid. Spike Lee's *Malcolm X* (1992) is a powerful film version of the autobiography that shows the hero's progress from childhood, to petty crime and prison, to nationalist agitation as a Black Muslim, to the final embrace of orthodox Islam with a more global and universal understanding of struggle against oppression. *Panther* (1995) offers a sympathetic portrait of a movement that combined ideologies of socialist revolution with those of cultural nationalism, modeling itself on Third World revolutionary movements. Many documentaries covered various aspects of the Civil Rights movement and the work of Martin Luther King, Jr. A particularly outstanding and comprehensive one is *Eyes on the Prize* (1987), made for public television.

The war in Vietnam sparked a number of films in the United States, mostly told from the point of view of Americans. In that respect they are less about social movements than about the fate of men caught up in the effort to suppress a movement. Examples include *The Deer Hunter* (1978), *Apocalypse Now* (1979), *Full Metal Jacket* (1987), *Platoon* (1986), and *Coming Home* (1978). For the student of social movements, the most interesting of these films probably is *Born on the Fourth of July* (1989), based on the story of a Vietnam veteran, disabled as the result of "friendly fire," who became a leader in the antiwar movement. Unlike most of the U.S. feature films, the thirteen-segment public television documentary *Vietnam* covers the origins of the national liberation movement, the Japanese occupation, the Viet Minh war against the French, and the expanded conflict in Southeast Asia as the United States entered the scene. Based on interviews with leaders and ordinary people on all sides, it is a remarkably complete and balanced document. More polemical is *Hearts and Minds* (1974), clearly made from an antiwar position.

The New Left, the student movement, and the counterculture were the subjects of surprisingly few films, considering the way they had captured the imagination in other media, such as music and print. *Woodstock* (1970) documents the giant rock festival, and *Gimme Shelter* (1970) the disastrous Rolling Stones concert that ended in a murder by a member of the Hells' Angels, who were recruited as security guards. *The Doors* (1991) is a somewhat overblown re-creation of the drug culture and the fortunes of Jim Morrison, a rock musician and countercultural icon. Two opposing views of the post-1960's era are offered by *The Big Chill* (1983), a box office hit that portrayed the growing cynicism and disengagement of the activist generation, and the less well-known *Return of the Seacaucus Seven* (1980), in which John Sayles shows how commitment and idealism continued in new forms, adapted to new issues and opportunities. *Running on Empty* (1988) traces the difficulties of a family whose involvement in terrorism led them to hide underground, in a shadowy existence of false identities and constant flight. More lighthearted is Alain Tanner's *Jonah Who Will Be 25 in the Year 2000* (1976), a portrayal of people living in communities of the European New Social Movements.

One post-1960's type of activism was the making of documentaries that explored conflicts and movements in the American past. Noteworthy among these documentaries are *Seeing Red* (1983), a documentary and interview-based reflection on Communism in the United States; *Union Maids* (1977), life narratives of three female union organizers in the 1930's; *With Babies and Banners* (1979), the role of women in the industrial union drives of the 1930's; and *Harlan County, U.S.A.* (1977), on unions, strikes, and industrial conflict in the mining region of eastern Kentucky. Similar in mood and subject, though fictionalized rather than documentary, is John Sayles's *Matewan* (1987), the story of a long strike and a violent showdown in the West Virginia coal fields. Documentary filmmakers also returned to key places and moments of the student movement, for example Berkeley in the 1960's and the Kent State college campus where demonstrating students were killed by National Guard fire. The public television series *The American Experience* includes a number of documentaries about movements in the United States such as the Underground Railroad.

No discussion of "social movement films" would be complete without a mention of Bertolucci's *The Last Emperor* (1987), in which Bertolucci uses the true story of Henry Pu Yi and China itself, brought to the screen as a mythical place of the imagination, in order to chart the most violent and state-transforming movements of the twentieth century—nationalism, fascism, and communism. The title character of *Forrest Gump* (1994), a box office smash and multiple Oscar winner, is a postmodern and characteristically American "last emperor." Like the unfortunate Pu Yi, Forrest Gump lives through and suffers in the major movements and upheavals of his time and country, preserving his innocence, making a virtue of his fundamental apoliticalness, and closing his life in the tending of a garden. Postmodern films are not always apolitical; they can celebrate postmodern forms of activism, of playful and pervasive (and sometimes perverse) resistance to oppression in all institutional and interactional settings. It is a long way from Lenin and the October Revolution to *Pump Up the Volume* (1990), Happy Harry Hard-on, and his one-person radio station, from which he subversively broadcasts desires, dreams, and unbending opposition to surveillance and disciplinary power in the schools.

Novels

Social movements often are addressed in utopian and dystopian novels that project the ideals of a movement into an imagined future society. Probably the most famous of these is *1984* (1949), George Orwell's grim depiction of a Stalinist world order in which language and memory themselves are irreversibly in the grasp of a totalitarian party. An earlier and more favorable portrait of socialism is offered by Edward Bellamy's *Looking Backward* (1888). Margaret Atwood's *The Handmaid's Tale* (1985) depicts a terrible society ruled by misogynist fundamentalist militarists. In Marge Piercy's *Woman on the Edge of Time* (1976), the future is portrayed in a more open-ended way, as a set of possibilities in the present, one of which leads to a wretched and authoritarian patriarchy, the other to utopian communalism in which the iron cages of gender and race are turned into a celebration of multiple, harmonious, freely chosen differences.

More realistic narratives about social movements were produced in the era of the mortal conflicts between fascism, communism, and liberal democracy. Andre Malraux's *Man's Fate* (1933) deals with the struggles between communists and nationalists in China. The resistance to the Nazis inspired many works of literature, among them Jean-Paul Sartre's drama

Dirty Hands (1948) and Ignazio Silone's *Bread and Wine* (1937). The postwar dissolution of the forces that formed the resistance was woven into Simone de Beauvoir's *The Mandarins* (1956), a novel about French intellectuals.

In the United States, novelists often took a critical view of the Communist Party. This was especially the case in two major works about the relationship of the party to African Americans, Richard Wright's *Native Son* (1940) and Ralph Ellison's *Invisible Man* (1952). Eastern European dissidents took a distinctly unfavorable view of communism. Aleksandr Solzhenitsyn's *One Day in the Life of Ivan Denisovich* (1963) and *The Gulag Archipelago* (1974-1978) are epics that reveal the horrors of Soviet labor camps. More wry and ironic, though no less critical, are Milan Kundera's *The Joke* (1969) and *The Unbearable Lightness of Being* (1984), two novels that describe the life of Czech dissidents and exiles.

The New Left in the West produced more journalism than noteworthy fiction; in fact, journalism was overwhelmed by a new personalized, anti-objective, and often self-displaying style, exemplified by writers such as Hunter Thompson, Tom Wolfe, and Norman Mailer (especially in the 1968 *The Armies of the Night*, his account of an antiwar march). This style to some extent replaced more conventional works of fiction. The boundaries between fiction and nonfiction blurred as authors such as Don DeLillo imagined the lives of such historical figures as Lee Harvey Oswald (in *Libra*, 1988) or mixed real and fictional characters. A novel that follows a relatively conventional narrative form but includes radical reflections on U.S. society is Agnes Bushell's *Local Deities* (1990), a gripping fictionalization of the underground lives of left-wing terrorists.

Latin America has produced a wealth of novels based on collective action. The ones that are translated in a way most likely to appeal to the North American reader include Isabel Allende's *The House of the Spirits* (1985), a multigeneration saga that uses the life of one family to draw the reader into the history of Chilean class structure and social movements. In many ways, its story of the changing fortunes of the landlord class, radical insurgencies, peasant organizing, and military repression expresses themes common to much of Latin America. Gabriel García Márquez's *The General in His Labyrinth* (1990) traces the last months of Simon Bolívar, as he realizes that his dream of a powerful, unified Latin America will not come into being. A similar tone of disappointment pervades Carlos Fuentes' *The Death of Artemio Cruz* (1964), about the life of a Mexican revolutionary whose compromises lead him into personal bitterness and symbolize the frozen character of the revolution itself.

NAME INDEX

SUBJECT INDEX

Abolitionist movement, 219, 253. *See also* Slavery

Abortion, 35, 79, 214

Afghanistan, 174

Africa, 111, 188. *See also* Central Africa *and individual countries*

African American community and movements, 27, 31, 44, 81, 107, 110, 134, 137-138, 142, 144, 147, 153, 163-165, 218-219, 238, 252, 255

Agency and structure, 47, 93

Albania, 250

Algeria, 91, 151, 183, 251

Alienation, 11, 16

Amnesty International, 140-142

Animal rights movement, 235

Anomie, 11, 16

Anthropocentrism, 234

Anti-Communism, 9, 15-16, 250

Antinuclear and pronuclear activism. *See* Nuclear power

Anti-Saloon League, 109

Anti-Semitism, 14, 197-199, 201. *See also* Ethnonationalism; Genocide; Racism

Arab nationalism, 193. *See also individual countries*

Argentina, 121, 143, 148, 164, 167, 169, 194-195, 210, 212, 251

Aryan Nations, 199, 202

Australia, 187, 192, 205, 238, 240

Authoritarian personality, 14, 63

Authoritarian populism, 123, 131

Authoritarianism, 14

Banditry, 75-76

Bangladesh, 223

Batista regime, 251

Berkeley Free Speech Movement, 109

Biocentrism, 234

Biological warfare, 245

Black. *See* African American

Black Panther Party, 31, 44, 106, 252

Bolivia, 148

Bolshevik Revolution, 148-150, 157, 162, 164, 249. *See also* Lenin, V. I.; Stalin, Joseph

Bolsheviks, 148, 151-152, 220. *See also* Lenin, V. I.; Stalin, Joseph

Brazil, 85, 121, 148, 160, 168, 178, 228

Britain. *See* England; Great Britain; United Kingdom

Buddhism, 179

Bulgaria, 197

Burundi, 192

Campaign for Nuclear Disarmament, 236

Canada, 131, 187, 192, 209, 236

Capitalism, 26, 28-29, 70, 91, 98-100, 103-104, 122-123, 135, 145, 158, 160, 200, 202-203, 212, 238-239. *See also* Class and class structure; Economic change and economic restructuring

Catholicism, 113, 174-175, 177, 181, 186. See also Liberation theology

Central Africa, 175

Central America, 110, 177-178, 234

Central Asia, 224

Central Europe, 143

Charismatic authority, 90, 200-201

Charismatic leadership, 13

Chicago School, 7, 13

Chicanas, 228

Chicano cultural nationalism, 228

Chile, 32, 159, 186, 212, 251, 255

China, 32, 72, 86, 91, 141-142, 144-145, 151, 159, 161, 227, 252, 254

Chinese revolution, 32, 252. *See also* China; Communism; Revolution

Christian Anti-Communist Crusade, 181

ABOUT THE AUTHORS

Roberta Garner is a professor of sociology at DePaul University and teaches in the international studies and women's studies programs. She is the author of three books on social change and social movements: *Contemporary Movements and Ideologies* (McGraw-Hill, 1996), *Social Change* (Rand McNally, 1977), and *Social Movements in America* (Rand McNally, 1972 and 1977; Markham, 1972). Among her articles are two with Mayer Zald, "Social Movement Organizations" (1966) and "The Political Economy of Social Movement Sectors" (1985). With Larry Garner, she has published on the Italian Communist Party and comparative issues in European political sociology. In 1994, her article "Transnational Movements in Postmodern Society" appeared in *Peace Review*.

John Tenuto received his bachelor's and master's degrees from DePaul University and teaches at DePaul in the areas of popular culture and criminology, as well as general sociology. His course on the juvenile court draws on eight years of experience in the State's Attorney's office. His master's essay analyzed the characters of Superman and Lois Lane to discuss changes in gender representations in popular culture.

DATE DUE